CHICAGO APARTMENTS

URBAN DOMESTIC ARCHITECTURE SERIES

CHICAGO APARTMENTS

A Century of Lakefront Luxury

Neil Harris

preface by Sara Paretsky

ACANTHUS PRESS
NEW YORK 2004

ACANTHUS PRESS LLC

Barry Cenower, Publisher
48 West 22nd Street
New York, NY 10010
212-414-0108
www.acanthuspress.com

COPYRIGHT © 2004 NEIL HARRIS

All images are copyrighted to the photographers and firms listed.
All institutions hold the rights to their photographs.

Every reasonable attempt has been made to identify the owners of copyright.
Errors of omission will be corrected in subsequent printings of this work.

All rights reserved. This book may not be reproduced in whole or in any part
(except by reviewers for the public press) without written permission from the publisher.

LIBRARY OF CONGRESS CATALOGING-IN-PUBLICATION DATA

Harris, Neil, 1938–
   Chicago apartments : a century of lakefront luxury / Neil Harris ; preface by Sara Paretsky.
     p.   cm.
Includes bibliographical references and index.
ISBN 0-926494-25-2 (alk. paper)
1. Apartment houses--Illinois--Chicago. 2. Upper class--Dwellings--Illinois--Chicago--Designs and plans.
3. Room layout (Dwellings)--Illinois--Chicago--Designs and plans. 4. Architecture--Illinois--Chicago--
20th century. 5. Chicago (Ill.)--Buildings, structures, etc. I. Title.
NA735.C4H37 2004
728'.314'0977311--dc22

                                            2004010641

Frontispiece: 229 East Lake Shore Drive. Detail of door, 1986.
(Bob Thall, courtesy Commission on Chicago Landmarks)

Book design by Jeanne Abboud

PRINTED IN CHINA

To Teri With Love

ACKNOWLEDGMENTS

THE ADVENTURE OF WRITING almost any book would be impossible without the aid of others, and it is with great pleasure that I acknowledge my debts to those whose help, encouragement, and accomplishments have meant so much. I am grateful to all of them, and I apologize to any whom I have inadvertently omitted. First of all, to scholars like Daniel Bluestone, Celia Hilliard, Wim de Wit, and above all, Carroll William Westfall, who have undertaken so much fundamental research into the history of the Chicago apartment house. Then to Barry Cenower who suggested this project and to Sara Paretsky for her elegant preface. Next, to a group of friends and acquaintances who have been generous in supplying me with leads, information, connections, and observations: Bob and Joan Feitler, Jean and Steven Goldman, Mary Gray, David Hilliard, Anne Hokin, Andrew and Moira Griffin, Rose Dyrud, Earl and Brenda Shapiro, Lee Koontz, Richard Robin, Shirl Tole, Michelle De Roche and Billy Wiley, Alyce K. Sigler, Mary Marks, Charlie Clark, Jay Strauss, Bob Loveman, Julie and Richard Wright, Killean Walsh, Robert and Wilma Hanson, Murray Wolbach III, Diane Kelly, Barry Karl, Jim McDaniel, Joan Armstrong, Janys Harvey, George and Vicky Ranney. And then, to the architects and developers who have given me access to plans and photographs: Helmut Jahn, John Vinci, Will Hasbrouck, Alex Kirkhaar, Ron Krueck, Mark Sexton, Lawrence Booth, Lori Carmichael, Stanley Tigerman and Margaret McCurry, Chungho Min, Richard Robin, John Buenz, Kimber Sipperly, Linda Searl, Lucien Lagrange, Christine Miller, Peter Bazelli, Steve C. Anrod, Christina Kuras, and Michael Tolentino, And finally, most of all, to archivists, collectors, and colleagues who have made their collections and libraries available and accessible, and who supplied me with the materials that were indispensable to this project: Russell Lewis, Rob Medina (especially), and Don Friedman of the Chicago Historical Society; Jack Brown, Mary Woolever (most particularly), Amy Bissonette, Peter Blank, John Zukowsky, Martha Thorne, and Kate Butterly of The Art Institute of Chicago; Meredith Taussig at the Commission on Chicago Landmarks; Tim Samuelson, Robert Shimer of Hedrich Blessing, Bob Sideman, for his meticulous reading of large portions of the manuscript and his many suggestions; and, for his generosity, Dave Phillips of Chicago Architectural Photography. I wish also to thank David E. Spatz and Michael Wakeford for their research assistance, and Sophie Bidek, for expertly redrawing a series of plans.

My major debt to my wife Teri Edelstein is acknowledged in the dedication. She has been a full intellectual partner in this venture, whose contributions on every level have been immeasurable. I could not have managed this book at all without Teri's continuous involvement and energetic interventions, her technical advice, careful readings of the manuscript, constructive criticism, and general management of a blizzard of pictorial materials, all of which immeasurably speeded up my hours of work, even while they added to hers.

CONTENTS

Acknowledgments	6
Preface	11
Chicago's Luxury Apartments	13
Note to Reader	35

SOUTH SHORE

6700 South Crandon Avenue	38
6901 South Oglesby Avenue	40
2666 East 73rd Street	THE COASTLAND	42
2231 East 67th Street	SHORELINE HOMES	44
7000 South Shore Drive	46
7321 South Shore Drive	WINDSOR BEACH APARTMENTS	48

HYDE PARK—KENWOOD

5000 South Cornell Avenue	52
5421 South Cornell Avenue	54
5801–11 South Dorchester Avenue	THE CLOISTERS	56
5000 South East End Avenue	58
5555 South Everett Avenue	JACKSON TOWERS	60
1640 East 50th Street	THE NARRAGANSETT	64
1648 E. 50th Street–4950 South Chicago Beach Drive	THE POWHATAN	66
1321 East 56th Street	TOWER HOMES	72
1644 East 56th Street	THE WINDERMERE	74
5454 South Shore Drive	THE SHORELAND	78
5490 South Shore Drive	JACKSON SHORE APARTMENTS	82
5530–32 South Shore Drive	THE PROMONTORY	86
5830–44 South Stony Island Avenue	VISTA HOMES	90

CONTENTS

NEAR NORTH SIDE

1200 North Astor Street | MCCONNELL APARTMENTS	94
1209 North Astor Street	96
1260 North Astor Street	98
1301 North Astor Street	105
1325 North Astor Street	112
20 East Cedar Street | BRADLEY APARTMENTS	118
70 East Cedar Street	122
40–50 East Chicago Avenue | HOTEL ST. BENEDICT FLATS	124
161 East Chicago Avenue | OLYMPIA CENTRE	126
1366 North Dearborn Parkway | THE DEARBORN SCHILLER	130
132 East Delaware Place–900 North Michigan Avenue	132
175 East Delaware Place | JOHN HANCOCK CENTER	137
257 East Delaware Place	142
55 East Erie Street	144
65 East Goethe Street	146
179 East Lake Shore Drive | DRAKE TOWER	148
199 East Lake Shore Drive | THE BREAKERS	152
209 East Lake Shore Drive	156
219 East Lake Shore Drive	160
229 East Lake Shore Drive | THE SHORELAND APARTMENTS	162
505 North Lake Shore Drive | LAKE POINT TOWER	164
680 North Lake Shore Drive | AMERICAN FURNITURE MART	168
860–880 North Lake Shore Drive	170
936 North Lake Shore Drive	178
999 North Lake Shore Drive | LAKE SHORE APARTMENTS	182
1040 North Lake Shore Drive | THE CARLYLE	184
1100 North Lake Shore Drive | MARSHALL APARTMENTS	186
1120 North Lake Shore Drive	188

1130 North Lake Shore Drive	190
1200 North Lake Shore Drive | STEWART APARTMENTS	194
1242 North Lake Shore Drive	196
1418 North Lake Shore Drive	200
1420 North Lake Shore Drive	202
1430 North Lake Shore Drive	206
1448 North Lake Shore Drive	208
1500 North Lake Shore Drive	210
1540 North Lake Shore Drive	220
2130 North Lincoln Park West	226
2300 North Lincoln Park West | BELDEN–STRATFORD HOTEL	230
6 North Michigan Avenue | MONTGOMERY WARD TOWER BUILDING	232
800 North Michigan Avenue | PARK TOWER	236
900 North Michigan Avenue	238
919 North Michigan Avenue | PALMOLIVE BUILDING	242
940–980 North Michigan Avenue | ONE MAGNIFICENT MILE	248
180 East Pearson Street | WATER TOWER PLACE	250
200 East Pearson Street | CAMPBELL APARTMENTS	254
400 East Randolph Street | OUTER DRIVE EAST	256
60–70 East Scott Street	260
300 North State Street | MARINA CITY	262
1320 North State Parkway	268
1530 North State Parkway	270
1550 North State Parkway	274
1244 North Stone Street	276
220 East Walton Place | CASTELLANE APARTMENTS	278
232 East Walton Place	280
233 East Walton Place	282

CONTENTS

NORTH SIDE

2920 North Commonwealth Avenue | COMMONWEALTH TOWERS	286
325 West Fullerton Parkway	288
399 West Fullerton Parkway	290
660–700 West Irving Park Road | THE PATTINGTON	292
3240 North Lake Shore Drive | SHERIDAN–MELROSE APARTMENTS	294
3300 North Lake Shore Drive | SHERIDAN–ALDINE APARTMENTS	296
3314 North Lake Shore Drive | LE GRIFFON	298
3400 North Lake Shore Drive | HARBOR APARTMENTS	300
3500 North Lake Shore Drive | CORNELIA APARTMENTS	302
3750 North Lake Shore Drive	304
3800 North Lake Shore Drive | SHERIDAN–GRACE APARTMENTS	306
3920 North Lake Shore Drive | LAKE SHORE TOWERS	308
2430 North Lakeview Avenue	310
2440 North Lakeview Avenue	316
2450 North Lakeview Avenue	318
2600 North Lakeview Avenue | MARLBOROUGH APARTMENTS	322
5000 North Marine Drive | THE AQUITANIA	324
421 West Melrose Street | THE EDDYSTONE	326
2800 North Pine Grove Avenue | THE BREWSTER	329
3000 North Sheridan Road	332
3100 North Sheridan Road | BARRY APARTMENTS	334
5510 North Sheridan Road | THE RENAISSANCE	336
5555 North Sheridan Road | EDGEWATER BEACH APARTMENTS	338
442 West Wellington Avenue	342

Selected Bibliography and Building References	344
Index	347

PREFACE

by Sara Paretsky

I SPENT MY EARLY YEARS in Chicago in small spaces, often sharing them with a few thousand cockroaches. One winter I lived in a three-flat without heat; another summer my next door neighbors were some pretty sad prostitutes. I had a wistful yearning for luxury, the kind of feeling that doesn't approach envy because the longed-for life seems too remote. I would wander around town, picking out buildings that looked especially inviting from the outside, imagining the interiors—Persian rugs (I'd seen some in museums), delicate sideboards, marquetry tables (British crime fiction of the thirties), grand staircases and bedrooms as large as football fields (Carole Lombard's in *My Man Godfrey*). I would choose one or another building as the place I would live if I ever got rich.

For a long time, my favorite fantasy home was one of the Fugard & Knapp apartments pictured in *Chicago Apartments*. I saw myself inside, looking out, watching the waves crash on stormy nights, while behind me wood burned in the Italian-marble fireplace, champagne cooled in the built-in wine cellar, and Prince Charming entertained me with a flow of witty conversation. I never had to vacuum or do dishes: the prince and the palace were kept in perfect order by someone like Peter Wimsey's Bunter.

One day I confided my fantasy to a friend, whose husband was a lawyer. It turned out his firm handled my fantasy building's legal affairs and he urged me to give up the daydream. Aside from the fact that the smallest unit was (and, as I learned from this book, still is) beyond my means, he said the tenants spent a lot of time suing each other over infractions in the building's by-laws—Mrs. Smithers' grandson left his tricycle in the hall; Mrs. Helefunt put wet trash in the garbage chute.

When I started writing crime fiction, I put my criminals into luxury buildings like those of Fugard & Knapp. This wasn't just because of the tiresome tenants in my dream building, but because it's an American hard-boiled convention, that the poor may not be virtuous, but the rich are definitely corrupt. In British crime fiction of the twenties, the wealthy were the guardians of society and justice. Peter Wimsey lived in an elegant flat over-looking Piccadilly, which must have resembled any number of the buildings in *Chicago Apartments*. In American crime fiction, the wealthy are the subverters of justice. It's a convention that goes back to the westerns of the 1890s, that the wealthy have used their power and position to buy the police, the courts, and the press in order to use them at the expense of ordinary people. Luxury apartments therefore become the setting for lies, secrets, and villainy.

In my fifth book, *Blood Shot*, the villain lived in an imaginary building next to the Fugard & Knapp of my dreams. When I wrote the novel, I hadn't seen any of the floor plans in *Chicago Apartments*, but after reading the descriptions here, I think my imagination must have been similar to that of the architects and building designers of the twenties.

Preface

(A doorman leads V I into the lobby)

Most buildings going up for the rich these days feature glass and chrome lobbies with monstrous plants and hangings, but the Roanoke had been built when labor was cheaper and more skillful. The floor was an intricate mosaic of geometric shapes, and the wood-paneled walls were festooned with Egyptian figurines.... The elevator opened onto what might have been the foyer of a mansion. Gray-white marble tiles showing streaks of pink were covered here and there by throw rugs that had probably been made in Persia when the Ayatollah's grandfather was a baby.

Without thinking about it consciously, I was in love with the buildings put up between 1915 and 1930. Neil Harris gives a brief history of the changes in money, tastes, and design between that period and the modern—the ones V I Warshawski characterizes as having "glass and chrome lobbies." My villains always live in the buildings I aspire to. In *Blacklist*, it's a twenty-room apartment on the Gold Coast, again similar to a Fugard & Knapp co-op, while in *Total Recall*, the Rossy family lives in something like an L. G. Hallberg building on Lake Shore Drive—the outside festooned with balustrades, cartouches, scrolls, and carvings, the inside holding eighteen-room, five-bath apartments.

I wish I had had *Chicago Apartments* before I wrote these books: like me, V I would not have known what a cartouche was, but she might have expressed as much sardonic amazement at these beautiful exteriors as she does at the opulent interiors.

One of the many fascinating tidbits I learned from *Chicago Apartments* was the history of the luxury apartment, how the very wealthy were persuaded to leave mansion living precisely because they could have a mansion within a building—as Gustav Humboldt does in *Blood Shot*—and also have access to the lake and the parks.

V I herself lives in the kind of apartment building that the wealthy disdained. It's a four-room, railway-style apartment in a six-flat, in what used to be a blue-collar neighborhood near Wrigley Field—although current changes in Chicago's demographics have made her neighborhood the fastest-growing community in the city and she probably will not be able to afford the taxes much longer.

V I is resolutely in the blue-collar world from which I'm descended, but she does have wealthier friends. In *Total Recall*, one of them, Dr. Lotty Herschel, has actually bought a condo on North Lake Shore Drive, in another building whose outside I've always loved for its cartouches and so on.

Along with the depravity of the wealthy, another characteristic of the American hard-boiled novel is its effort to provide authentic descriptions of place. Thanks to *Chicago Apartments*, I will be able to add bits of authenticity to Lotty's building—as well as to the next lakefront home some super-rich bad guy inhabits.

My current favorite fantasy building at 1550 N. State Parkway is included in this volume; from it, I learned that 1550 was the most important of all the early luxury buildings—meaning, alas, that I will never be able to afford to live in it, to use its concrete wine and preserve closet, or the built-in refrigerator that opens from opposite sides (I imagine one door opening into the kitchen, the other into my study so I could always be close to some nourishing snack). Still, V I will no doubt have the chance to see a building much like it, perhaps even be served some haut-Margaux from that concrete wine closet. And to speak scathingly of it, so that readers won't guess that in her heart of hearts, she longs to live there.

CHICAGO'S LUXURY APARTMENTS

by Neil Harris

CHICAGO IS A LAKEFRONT CITY. For much of its length, a wall of buildings looms over Chicago's lake-lined parks, beaches, and its most celebrated boulevard, Lake Shore Drive. Strictly speaking, Lake Shore Drive is not a boulevard, but its low speed limits, non-commercial character, and scenic borders differentiate it from most other eight-lane highways. The views from this strip of road define a popular sense of the larger city and, except for a quarter-mile stretch that parallels the ribbon of Michigan Avenue office buildings, the western vistas consist largely of apartment houses. Even some of the Michigan Avenue buildings themselves are undergoing residential conversion. Rhythms change as one moves south to north: parks and hotels alternate with the towers of South Shore and Hyde Park, after which the tracks of the Illinois Central Rail Road divide the roadway from neighborhoods just beyond. North of the Loop, a veritable wall of buildings begins, soon thereafter making a brief east-west angle before resuming its relentless northward movement. Lincoln Park intervenes, with glimpses of more tall residences beyond, and then a new, tighter wall begins, and continues, sometimes with extraordinary density, until the Drive ends at Hollywood.

Thousands and thousands of windows look out on Lake Michigan, and behind them are the residents of an apartment city. Chicago is also a city of bungalows, and a city of three and six flats, and a city of El tracks and warehouses and factories. Yet, its glamour lies heavily in those high-rise apartment houses, many of which are more than 80 years old and flaunt their pinnacled and ornamented fronts with an assurance undiminished by more recent stylistic changes. The most luxurious among them boast spaces and features that match the richest fantasies.

The pre-history of these buildings begins in the 1880s and 1890s, during years of enormous growth for the city. Marking a recovery from the Great Fire of 1871, a series of freshly built flats, hotels, and apartment houses beckoned to wealthy Chicagoans. This marked a new era for Chicagoans who, like other Americans, had associated respectability with control of vertical space. While attached row houses were entirely acceptable for the fashionable in late 18th and early 19th century eastern cities, living above or below other families signified a loss of control, privacy, and above all, status. For much of the 19th century, and even beyond in certain places, such arrangements were relegated to those without choice or resources. A continuing identification of family stability and civic virtue with rural or small town life, at least rhetorically, also didn't help the reputation of the apartment house. It had many prejudices to overcome before cementing the allegiance of the upper-middle class. Even after doing so, developers and designers hastened to emphasize, by language, plan, and appearance, the most fundamental domestic associations. "Apartment homes" moved from being an oxymoron to becoming an acceptable reality.[1]

Chicago's early luxury apartment buildings were not invariably close to the lake. They were still relatively low in height and, while spacious within, contained small numbers of units. Some lacked elevators. As the 19th century became the 20th, the buildings, along with Chicago, began to grow in number and refinement. By the time World War I broke out, the city was home to almost two million people, and much of its social elite had made the move north from the avenues of the near south side to the Gold Coast of the near north side, close to or actually on the newly enhanced lakeshore. After the war, the scattered 10- and 12-story apartment buildings were joined by dozens of others—taller, more capacious, still more elaborate, and differently financed and administered.

It was, in fact, during the 1920s that the lines of buildings along Lake Shore Drive—up through Irving Park Road or thereabouts—were filled out, along with the south side's more scattered towers. In what remains an astonishing burst of architectural and developmental energy, Chicago received a staggering housing legacy. More than 60 of the approximately 100 structures in this book were built in a five-year period ending about 1929. They, and their immediate predecessors, were not part of Chicago's stylistic insurgency—the "Chicago School" vernacular revolt forever associated with Louis Sullivan, Frank Lloyd Wright, William Le Baron Jenney, and the early buildings of Daniel Burnham and John Root. Few among them demonstrated independence from the architectural styles of the past. They flaunted, instead, the trappings of Continental Europe and "olde" England: turrets, balustrades, swags, garlands, pediments, colonnades, rustications, and flying buttresses festooned their facades and enlivened their silhouettes, earning the contempt of modernists like Lewis Mumford, who wrote in 1927, "Today the architecture of Chicago is lost in a deluge of meaningless vulgarity."[2] Behind their elaborate facades, these buildings enclosed apartments that were simultaneously spacious, modern, domestic, and expensive: multi-roomed, high-ceilinged, soundproofed residences, with

Lake Shore Drive, looking north, c. 1930. (Courtesy collection of David R. Phillips)

views and appointments that excited the respectful awe of newspaper journalists.

This era, of course, came to an abrupt end with the Great Crash of 1929 and the economic depression that followed. During the 1930s and most of the 1940s, private construction, especially luxury apartment building, came to a halt everywhere. Public housing projects were designed for different constituencies. The pent-up housing shortage succeeding World War II, combined with memories of earlier collapse, rent control, and investor caution, expanded federal government involvement with housing, vastly multiplying Federal Housing Authority insured mortgage loans. These loans stimulated an apartment house construction boom in Chicago and elsewhere. However, Federal regulations precluded the lavish room sizes and appointments that had highlighted the earlier luxury market. With exceptions here and there, the apartments of the 1940s through 1970s, however innovative in construction method, efficient in management, and modern in appearance, and sited as they were on prime pieces of lakefront or near lakefront property, were tighter, smaller and much more modest in appearance than their 1920s ancestors. The trade-off of space for location and traditional decorative detail for modernist austerity appeared to satisfy many of the new residents in what some historians have called a democratization of the lakefront. Exceptions here and there only seemed to prove the rule. The grand luxury buildings were period pieces, reminders of an increasingly distant past.

Then in the 1980s, and even more in the 1990s, a change occurred. As Chicago's urban temptations lured suburban émigrés back to the city, as condominiums became instruments of investment, as apartment owners worked to combine separated units, and as building re-use began to shape new tastes, architects and developers started to reclaim some of the ground lost half a century earlier. There were many modifications and compromises, and the eruption of new buildings raised aesthetic and density issues. It was apparent by 20th century's end that changing expectations had taken hold. Whether the traditional American triad of rise, fall, and resurrection could cover all this was not absolutely certain. However, a third act to the luxury apartment drama seemed to be in course of formation.

Such is the story line of this book, although it will be demonstrated more explicitly in images than in words. Because the buildings are organized geographically rather than chronologically, and recognizing that even pictures need something more than captions, what follows is an effort to introduce some of the players, trends, and above all, buildings, before addressing their individual stories.

THE BUILDINGS

In Chicago, the luxury apartment era began, to all intents and purposes, in the 1880s and 1890s. A series of accomplished architects designed a set of large, lavishly appointed, and technologically modern suites in buildings. Sometimes they were called hotels—often for legal reasons—but they also unashamedly bore the title of apartment building. Most of them no longer stand in anything like their original condition, but photographs, prints, floor plans, and an occasional survivor, demonstrate their ambition and their elegance. They hosted some of the city's leading families. Lawrence Hallberg's Mentone Flats of 1882, and Treat and Foltz's Ontario Flats just two years later, were prominent early examples of the genre; another somewhat lower structure was the celebrated Mecca Flats, a courtyard complex whose open area hosted elaborate parties. *The Elite Dictionary and Club List of Chicago*, published in the late 1880s, listed as separate establishments six flats and hotel buildings, including the Mentone, the Hotel St. Benedict, and the Ontario Flats.[3]

Decidedly European in stylistic inspiration, some of them distinctively Parisian in appearance, these buildings were succeeded by dozens of luxury hotels and apartment houses as the 1880s became the 1890s. They included Clinton J. Warren's Virginia Hotel of 1888, a particularly popular establishment; in the early 20th century Horatio Wilson's Raymond Apartments, which stood on Walton Place and Michigan Avenue, in the heart of what would, many years later, become the city's premier shopping district; and Solon Beman's Bryson, the south side's most luxurious flat building, on Lake, now Lake Park Avenue. Apartments here could run as large as 12 or 14 rooms, offering a range of conveniences and comforting levels of service and security. Normally no higher than six or eight stories, they especially appealed to those fleeing the inconveniences of household management; by the 1920s, hundreds of

The Bryson Hotel, c. 1925.
(Courtesy collection of
David R. Phillips)

residential hotels, from small family-run enterprises to imperial operations like the Shoreland and the Belden-Stratford, served this market.

Defenders of flat living grew increasingly lyrical about its virtues. "It embodies the accumulated architectural achievements of the past, the skill of the world's best engineers," exclaimed one rhapsodic 1912 realtor. "The plutocrat may search the world for comforts, but all his wealth can add but little to the comforts of the modern flat."[4]

Whatever the rhetoric, a growing market of upper-middle-class consumers did find apartment life appealing, for Wilson and Warren and Hallberg were joined by other notable local architects—Benjamin Marshall, Andrew Sandegren, John A. Nyden, Howard Van Doren Shaw, and William Ernest Walker among them—producing by the outbreak of World War I a set of significant, handsomely appointed structures. Some of the most luxurious among them were still no more than three or four floors high and had no elevator. One impressive example was J. E. O. Pridmore's fabled Gables Apartments of 1914, on Kenmore and Hollywood Avenues. This four-story Elizabethan building contained nine 10- and 12-room apartments, each differently laid out, along with three individual ballrooms. The apartments rented for up to $3,000 a year.[5] Pridmore's Manor House, not far away, also in Tudor dress, was even more luxurious: its six apartments contained up to 16 rooms, with billiard rooms, libraries, and ballrooms. Other opulent small apartment buildings lay scattered through Chicago, but increasingly, as the 20th century proceeded, height assumed special significance. Benjamin Marshall's stunning achievement at 1550 North State Parkway, for example, was the last word in contemporary elegance, and stood 12 stories high.

Architectural historians have divided Chicago's pre-World War I apartments into phases representing building rhythms and styles. Limitations of space and the presence of some excellent analyses preclude such discussion here. Certainly by 1910 or 1912 scale and splendor had risen, although again, there had been earlier precedents. With understandable exaggeration and with some inaccuracy, the real estate brokers A. J. Pardridge and Harold Bradley, who produced in 1917 the first systematic guide to such establishments, declared that until "the last half-dozen years, there were almost no apartment buildings which would be considered as satisfactory domiciles in comparison with houses."[6]

Such newer buildings had rich appointments and emphasized both space and privacy. Announcing a new south side apartment house in 1903, *The Economist* stated that each unit's public rooms were arranged as to "open into each other, giving it the appearance of a private house."[7] Porcelain bathtubs and iceboxes, silver safes, built-in buffets and bookcases, fireproof construction, servants' rooms, carved mantels, paneled libraries, marble lobbies, even an occasional garage, in short "everything that appeals to comfort and taste" were among their amenities. At Marshall & Fox's 199 East Lake Shore Drive the modern conveniences included "a private filtration plant on the premises, garbage chutes in each kitchen to an incinerator, vacuum cleaning installation," among others.[8]

The world of flats and apartments was not inconsiderable in this period. After the "flat craze" in the 1880s and 1890s, between 1910 and 1915 flat building in Chicago moved from consuming about 35% of all buildings to more than 60%, almost 60 million dollars worth in 1915.[9] This constituted the single most significant category of local building, larger than factories, warehouses, and office buildings put together, and added in those six years alone some 28,000 units to the city's housing stock.[10]

The class of consumers who rented luxury flats was not very large in number, compared to the hundreds of thousands of flat dwellers living in the city. However, their wealth and status brought them considerable visibility in the press and their purchasing power made them highly desirable clients for both architects and developers. Apartment house life before World War I is difficult to label, considering its diversity of style and size. By 1910 there were signs of change in any event. But for the most part, the luxury elevator buildings were speculative investments of relatively small scale. Of the 68 apartment buildings listed by Pardridge and Bradley in 1917, only about 18, one-quarter of the total, had six floors or more, and none went beyond 12. Most of these had been constructed in the previous half-dozen years. There was occasional talk of much larger buildings, but little action was taken toward that end.

At their most polished, such apartments were impressively finished inside and out and were extremely expensive. The Pardridge and Bradley guide offered 15 buildings where apartments rented

Exterior, the Manor House. (Pardridge and Bradley, *Directory of Apartments*)

for more than $3,600 a year, several times the annual income of a typical American family at that time. They included 1550 North State at $8,400, 1100 North Lake Shore Drive at $5,000, and 936 North Lake Shore Drive, whose rentals ranged from $4,800 to $5,600 annually. High ceilings and large rooms were standard. What the brokers called a "medium-sized" apartment at 230 East Delaware Place contained two maids' rooms and two bedrooms and occupied more than 2,500 square feet. The grandest of all, 1550 North State, cleverly separated the living, sleeping, and service sections from one another, and permitted a clear space of more than 100 feet in length for entertaining. Its kitchen and butler's pantry, designed by a New York chef, featured a refrigerator that opened from opposite sides, a concrete wine and preserve closet, and three broilers. It would be hard for any apartments to equal either the dimensions or the facilities of 1550 for decades to come.

The standards of apartment life for the prewar years were set by the dimensions and capabilities of town mansions, which in Chicago on the near north and south sides offered multiple levels of high-ceilinged rooms, and on Prairie Avenue and surrounding streets, patches of lawn, gardens, backyards, and carriage houses or stables. On the south and west sides of the city such mansions were abandoned with increasing frequency in the late 19th and early 20th centuries, as the Gold Coast consolidated its domination and wealthy home owners moved north.[11] There was less space to build there, however. Apartment buildings did not present much in the way of outdoor amenities, but placed near parks or the lake shore, as so many of them were, they offered some compensations. As the automobile era took off in the first decade of the new century, they could provide their own garages and automobile entries, rooms for chauffeurs, or easy access to nearby garages.

No easy line of demarcation separates the first luxury flat era of genteel intimacy from that of the second, which emphasized vertical magnitude. A rough sense of contrast may be obtained from the bible of this next age, *A Portfolio of Fine Apartment Homes*, the grandest and most ambitious effort to bring together the city's most distinguished apartment houses.[12] Baird & Warner, the issuer, had become by the mid-1920s one of Chicago's most prominent managers and developers of real estate and the lavish volume that appeared in 1928 was meant to present wealthy buyers or renters with a range of opportunities. Much larger in format than the Pardridge and Bradley book, at 19 by 12 inches in size, beautifully designed and gracefully printed, the *Portfolio* did not include by any means all of Chicago's fine apartments. For one thing, it was confined to the North Side and Evanston. And even here it omitted, for unclear reasons, some well-known addresses.

Nonetheless, its accomplishment was considerable, and the contrast between it and Pardridge and Bradley clearly showed the changes of ten years time. The *Portfolio* included some 93 Chicago buildings (sharing only a few with Pardridge and Bradley); of them, 36, more than one third, were 12 stories or higher, and 26 were 15 stories or more, culminating in the 30-story Drake Tower, Chicago's tallest apartment house before World War II. Almost all had been built during an extraordinary five or six year period just preceding publication, an era of astounding legal, financial, architectural, and technological energy in Chicago.

The changes in scale and character were widely acknowledged. "A 1929 Rip Van Winkle," Ruth Bergman wrote in *The Chicagoan*, "would not recognize the current standard in Chicago apartments." Twenty years ago "the little gray home in Chicago had a light in the window and a child waiting at the gate; now it has an electric sign on the roof and a uniformed attendant at the door."[13]

The new lakefront skyline of tall apartment buildings contained some surprising internal variations and an unending set of novelties. "The person who insisted upon always having the *dernier cri* in apartments would have to move about once a week," Ruth Bergman observed.[14] Externally, there were many similarities. The 12, 15, and 20-floor structures typically adopted a repertoire of traditional European stylistic vocabularies: Tudor, 18th-century English, Italian Renaissance, and French classicism were the most consistently summoned, although more idiosyncratic adaptations of Spanish, Moorish, Byzantine, and German traditions were also represented. Ornamental details concentrated around the entry and base, the roofline, and selected window courses. Brick and stone were the preferred surface materials, covering frames of concrete and steel. Although brickwork could sometimes be deployed in unusual colors and was occasionally inventive in pattern, especially in neighborhoods away from the lake, this was more commonly done in smaller buildings. A relatively narrow range of reds dominated the luxury high rises that used brick.[15] Their expensive and elegant limestone trims often came from nearby Indiana quarries, and quite a few buildings were clad completely in stone. The surge of terra-cotta manufacturers, including local firms like Northwestern Terra Cotta, meant that stock details abounded, in a variety and ingenuity that remain impressive today.

Rich facade details, however, did not necessarily correlate with luxurious building interiors. Throughout Chicago there are colorfully decorated residential hotels and inexpensive apartment complexes—Raymond Gregori's buildings on West Wrightwood for example, Leo Steif's 10 West Elm, Leon Urbain's Poinsettia on Hyde Park Boulevard, Maurice Bein's Cornell Towers, Paul Frederick Olsen's Jeffery Avenue extravaganzas, William Doerr's south side hotels—that are more inventive, modernistic, and ornamentally memorable than their more expensive and expansive counterparts. Indeed, it could be argued that designers of some of the more modest interiors over-compensated in their efforts to command attention.

The luxury buildings tended, with some notable exceptions, to emphasize dignity and moderation, or to use John Craib-Cox's phrase, a "restrained sumptuosity."[16] With so many set on the shoreline, their wider spatial aprons permitted more sustained and better-framed viewing. By the end of the 1920s, some of their architects—notably Philip Maher and Charles Morgan—challenged dominant stylistic conventions and invoked the approaches of European modernism in a stripped down approach to ornament and an emphasis upon structural form, but they were few in number. For most of this period, Chicagoans preferred their grander apartment residences to be accompanied by canonized systems of embellishment and references to admired European traditions.

This stock of 1920s residential towers, which forms the backbone of the present volume, retains for many of today's Chicagoans a viewer-friendly feeling, emphasized by contrast with their under-detailed and massive successors. Their rediscovered popularity reflects a number of things: the generous interior room dimensions, the locations, the amenities, the construction quality, personal associations, and preservation interests. But one element, no doubt, is their appropriation, on a grand scale, of stylistic elements that are simultaneously recognizable and valued.

Nostalgia and admiration aside, the enlarged scale of these buildings brought some criticism, contemporaneous and subsequent. Moving from 10 or 12 stories to 20 or 25, they changed the character of the pedestrian experience and challenged the charm of neighboring streets. Carroll William Westfall, the most careful and authoritative historian of Chicago apartments, finds, for example, Robert De Golyer's 1120 Lake Shore Drive (1925) flawed. Despite its much larger bulk, it failed to adapt its architectural details to a much stretched-out reality. Window surrounds, moldings, and string courses, Westfall argues, had become awkwardly proportioned. "Dozens like it" soon appeared, Westfall goes on, "all of them too large relative to their neighborhoods and to the requirements of coherence in design." Their builders "were in pursuit of financial gain, … untempered" by older concerns of "image and manners."[17]

There is much to these charges of mercenary ambitions and violation of building height etiquette. But during the 1920s, at least, building "manners" meant something different from the number of floors or the sheer bulk of the structure. Newspaper reviewers, architects, and developers, repeatedly and quite specifically, spoke about building etiquette, for apartment houses especially. But they were most concerned with the materials used on side and rear walls, and with the character of roof lines. Again and again, *Chicago Tribune* columnists inveighed against "shirt front" or "dickey" buildings which used expensive materials only on their main facades, and employed inferior brick for their other sides. Doing so, wrote Philip Hampson, resembled "a gentleman who is dressed in evening clothes and wears a top hat, but who has been chary of using soap back of his ears and on the neck."[18] John Nyden, a prolific designer of apartment houses and hotels, extended the simile, declaring "there is no more reason for having rich material on the front and poor material on the rear sides than there is for making the front of a man's coat of rich material and the back of inferior quality." Nyden insisted that he had educated his clients "to play fair with their neighbors by making all sides the same."[19] Al Chase, chief real estate reviewer for the *Tribune*, commenting on Walter Ahlschlager's pledge to use the same brick and stone on all sides of the south side's Jackson Towers, said essentially the same thing. "Making a tall building outside the Loop the same on all sides is especially imperative from the standpoint of good taste, attractiveness, and fairness to the neighborhood in general."[20]

Buildings were also considered respectful of their neighbors if they hid what were termed "rooftop atrocities"—their water tanks, elevator penthouses, and other utilitarian devices—behind parapets, towers, mansards, set backs, or appropriately shaped shields of one kind or another. In a typical comment, Al Chase noted approvingly of one Sheridan Road building that "the usual group of unsightly penthouses which so many Chicago architects like to scatter about on the roof are to be hidden in a set-back on the top." He went on to observe that "the usual tank atrocities will be concealed in two towers."[21] Letter writers complained about the "chicken coops" disfiguring the tops of important buildings. Pledging to disguise such appendages, owners, developers, and architects committed to community standards and to civic ideals of harmony and control.

Such attitudes were, in part, a legacy of City Beautiful reforms that had, since the Progressive Era, centered on the creation of new city plans, the passing of smoke abatement legislation, improvements in street furniture, and more recently, the adoption of zoning ordinances, among other accomplishments. Increasingly the good or bad manners of a building were considered to reside in its materials and its cosmetic disguises—its code of public appearance. Height restrictions seemed more a function of public safety and health than of civic etiquette. Admiring journalists described the new apartment blocks as "cliffs," invoking other geographical features as metaphors to naturalize the new cityscape.[22]

Luxury apartment life in the 1920s was nurtured, in Chicago and elsewhere, by moving pictures—Hollywood stars may have lived in swimming-pool favored Beverly Hills mansions, but the high life characters they played moved through

Chicago, looking west to near north, c. 1925. (Courtesy collection of David R. Phillips)

glamorous New York penthouses with enormous, high-ceilinged rooms and landscaped terraces. Settings for romance and intensely polished glamour, the penthouse, as James Sanders suggests, was a place where hard-edged boundaries—between inside and outside, between country-like nature and steel-framed technology—dissolved into partnerships.[23] New York's famed 1916 zoning law, which encouraged setbacks on higher floors in the interests of light and air, underwrote the creation of many of the penthouse terraces. Such setbacks, and the terraces they supported, were relatively rare in Chicago, where different building regulations held sway. Yet they occasionally made an appearance, along with the penthouses, to approving newspaper comment, and the sparkle of Hollywood-inspired apartments cast a promotional glow on the high rises of the inter-war era.[24]

Looming like skyline ghosts are the innumerable projects that were never constructed, many of them still taller and grander than their realized colleagues. The unbuilt Chicago of the 1920s was meant to have apartment buildings of 40 and 50 stories or more, concentrated complexes offering a series of elaborate services, high-speed elevators whisking tenant-owners from their multi-level garages directly to their large apartments. "Gothic Goliath" was the newspaper label for a 1927 41-story apartment tower designed by Holabird & Roche at 900 Lake Shore Drive, to be financed by the McCormick interests.[25] It was one of many designs that came to nothing. Optimistic fantasies are the lifeblood of real estate history, but they were never more grandiose and apparently attainable than in the late 1920s, when Chicago's shoreline, north and south, seemed destined to hold an uninterrupted line of luxurious high rises.

Leaving aside such losses, the actual accomplishment of the architects in just half a dozen years or so was still very impressive. The exuberance of these eclectically styled buildings remains a strong presence today. The French Renaissance facade of 1500 Lake Shore Drive contrasts with the Gothic-topped 1448 just across Burton Place and is flanked by the steep-roofed classicism of 1540 on the other side; the broadly curved Tudor-style 3800 Lake Shore Drive faces 3750, its massive Georgian-detailed neighbor to the south. In the two elegantly modernist, limestone-faced Astor Street towers of Philip Maher, the exuberant exoticism of Walter Ahlschlager's Jackson Towers or the idiosyncratic massing of Robert De Golyer's 7321 South Shore Drive, among others, there are dozens of buildings that exemplify, in various ways, the decade's achievements. Developer rhetoric competed with architectural ingenuity for consumer attention. But the ambition and animation quickly disappeared in the aftermath of the Great Depression and were distant memories by the end of World War II. The stock phrase, "an era had ended," for once might seem apt.

Of course, almost all construction went into a tailspin as the 1930s began. Both nationally and in Chicago, the figures remain arresting in their dramatic and instant collapse. There had been signs of contraction well before the crash, but the first six months of 1930 reveal that Chicago's building permits evaporated to one-third the level of the previous year, and things got worse from there. By 1933 new residential construction of all kinds had practically disappeared. In 1925, American builders created almost one million non-farm dwelling units; in 1933 the same category included little more than 90,000 throughout the entire country. In Chicago only 137 new dwelling units were added that year.[26] Between 1929 and 1933 the stated value of new building permits nationally was reduced by 90%. Private construction capital could hardly be found. In 1925, Chicago issued 17,501 building permits. That figure would not be equaled for more than thirty years. Indeed, the total number of permits issued between 1930 and 1939, ten years' worth, would not match the single year of 1925.[27] By 1932, the 17,501 permits had become 467.[28]

Chicago's apartment house architects confronted 20 years of famine. Some retired, disappeared from professional practice, or died. Others went on with non-residential construction. And a few—Robert DeGolyer, Philip Maher, Ralph Huszagh among them—found work designing public housing projects like the Jane Addams Houses, the Julia Lathrop Homes, the Ida B. Wells Homes, and Trumbull Park Homes. These massive complexes contained some highly original planning elements and, whatever their eventual fate in later decades, represented a moment of commitment to and enthusiasm for government-funded housing efforts. But their austere, largely undecorated exteriors, and small interior spaces contrasted emphatically with the glories of the apartment era that had gone before.

Governmental intervention into the housing market did not end with the Depression and World

War II. As we will see shortly, the financing of housing on almost all levels relied heavily on the availability of publicly funded mortgage insurance, which dictated a range of technical requirements. The high ceilings of another era were no longer possible for most buildings. Here and there, in the 1940s and 1950s, luxury rentals and co-ops were built in Chicago. They obeyed a new aesthetic and emphasized very different things than their predecessors. The buildings tended to hold more apartments, to make less space available for individual units, and to compensate by providing recreational facilities, small terraces and balconies, and newer mechanical contrivances. Along North Lake Shore Drive and North Sheridan Road, on South Shore Drive, and across a wide swath of neighborhoods a series of 30- and 40-story apartment houses were built with almost identical interior arrangements. It was hard to find a single duplex or "roof-top bungalow" among them, although developers or architects sometimes arranged for a single example for themselves.

Several of these buildings had considerable architectural distinction about them, most notably the highly influential Mies van Der Rohe projects, starting with the Promontory (1949) on the south side, and continuing with the Glass Houses (1951) on the north. There was little interior opulence to them, and while the elegance of certain details confirmed the modernist sympathies of many critics-- and building residents--and the compact efficiency of their glass-walled interiors pleased a new generation of apartment dwellers, their distinction did not rest on lavish spaces or appointments. Location, views, and certain collective conveniences were what sold. Apartment units shared collective laundries; bathrooms and kitchens shrank in size. Indeed all room dimensions became tighter. Dining rooms were now 8 by 10 foot areas that were, in essence, part of the living rooms. Servants' rooms disappeared, along with servants. The two-bedroom, middle-class apartment might be under 1000 square feet, its ceilings 8 feet high.

A few luxury buildings appeared as early as 1949 or 1950. Leo Hirschfeld's 16-story 1335 North Astor cooperative with large two- and three-bedroom apartments and two penthouse apartments on the top opened in 1951, about the same time as another, 1350, just across Astor Street. With modern conveniences like radiant heating, freezers, electric dishwashers, and special television outlets, it incorporated the wrap around, corner glass windows and light colored brick that had been featured by New York architects in the 1930s. Nevertheless, there were relatively few luxury buildings constructed in Chicago in the 1950s.

This was an era, of course, when suburban life styles lured large numbers of middle-class Americans from the cities; Chicago already enjoyed a string of fashionable suburbs, primarily west and north; developers enlarged them and created others. The critical mass of well-to-do urbanites who had supported the construction of new luxury buildings in the 1920s had shrunk considerably. A new class of clients, particularly for prime lakefront and Gold Coast sites, was willing to sacrifice the grander spaces of earlier years for more affordable views and modern conveniences.

Some of the most ambitious developments of this period aimed to prove that the trade-off could work. Outer Drive East and Marina City, which opened within a year of one another in the mid 1960s, were immense concentrations of apartments by prewar standards. They featured dramatic locations and innovative, cost-effective construction methods, along with automobile and recreation-friendly features, to attract constituencies that some feared might permanently flee the city.[29] The size of individual apartments in these complexes or in the Mies Glass Houses, would have disappointed the tenants of an earlier day. However, their success encouraged other developers, and vertical ambitions climbed. For example, 1964 saw the opening of the 55-floor 1000 Lake Shore Plaza, claiming title to the tallest reinforced concrete building in the world when it opened.

In fact, in the years following World War II the apartment house sector as a whole moved forward more rapidly than did industrial and commercial real estate, partly because of a long pent-up demand for housing, and partly because its public financing, in the form of mortgage insurance, was enticingly present. Throughout the 1950s, 1960s, and 1970s a whole series of major apartment complexes were constructed throughout the city; some of the largest were along Sheridan Road, near the north lakefront, an area once dominated by single-family residences. With rather different results, Sheridan Road recapitulated the Gold Coast's experience of the teens and 1920s. Now buildings of 30, 40, and 50 stories rose: Granville Tower (1965), 29 floors, at 6166 Sheridan; East Point (1967), a few doors away, by the Arpen Group, with 43 floors; Malibu East (1970) at 6033 North Sheridan, by Hausner & Macsai, just a little higher; Park Place Tower (1971), by Loewenberg & Loewenberg on West Irving Park Road, 56 stories. These buildings displayed an impressive amount of external variation: some with rounded glass corners; others with long strings of balconies; still others, with surprising touches of color. Architectural historians and critics have singled out individual buildings for particular praise or contempt. What they shared, aside from height and their large numbers of units, was an emphasis on panoramic views, athletic facilities, and tight floor plans. The more ingenious architects played with methods that maximized efficiency within the studios, one bedroom, and two bedroom apartments that dominated, but there were limits on what could be done with eight-foot ceilings and 1,000 square feet.

Changes in expectation were slowly taking place however. One source, to be described shortly, came from the condominium movement, made possible by new state legislation in 1963.[30] Leo Hirschfeld, the architect of 1335 North Astor, produced the first high-rise luxury condominium, the Carlyle, just half a dozen years later. High rises constructed for tenant-ownership began to indulge in some of the niceties that had been boasts of the cooperatives some 40 years earlier, although still on a somewhat reduced spatial scale. When combined with commercial and office developments, as they would be in the years that followed, the results could be arresting.

Of even more significance, perhaps, was the growing experience of building conversion: the transformation of commercial and industrial spaces into housing units. Preservation buffs and urban pioneers had been taking over warehouses, industrial lofts, even storefronts and churches, since the 1960s and 1970s in Chicago. Federal tax legislation from 1981 and earlier helped this process. Areas south and west of the Loop began to demonstrate the impact of these conversions by the 1980s, and they had a profound effect on the ecology of the whole city. More than that, loft conversion opened up a new set of spatial possibilities to those whose notion of apartments had been defined by the ceiling heights and room dimensions of the postwar era; they whetted the appetite for more. The current dispersion of a "faux loft" taste to cities, such as Houston, that did not experience much actual loft conversion, may demonstrate the wider presence of this sensibility.[31]

The pace of conversions quickened in the 1980s when the first of a series of Chicago office and showroom buildings began their shift toward apartment residency. The famed Manhattan Building, a Chicago School classic by William Le Baron Jenney (1891), at 16 stories briefly the tallest building in the world, was renovated into apartments by Hasbrouck, Hunderman in the early 1980s. The Manhattan's conversion took place while the American Furniture Mart was undergoing a somewhat lengthier transformation; these would be followed by a series of other such projects. A set of buildings on South Dearborn — John Van Osdel's Terminals Building of 1892 among them — and the transformation of the Reliance and Union Carbide buildings into hotels, are notable illustrations. Remodelings of Montgomery Ward's Michigan Avenue Headquarters' building and its great riverfront warehouse complex, the Singer Building, and the Palmolive Building, constitute a few more prominent examples. With unusual dimensions, higher ceilings, and dramatic spatial possibilities evident, such complexes appeal to buyers or tenants who find traditional layouts constricting or want studio or library space or extensive home offices, or who simply wish to occupy celebrated structures.

The taste nurtured by conversions, suburban house living, and, in the 1990s, by prosperity-driven higher expendable incomes, led to the first significant revival of grand luxury interiors in Chicago since the 1920s. With just a couple of exceptions, local architects and developers had avoided creation of high-ceilinged units of 4,000-6,000 square feet; potential purchasers needed to choose from among vintage buildings for such apartments. During the previous two decades residents had often joined existing apartments to obtain more space, and a number of newer buildings had more than one penthouse available. But the creation of totally new apartments which could be customized in fundamental ways and contained many good-sized rooms awaited the 1990s. Lucien Lagrange was one architect who identified this niche; other buildings serving it include the Elm Tower (2003) and the not yet completed Maple Tower, both by A. Epstein & Sons International. The size or longevity of this market demand remains unclear. However, the lavish, eclectically styled towers of the 1990s

Bond. (Courtesy Ryerson and Burnham Libraries, McNally and Quinn Collection, The Art Institute of Chicago. All rights reserved.)

along with the wider variety of idiosyncratically spaced interior plans that flowed out of the new experience, represented something that had not been seen in the city for almost 70 years.

FINANCING REAL ESTATE

All building construction is linked intimately to larger business cycles and the willingness or enthusiasm of developers to assume risk in the interest of profit. In Chicago's case, these rhythms were further defined by the shifting role of government and changes in opportunities to own or invest in apartment houses. Four large periods reflecting these issues can be discerned over the last century. The first ran from the 1880s to the early 1920s and was dominated by a simple legal fact: Illinois law forbade the formation of corporations whose purpose was the purchase and improvement of real estate. Passed after the Great Fire of 1871 to discourage speculative exploitation and frequently amended in the decades that followed, Illinois law contrasted with New York's more permissive legislation, and by the second decade of the 20th century it stood out even in the Middle West. Without the legal advantages of incorporation, the cooperative ventures that built some of New York's great buildings were impossible, although occasionally tenant cooperatives were formed after a building had been completed. By the early 1920s, however, legislative changes had transformed the real estate scene, and the cooperative apartment house became a dominant type in the luxury market. Most of the lavish 1920s buildings featured in this book were conceived as cooperative ventures, although they too could be divided into various types.[32]

One source of division lay in origins. A syndicate of wealthy investors could determine that they wanted to build a structure to house themselves and their friends. Developers and architects would be brought in to assemble, administer, and design a project, and the opportunity to buy shares would be advertised, but often many of the units would be gone before the building was finished. More typically, developers would assemble a tract of land, sometimes by purchasing and demolishing existing residences, then hire designers, builders, and agents, and construct the building as an act of speculation. Shares of ownership, again, would be advertised and sold, but there was no core of pre-sold units.

A second distinction lay in organization. One-hundred per cent cooperatives, as they were called, were self-explanatory. Every unit in the building was up for sale and every tenant was an owner. These were touted as absolutely secure financially. Partial cooperatives, or group ownership cooperatives, or modified cooperatives—there were many terms—on the other hand, assumed that a portion of the building, sometimes the vast majority of units, would remain as rentals. This income supported the maintenance of the building and reduced the assessments of the minority of residents who were stockholders in the corporation. However, not all investors in such buildings necessarily lived in them and there were variations, which cannot be described here, in which trustees were given the responsibility of management.

In either case, among tenant-owners or corporate stockholders there was responsibility for an underlying building mortgage, which in many cases amounted to 75% of project costs. Mortgages were issued by banks and loan companies, which could produce individual bonds whose collateral was the building itself. Such bonds, often adorned with an elegant rendition of the apartment house and accompanied by a prospectus that detailed the building's costs and features, constitute an indispensable source of information. Generally they were issued by important local institutions, such as Greenebaum Sons Investment Company, Garard Trust, Union Trust, and H. O. Stone & Company. The bonds were presented as suitable options to conservative investors who were willing to forgo the higher return rates promised on the stock market in favor of these regular and apparently secure 5% or 5.5% or even 6% returns.

Luxury cooperatives appeared to possess advantages over rental buildings. Since they were built for prospective owners, they tended to offer larger and finer apartments than rentals did, and many could be customized for individual needs. Their blessings were trumpeted by a whole crew of publicists and promoters, who pointed to their economy, tax benefits, social selectivity, and moral significance.[33] Earnest Elmo Calkins, the New York advertising innovator, wrote one classic essay, "On Buying A Cooperative Apartment," which was reprinted by the Kirkham–Hayes Corporation, a Chicago developer. Cooperative floor plans made the "apartment as much like a home as possible," Calkins argued, going beyond the "deadly uniformity of the old-time rented apartment." His own Park Avenue building, Calkins reported, "is run something like a club."[34] Home ownership, declared Elmer A. Claar in 1926, who managed the cooperative division of Baird & Warner, "is an expression of the innate desire to possess a fireside, a desire which is beyond the financial reach of most of those who must dwell in the thickly-populated, highly-developed communities" that are large cities. The cooperative apartment "costs less to purchase, requires a smaller original payment without speculation, and costs less to operate than an individual dwelling with similar accommodations in the same neighborhood."[35] Put more succinctly, a booklet issued by the newly organized Co-Operative Association of Chicago defined a cooperative building as "a highly restricted community of homes under one roof."[36] Articles, pamphlets, and broadsides beyond number featured cooperative ownership as a panacea for city living. The Chicago Real Estate Board in 1925 established a separate Cooperative Apartments Division to recognize the trend, the same year that realtor H. H. Decker predicted that more Gold Coast residents would own cooperative apartments than houses within 5 years. During a seven-year stretch, at least 100 cooperatives were built housing some 20,000 people, with a total investment made of more than $80 million.[37] "No bond, insurance company loan or any other mortgage on a 100 percent cooperative apartment has ever gone into receivership," a 1930 survey by the Chicago Real Estate Board insisted.[38] The names of society leaders, bankers, and prominent professionals who had purchased cooperative apartments were published to reassure doubters and skeptics about the safety or propriety of such an investment. The fact that some early cooperatives, such as 1120 North Lake Shore Drive, completed in 1925, were offering rebates and distributing excess revenues to tenant-owners by the end of the decade, made for good news.

The happy cooperative story came to an end, at least temporarily, by the fall of 1930. Over the next several years many, indeed most, of the luxury cooperatives erected in Chicago, particularly the partial cooperatives, failed. Their apartments were put up for rent "at prices *revised for the times*," as one realtor phrased it. With so many apartments unsold in the newer buildings, and a shrinking rental market for expensive units in the partial cooperatives, the heavily leveraged developers—or the cooperative corporations—could not pay their mortgage interest. Individual tenant-owners were unable to shoulder an ever-larger share of the debt, so foreclosures were inevitable. Indeed, Chicago's real estate foreclosures rose 50% from 1929 to 1930. Lawyers stepped in to mediate the mounting claims of debtors and bondholders, and speculators purchased the distressed buildings at a fraction of their cost.[39] Exorbitant legal fees, or so protestors claimed, and deceptive practices added to the general woe.[40] Barely a year or two into their ponderous multi-year loans when the Great Crash occurred, the financial challenges for cooperatives were staggering. More than $600 million of bonds in Chicago had defaulted by 1933.[41] While some 100% cooperative buildings did weather the storm, they were in a minority. Collapse became so common that some banking houses entered the specialized field of refinancing defaulted bond issues.[42] This story has not yet been fully told, and it encompasses a blend of dashed hopes, disappointments, frustrations, and severe hardships, as many equity holders lost their entire investment and were forced to rent, if they could afford even that. Real estate hosannas were replaced by dirges. However, by the early 1940s, and picking up even more after the close of World War II, a number of luxury buildings were purchased back by their tenants, and became cooperatives once again. By then, a third phase of financing had become a significant influence on the apartment house market.

This third era of apartment investment was marked by the heavy involvement of the federal government. Fifteen years of war and depression had left in their wake severe housing shortages across the country. With national rent control still in place, congressional appropriations expanded the Federal Housing Authority's mortgage loan insurance program, itself a New Deal creation. If buildings met certain mandated requirements — strictures that limited rental schedules, ceiling heights, room sizes, and heating systems—the federal government pledged to guarantee mortgage repayment to the funders. Developers and architects rushed in to service the new market and the changed standards. In Chicago, tens of millions of dollars of mortgage debt insured by the FHA in the late 1940s and 1950s resulted in a stream of large apartment structures, many of them on prime lakefront sites. While here and there cooperative or luxury rentals were constructed, developer energy was concentrated on FHA-linked projects. The failure of so many luxury cooperatives a few years earlier did not encourage a resurrection of the type.

The memories of cooperative collapse contributed, in part, to the fourth and final phase of apartment investment, which came with the Illinois legislature's condominium legislation of the early 1960s. The law made possible the sale and purchase of individual apartment units financed by individual mortgages. The security of such an investment, promoters argued, resembled home ownership. Since the purchasers owned their property, they could sell to whomever they chose, although condominium boards generally possessed the right of first refusal. From a trickle in the mid-1960s the condominium enthusiasm grew to a flood in the following decades. By 1980 Illinois ranked just behind Florida and California in condominium units. Rental buildings, large and small, were converted to condominium ownership as renters sought to profit from tax advantages and other benefits that had in the 1920s been the prerogative of cooperatives. Increasingly, developers turned from constructing rental buildings to planning those specifically designed for condominium ownership. While some older building retained the cooperative mechanism of ownership, as a device for new buildings it practically disappeared. The impact of condominiums on growth, neighborhood stability, and apartment living in general was widely debated; the problem of gentrification was quickly acknowledged, although the terminology developed somewhat later.[43] Yet condominiums did permit the planning of more lavish apartment interiors, such as in the Carlyle (1967) and the Warwick (1974) on North State Street and thereafter in the multi-use complexes that girdled North Michigan Avenue. Almost without exception, they became the instrument of choice for developers serving a high-end clientele, although room sizes, ceiling heights, and layouts, for the most part, were surprisingly restrained until the late 1980s and 1990s. That the 5,000 and 6,000 square foot apartments reborn in this later era would, without question, be marketed as condominiums, testified to the absolute dominance of this realty instrument.

IMPROVEMENTS, DEVELOPERS, ARCHITECTS

As in any city, apartment house growth and location reflected broader shifts in taste and policy. Since so many of the luxury apartment houses would be built close to the shores of Lake Michigan, the immense development plans of the Chicago Park District in the 1920s, which included the extension of Lincoln Park northward and the expansion of Lake Shore Drive north and south, energized real estate development there. Improved travel times to the Loop, particularly from the far north and south sides, accessible golf courses and tennis courts, children's play areas and park promenades, all whetted developer appetites in the 1920s. The aggressive marketing of large property holdings—the Lehmann and Leon Mandel estates, the Potter Palmer and Edith Rockefeller McCormick interests primary among them—threw open prime lakefront or near lakefront lots. Rising land values attracted the interest of homeowners whose family mansions had been built only one generation earlier, and when developers came calling, they were ready to sell.

The developers of luxury buildings and a number of the architects with whom they worked merit further study. A whole series of prominent characters and dominating firms—the notorious William C. Bannerman, Herbert Greenwald, the Drake Brothers, Draper & Kramer, Baird & Warner, John Buck, Albert Robin, John Mack, and Raymond Scher—have been described in Miles Berger's massive book, along with a few of the architects, such as Benjamin Marshall, who were important developers themselves.[44] Many of the most significant figures of 20th century Chicago's housing market—Philip Klutznick, Arthur Rubloff, Bernard Weissbourd, for example—had ambitions broader than serving a middle or upper-middle-class market, and their deployment of multi-family housing in the interests of urban renewal constitutes a large story on its own. The impact of schemes like Sandburg Village or Dearborn Park on the socio-economic history of Chicago is immense.

But many other figures—Peter F. Reynolds, Edward Carson Waller, Jr., the Hoguelet brothers, Charles F. Henry, Harold Costello, Thomas Collins, G. H. Gottshalk—remain obscure, and the role that the architects themselves played in financing luxury high rises is largely unexamined. Favorites such as Robert De Golyer, Philip Maher, McNally & Quinn, and Paul Frederick Olsen were often paid, in part or in full, by shares in the buildings they designed. Others—Walter Ahlschlager, John Nyden, B. Leo Steif, Benjamin Marshall among them—were significant real estate investors, and a few lived rather flamboyant life styles. Marshall's lavish North Shore estate was legendary, while Ahlschlager purchased, for $100,000, a country house on 21 acres adjoining the spread of A. Watson Armour.[45] Andrew Sandegren captured newspaper headlines when a drinking party in his near north studio ended in gunshots—fired by him.

The Great Depression hit the architects as hard—sometimes even harder—as it did the developers themselves. A number of architects had links, family or other, with the construction firms and contractors that participated in the building process. In some cases owners and building contractors were the same—the Hugh McLennan firm, with a string of buildings in Streeterville was one of several examples—and they often possessed direct lines of political influence that were vital in mastering the labyrinthine world of zoning and permits. Although national and out-of-state construction firms were active in Chicago, particularly after World War II, many if not most of the buildings in this book were built by Chicago outfits. Some, like Avery Brundage or Paschen Brothers, were important players on the local scene. A large and well-trained network of engineers, artisans, skilled craftsmen, and decorators collaborated with the designers and developers, and were largely responsible for the longevity and livability of the pre-Depression structures. Their stories cannot be told here, but their talents and judgments were fundamental elements of the apartment house saga.

SELLING THE APARTMENTS

Once developers or syndicates had assembled the land parcels and arranged the financing, architects had devised their plans, and contractors had begun construction, the tasks of selling and renting began. A great deal depended on the creation of effective marketing strategies. Developers and syndicates

Streeterville from East Lake Shore Drive, looking south, 1932. (Courtesy collection of David R. Phillips)

were aided, in the 1920s at least, by extensive newspaper coverage. Through the early years of that decade, in the *Chicago Tribune* at least, real estate news was limited to one page or less on Sundays as part of broader market reporting. There were occasional photographs and renderings, but the stories were short and the illustrations scarce. Starting in the fall of 1925, however, "because of increased interest in real estate development, in real estate news and real estate advertising," the *Sunday Tribune* dedicated a special section to real estate, with articles, maps, pictures, and news stories, all edited by Al Chase.[46] For the next three years or so, with occasional lapses, new construction and major real estate transactions were covered extensively and colorfully, in the same part of the newspaper. A squadron of talented architectural renderers usually employed by the architectural firms offered dramatic renditions of the new buildings. Charles Morgan, B. C. Greengard, S. Chester Danforth, and others portrayed these projects in striking poses, emphasizing height and elaborate detail. The late 1920s building boom, as Al Chase and Philip Hampson described it, became a larger strategy whereby "Dad Dearborn" sought to compete with his "Father Knickerbocker" rival to the East; the growing number of luxury high rises testified to Chicago's wealth and ambition, and the real estate journalists tended to endorse the most extravagant fantasies.

Developers, of course, did not leave their destinies in the hands of the press alone. They devised advertisements that ran in selected journals as well as newspapers, and they commissioned professionally designed and elegantly printed brochures, enlisting the talents of significant local artists and prestigious printers. Running occasionally to a dozen pages or more, they contained maps, photographs, floor plans, and debonair renderings. Some were impressive enough to gain entrance into annual exhibitions of fine printing.[47]

Lake Shore Drive, c. 1960, (Arthur Siegel, courtesy Chicago Historical Society)

While a few sought to capture the "Art Moderne" spirit in their prospectuses—227 Delaware Place, for example, despite its conventional architecture, sported a small but smartly designed booklet—most were more conservative and mirrored traditional aesthetic conventions. Type fonts and line drawings emphasized dignity and self-esteem, linking these with domestic associations—399 Fullerton (1927) and the Dearborn Schiller (1928) were typical in this respect. Rhetorical appeals could be practically interchangeable, as the delights of high living were paraded before potential clients, but there were interesting variations in typography and layout. Post-World War II apartment buildings also employed the prospectus as a publicity instrument, but few of them displayed the design refinements of the earlier period.

Buildings were also promoted with displays of model apartments, often furnished by noted decorators or local department stores—Colby's, Carson Pirie Scott, John M. Smyth—and by advertisements run by sub-contractors and suppliers—makers of boilers, stoves, bathroom equipment, insulation, elevators, roofs, utilities companies—illustrating buildings that featured their products. General Electric Refrigerators showed off pictures of 5510 Sheridan Road (1927) and 6700 Crandon Avenue (1928) to demonstrate its popularity among cooperative builders: Standard Plumbing featured the Shoreline (1928) at 2231 East 67th, and McQuay Radiators promoted 1430 Lake Shore Drive (1928). Planted articles listing the names of prominent purchasers or renters added to the "buzz" around specific projects, and columns by economists and real estate publicists sought to reassure nervous

Brochure cover, *3800 Sheridan Road*.
(Private Collection)

investors about the safety of cooperative investments or later, of condominiums.

Another device used to attract attention or cement loyalty lay in the practice of naming. Since the late 19th century owners and developers of apartment houses in the United States had lavished upon them distinctive and rather ambitious names, referring to figures, events, and locations hallowed in American or European memory, to exotic dreams of time and place, or sometimes simply to the immediate family of the builders.[48] In Chicago, building names shared this character or simply reflected neighboring streets—with Arms or Manor or Towers added to them. There were occasional contests sponsored by the developer to name a new building. Sometimes the name—as with the Native American designated Powhatan and Narragansett—set thematic possibilities for architects to develop. At other times, the very absence of a name could be significant. Obeying the observation of historian James Goode, "the grander the name, the less pretentious the apartment house," many of the north lakefront's most imposing buildings simply adopted their address as their name. Indeed, this became a signature device for Gold Coast residences. The risks involved with using showy foreign neologisms were indicated most recently by announcement of a new Sheridan Road condominium to be called the ParVenu.[49]

FLOOR PLANS

The most fundamental element of the apartment house, in the end, lay in the arranged varieties of its individual units. The skill of architects was best displayed in how they organized and manipulated the spaces they worked with into commodious, efficient, and engaging settings for those who slept, ate, entertained, and sometimes worked within them.

Debates about principles of organization for apartment layout go back, once again, to the 19th century. Through many decades, articles ran in American architectural journals evaluating various approaches, foreign and domestic, to exploiting the peculiarities of site shape and size, meeting the need for light, air, and privacy, establishing minimal sizes for kitchens and bathrooms, and providing clear separation of service, public, and private areas. The long, strung-out halls, bisecting apartments of an earlier era, were succeeded by more efficient and more elegant layouts, which varied according to budget and architectural skill. Extremely able planners were at work, particularly in the 1910s and 1920s, including Benjamin Marshall, John Reed Fugard, Andrew Sandegren, Robert DeGolyer, J. Edwin Quinn, Paul Frederick Olsen, and Roy France. They were succeeded in the years following World War II by firms such as Solomon Cordwell Buenz and Hirschfeld, Pawlan, and Reinheimer. The pressure from developers to squeeze every foot of buyable space from a building's footprint led architects in later years, even in luxury buildings, to emphasize different features. While bedrooms might grow smaller, closets and master bathrooms took up more space. The addition of washers and driers, media or family rooms, and home offices consumed the space that had once been allotted for live-in servants. The maids' rooms, so ubiquitous a part of the earlier floor plans, along with the occasional servants' hall, were absent from even the grandest schemes of the 1990s. Internal family privacy and self-containment took over from the kind of privacy ideal that had supported anti-apartment sentiment a century earlier. A common elevator landing today is more tolerable, apparently, than strangers in the household.

The approximately 100 floor plans illustrated in this book suggest both architectural ingenuity and changing social mores. What they cannot do is evoke the more subtle modulations induced by architects and decorators commissioned to design individual units. Photographs of work by David Adler, Walcott and Work, Samuel Marx, and others active in Chicago, suggest the range of possibilities. Successors like Vinci Hamp, Tigerman McCurry, Krueck & Sexton, Booth Hansen, and Searl and Associates have produced their own variations. Some commissions harmonized well with the apartment building's own architecture; others deliberately challenged it. A number of clients, for example, energetically resisted the logic of modern exteriors, preferring their decorators to provide them with highly traditional and eclectic arrangements. Others displayed avant-garde tastes within the most orthodox of buildings.

Photographic firms such as Raymond Trowbridge's and Hedrich Blessing recorded these interiors, many entirely vanished, and provide us with an inventory of preferences and ambitions. Sometimes the photographers transcribed a building's public spaces as well, recalling the comprehensive character of their design. Lobbies, elevators, swimming pools, roof gardens, lounges were, at one time at least, conceived as integral parts of a larger whole, their decorative details carrying out the structure's larger theme.[50] Some of the more extraordinary buildings had the same level of care lavished on their fittings that contemporaneous ocean liners enjoyed; unlike the liners, they are still in service 70 or 80 years later.

It is truly remarkable that these older apartment buildings have survived and continue to be viable in an era that has developed so many throw away landscapes. Such durability reflects well on the original builders and on those who have spent money and energy repairing, maintaining, and restoring what time, weather, and wear have eroded. Of course there have been losses, such as 900 North Michigan and the Walker buildings on Lake Shore Drive. The same energies and developmental urges that powered the grander structures could as easily be responsible for their future destruction in the interest of possibly more profitable successors. The same sense of privilege that attached itself to their creation has undoubtedly helped underwrite their longevity.

Once the stepchild of middle-class respectability, and variously the symbol of personal self-absorption, domestic irresponsibility, and corrupted taste, apartment houses "of the better sort" have emerged as anchors of stability for neighborhood growth and instruments of physical renewal. The course of post-World War II Chicago was powerfully affected by the planning of Sandburg Village and its high rises, for example. The ghettoized apartment buildings of the public housing projects, on the other hand, had an even greater and more malevolent impact on the city fabric. Their residents were never served as effectively as the tenants and owners of the luxury buildings.

If ill-planned, ill-maintained, or deteriorated apartment buildings can become sources of danger and infection to communities, so their rehabilitation may help to reverse active blight. Secure in their lakefront locations, most of Chicago's luxury high rises went largely unaffected by neighborhood change, and they did retain a community of reasonably prosperous inner-city residents during years when urban flight took on epic proportions. The repopulation of cities like Chicago is a complex phenomenon, but older and newer apartment buildings of quality have played a significant role in its development. The future of these buildings depends to a great extent on market forces, even if some are now protected by landmark status. Alongside most of the new towers sprouting skyward, the vintage structures look better and better, and seem destined to last.[51] But Chicago's history suggests that surprise is the only real constant.

APPENDIX

COSTS AND PRICES

ANY SURVEY OF LUXURY housing across more than a century must acknowledge its pricing levels. This book is studded with references to original rental figures, mortgages, and construction costs. How can they be translated into contemporary terms? Economists, historians, and statisticians have developed multiple, and sometimes competing, ways of comparing dollar values across historical time.[52] While it is important to place costs within some framework, it is also necessary to acknowledge the complexity of doing so and the very rough approximations that can result.

Although the Consumer Price Index (CPI) is often employed as a guide, it has been in use only since 1913, and it is not always the best indicator of meaningful change. Some economists use the unskilled wage rate, over time, to compare how long it would take laborers to earn a product's cost. Although there are other instruments as well, including the Gross Domestic Product per capita, I will rely only on the CPI and the unskilled wage rate for comparison here.

Using the CPI, if one begins just before World War I, the conversion factor for changing 1914 dollars into 2002 dollars stands at 18.3. In other words, what cost $10,000 in 1914 would cost $183,300 in 2002. Using a rough measure, then, an apartment renting for $8,400 a year in 1914—the rental for apartments in 1550 North State in 1912 just before it went cooperative—would cost, in today's terms a bit more than $153,000, or $12,750 a month. Similarly, an apartment selling for $20,000 would cost, in today's dollars, $366,000. Although there was no literal CPI for 1900 or before, various analyses suggest an even higher ratio. That is, what cost $10,000 in 1900 would cost $213,000 today.

The cost of living rose dramatically during World War I, an experience that nurtured the creation of upper-middle-class residential hotels to serve clients trying to avoid the cost of employing household servants. The CPI then declined somewhat, and was remarkably stable during the 1920s. The conversion factor, for that intense period of luxury apartment house building between 1924–1929, was about 10.5. Using the CPI index alone then, a 1920s apartment that cost $30,000 would be equivalent to $315,000 in 2002 dollars. Deflation accompanied the Depression, inflation developed during World War II, and for 1950, the conversion factor stands at 7.6. The CPI doubled over the next 25 years, so for 1975 the conversion factor would be 3.4. A $30,000 house in 1975 would, then, be priced today at slightly less than $100,000, using the CPI alone as a guide.

Such figures hide enormous variations in the relative value of various investments, as well as in wage power. Using unskilled wage levels as an indicator, the $10,000 of 1900 is actually worth more than $1 million today; $10,000 in 1912 equals some $850,000, and $10,000 in 1925 amounts to $363,000. To calculate in earning terms what a $30,000 apartment of 1925 might be worth in 2002, one would have to multiply its price by 36, and get a figure of $1,080,000. The CPI would produce just one-third this amount. Which of these figures is more meaningful to contemporary readers depends on their point of view. The CPI is helpful from the standpoint of studying inflation and dollar values; the wage rate is better at suggesting how much of the population realistically had access to these apartments. For comparison purposes, it is worth noting that in the 1920s, $30,000 could buy a 12- or 15-room mansion in Kenwood on the South Side, a highly desirable part of the city; that excellent hotels had rooms available for $2 a night; that Chicago apartments of three or four rooms might rent for well under $40 a month; that men's ties could be purchased from reputable retailers for under $1 apiece; and that a Model T Ford cost $290. In 1925 the average cost of a home in the United States as a whole stood at $4,800, and the average cost of an entire apartment house was $50,000.

Clearly, there is no infallible guide for precise calculation. At a time when a single apartment costing $40,000 in 1925 can have a price tag of $8,000,000 today, a conversion factor of 200, neither the CPI nor the wage scale can explain the differential by themselves or together. Yet, they remind us of the need to translate both price and value, even when, as usual, they are not the same thing.

NOTES

1. A number of historians have traced this evolution, none better than Carroll William Westfall, in a series of important essays, most notable among them "Chicago's Better Tall Apartment Buildings, 1871-1923," *architectura*, 21 (1991), 177-208. See also Westfall, "From Homes to Towers," John Zukowsky, ed., *Chicago Architecture, 1872-1922* (Munich: Prestel, 1987), pp. 267-289.
2. Lewis Mumford, "New York vs. Chicago in Architecture," *Architecture*, 56 (Nov., 1927), p. 245.
3. *The Elite Dictionary and Club List of Chicago, 1887-8* (Chicago: Elite Publishing, 1887), pp. 202-3.
4. Ivan B. Ackley as quoted in *The Economist*, 47 (Jan. 27, 1912), p. 222.
5. See *The Economist* 61 (Jan. 11, 1919) for the 1919 sale of the Gables.
6. A. J. Pardridge & Harold Bradley, *Directory to Apartments of the Better Class Along the North Side of Chicago* (Chicago: Pardridge & Bradley, 1917). The authors described themselves as real estate brokers.
7. "A Fine Apartment House," *The Economist*, 29 (Feb. 28, 1903), p. 277.
8. Pardridge & Bradley, *Directory to Apartments*, p. 17.
9. "Apartment House Construction," *The Economist*, March 11, 1916, p. 518.
10. "Building Statistics," *The Economist*, June 3, 1916, p. 1115. For more on national trends see the report issued by the U. S. Department of Labor, Building Expenditures 1921-27. *Trend Toward Apartment House Living In American Cities* (Washington: Government Printing Office, 1928). Between 1921 and 1927, according to this report, the percentage of Chicagoans living in multi-family dwellings went from 44 to 69%.
11. Note the reports of famous south side houses being sold in the *The Economist*, 42 (Nov. 20, 1909), p. 784. At this point they were being redeveloped for other purposes, as buildings or sites.
12. *A Portfolio of Fine Apartment Homes Composed By The Michigan Avenue Office of Baird & Warner* (Chicago: Baird & Warner, 1928).
13. Ruth G. Bergman, "Home, Suite Home," *Chicagoan*, 7 (Nov. 23, 1929), p. 36.
14. Bergman, "Home, Suite Home" *Chicagoan*, 7 (Dec. 7, 1929), p. 50.
15. Not in every case, however, as the brown brick of 179 East Lake Shore Drive, the Drake Tower, demonstrates.
16. John Craib-Cox, "Houses in the Sky," *Architectural Review*, 162 (1977), pp. 228-231. Craib-Cox suggests that the flashier hotels used their details to attract transient visitors, while the more staid luxury apartments sought to distinguish themselves from their garish neighbors.
17. Carroll William Westfall, "Chicago's Better Tall Apartment Buildings, 1871-1923," *architectura*, 21 (1991), p. 208.
18. Philip Hampson, "14 Story Co-op will rise on Astor," *Chicago Tribune*, March 27, 1927, part 3, p. 1.
19. *Chicago Tribune*, January 21, 1923, part 2, p. 11. Nyden was talking, in particular, of the Commonwealth Hotel being constructed on the corner of Diversey and Pine Grove. Note also the satirical cartoons of shirt front buildings featured in the *Chicago Tribune*, Dec. 13, 1925, part 3, p. 1. They were part of a contest sponsored by the Chicago Face Brick Association.
20. Al Chase, "South Side's Biggest and Newest 'Co-op,'" *Chicago Tribune*, June 15, 1924, part 2, p. 13.
21. Al Chase, "Start 3 million dollar Sheridan Road Co-op," *Chicago Tribune*, Feb. 4, 1927, part 3, p. 1. See also "Nimmons Puts Pep Into 'Roof Tank Tempest,'" *Chicago Tribune*, Aug. 9, 1925, part 2, p. 14.
22. For example, see the description of Sheridan Road's development, *Chicago Tribune*, Apr. 22, 1928, part 3, p. 1; *Chicago Tribune*, Jan. 16, 1927, part 3, p.1.
23. See James Sanders, *Celluloid Skyline. New York and the Movies* (New York: Knopf, 2001), pp. 243-251.
24. Note the Elise Seeds cover of the *Chicagoan*, 4 (January 14, 1928), showing a houseman shoveling snow on top of an apartment house.
25. Al Chase, "World's Tallest Apartments," *Chicago Tribune*, Apr. 10, 1927, part 3, p. 1.
26. Carl Condit, Chicago 1930-1970. *Building, Planning, and Urban Technology* (Chicago: University of Chicago Press, 1974), p. 37.

NOTES

27. *The Economist* annually printed a 25-year digest of permits. See, for example, *The Economist*, 123 (Jan. 28, 1950. p. 109.

28. The story is told most succinctly in Tables LXXXVI-LXXXXVII, Homer Hoyt, *One Hundred Years Of Land Values In Chicago* (Chicago: University of Chicago Press, 1933), pp. 474-476.

29. For comparison sake, one might note that Outer Drive East tripled the number of units in very large prewar luxury buildings like the Edgewater Beach Apartments, which had slightly more than 300 units, and quadrupled the major private apartment complex of the 30s, 5000 N. Marine Drive, by Oman & Lilienthal (1939-40), with its 202 apartments.

30. See *Realty & Building,* 149 (May 18, 1963), p. 5, for a description of the legislation.

31. See Simon Romero, "SoHo-Inspired Lofts With Views of Houston," *New York Times*, Aug. 9, 2003, pp. 1, B 14.

32. Some were modest and extremely cost conscious. Henry K. Holsman was one developer who emphasized this. See *Chicago Tribune*, Feb. 28, 1927, part 3, p. 1.

33. See "Promoting Co-Op Apartments," *The Economist*, 70 (Nov. 17, 1923), p. 1126.

34. Earnest Elmo Calkins, *On Buying A Cooperative Apartment* (Chicago: Kirkham-Hayes Corporation, n.d.), p. 7. The essay was reprinted from *The Spur.*

35. Elmer A. Claar, "Co-operative Apartments," *Western Architect,* 35 (Apr., 1926), p. 42.

36. As quoted in "Co-Operative Apartments," *The Economist*, 71 (Apr. 19, 1924), p. 969. The article contains a list of prominent cooperative buildings and some of their owners.

37. *Advantages and Development of Co-Operative Apartment Homes* (Chicago: Co-operative Apartment Division of The Chicago Real Estate Board, 1929). The peak year, for this survey of 100 buildings, was 1927. These were all 100% cooperatives. The pamphlet listed the names of some 300 owners, from lawyer Cyrus H. Adams of Isham, Lincoln & Beale, to industrialist William Wrigley, Jr.

38. As quoted in *Chicago Tribune*, July 27, 1930, part 2, p. 12.

39. See, for example, the summary in "Outstanding Real Estate Reorganizations in 1932," *The Economist* 89 (Jan. 13, 1933), p. 23, which details, among other collapses, 1430 Lake Shore Drive, 1540 Lake Shore Drive, Eddystone Homes, the Drake Tower at 179 Lake Shore Drive, and buildings including the Narragansett, Aquitania, and Windermere. The 1933 volumes are filled with articles discussing bondholder lawsuits, meetings, reorganization plans, legislative proposals, etc.

40. See *Chicago Tribune*, Sept. 13, 1931, part 1, p. 24.

41. *The Economist*, 89 (March 19, 1932), p. 186.

42. *Chicago Tribune*, July 26, 1931, part 2, p. 12.

43. For more on condominiums see the July 1979 report prepared by Schlaes & Co., *Condominium Conversions in Chicago: Facts and Issues.* This reported noted that 80% of Chicago's 1977 condominium conversions took place on the city's lakefront, and argued that "Conversion is highly localized, less likely to spread than many have believed." In fact, the movement would be far more sweeping.

44. Miles Berger, *They Built Chicago* (Chicago: Bonus Books, 1992), is an indispensable guide to the history of Chicago development. But while it has a very useful bibliography, it is otherwise not annotated.

45. *The Economist*, 75 (June 12, 1926), p. 1677.

46. See the announcement *Chicago Tribune*, Oct. 14, 1925, p. 35. The section was meant to begin Oct. 18.

47. See, for example, entries 10 and 16 in the *Second Annual Exhibition of Chicago Fine Printing* (Chicago: Society of Typographic Arts, 1928). I am indebted to Roger Whidden for this reference. Or see entry 10 in *Exhibit of Fine Printing Produced in Chicago* (Chicago: Chicago Chapter A.I.G.A., 1927). The McNally-Quinn collection in the Burnham Library, Art Institute of Chicago, is rich in examples of this extraordinary genre.

48. For more on apartment naming see Neil Harris, *Building Lives: Constructing Rites and Passages* (New Haven: Yale University Press, 1999), pp. 55-57. Architect John Nyden was one who named buildings after his children. See *Chicago Tribune*, Feb. 13, 1927, part 3, p. 1.

49. See "Coldwell Banker Previews, Spring, 2002," *Chicago Tribune*, March 17, 2002.

50. See the satirical piece, "Co-op 3931," *Chicagoan*, 4 (Nov. 3, 1928), p. 22, in which tenant owners insist that "the new doorman's costume must be wine red to match the upholstery of the tenant's car."

51. See Blair Kamin, "Monuments to Mediocrity," *Chicago Tribune*, Aug. 10, 2003, part 7, pp. 1, 6-7.

52. There is a large literature devoted to the subject. Explanations, definitions, and conversions are made possible on the informative web site run by Economic History Services, http:/eh.net/hmit/compare

NOTE TO READER

As this book is intended to be read both by Chicagoans and non-Chicagoans, some preliminary comments might be in order.

I have divided the apartment buildings into four geographical segments, whose broader identity may be familiar to locals. However, for strangers (and for locals) I have added very brief summaries describing each section.

Addresses of buildings reflect their current status, rather than the broader numbers which are part of building permits, or older street names. Building names, however, while usually still in use, normally reflect the intentions of the original builders, and may no longer be active. The arrangement, within geographical sections, is alphabetical by street address.

The dates provided reflect my understanding of the beginning and completion of construction. They, as well as the building contractors' and architects' names, are taken from a variety of sources: building permits, newspaper articles, notices in *The Economist* and *American Contractor*, and other places. I have used the word builder to refer to the general contractor or chief construction company. In a few cases, two are listed.

This information was not always consistent. The permits, for example, the official records, are filled with errors and misspellings, like many of the other sources. And, contrary to some popular notions, the permits do not include building plans. These have had to be individually unearthed from books, journals, and brochures. I have used my best judgment about all these details, but I'm sure I have erred in various places. I welcome corrections, but the areas of possible disagreement are surprisingly numerous and firm conclusions sometimes difficult to achieve.

The buildings chosen for inclusion reflect, ultimately, my personal decisions. I'm sure I have omitted structures that merit consideration, and included others that can be challenged. Some of my exclusions came from difficulties obtaining historical information, images, and floor plans. My objective was to identify approximately 100 elevator structures whose luxurious amenities, generous or unusual interior spaces, architectural features, locations, or innovations have made them significant in the history of Chicago apartment house life. While a few of them are no longer standing, my emphasis lay on buildings that are still functioning. I also selected small groups of residential hotels, multi-use buildings, and adapted structures that were originally intended for other purposes, because these reflect important moments or trends in the city's luxury high life.

This is not, by any means, a history of Chicago's multiple family dwellings as such. The thousands of two, three, and four-story flat buildings, some of them extremely opulent, most of them serving a different constituency, form another important story. And so does the history of multi-family public housing, which has been analyzed by a series of scholars but which justifies still more historical attention.

This text is far more limited. It focuses on buildings that were, on the whole, marketed to the upper-middle class and above, meant to suggest living options that were attractive, however expensive. It seems clear, for reasons requiring little explanation, that the housing needs of the rich were met far better than the housing needs of the poor, in Chicago as elsewhere, and that bankers, developers, architects, and engineers worked together to satisfy the wants of the economically privileged with far more enthusiasm than they did to serve any others. The contrast is one that many historians—most notably Carl Condit—have pointed out in eloquent and riveting prose.

In the end, this is a book about pictures and plans. A great deal of effort has gone into their assembly and reproduction. The text is designed to synthesize and contextualize them, as well as to suggest areas for further work. The introduction is modestly annotated. Those who are interested in learning more about specific buildings (perhaps their own) will find listed in the building references (pp. 345-6) some citations covering most building entries. They come from my primary sources, *The Economist* (later *Realty & Building*) and the *Chicago Tribune*. These are by no means exhaustive, but they should provide clues for further investigation.

SOUTH SHORE

South Shore Drive. (*Chicago Daily News*, courtesy Chicago Historical Society)

AS A NEIGHBORHOOD, South Shore extends from Lake Michigan to Stony Island Avenue and from 67th Street to 79th Street. Its history stretches back to the mid-19th century, but it began its rapid growth in the 1890s and fully blossomed in the 1920s, when real estate companies undertook the massive development of newly purchased land tracts. The bulk of these tracts was covered with bungalow and three- or four-story flat buildings, but two sectors in particular—Jeffery Avenue and the land bordering Lake Michigan—hosted some high-rise residential developments. A building boom was stimulated by convenient transportation access by both rail and, with the extension of South Lake Shore Drive, by automobile—along with spectacular views along Lake Michigan and Jackson Park. Helping, too, were the presence of nearby public golf courses and the panache of the South Shore Country Club, although the latter was emphatically private and restricted by race and religion.

The luxury high rises of this area boasted many of the same amenities as their north side counterparts, but their scale and opulence were somewhat more restrained. After World War II, more residential high rises were constructed in the neighborhood, and they reflected a spatial shrinkage and unit multiplication that occurred elsewhere in the city. Racial migration patterns decreased the area's appeal for upper middle-class whites who had lived in the older luxury buildings, but the spaciousness and siting of these buildings were permanent assets and appealed to a new generation of residents, many now African-American. Passage of the condominium legislation of the 1960s aided the survival and restoration of a number of these structures.

6700 South Crandon Avenue

Quinn & Christiansen, Architects | E. Edlund, Builder | 1927–28

Exterior, c. 1985.
(Courtesy Commission
on Chicago Landmarks)

This apartment tower was first occupied in late 1928, part of what was then termed the South Shore Country Club District, "the most desirable residential section of Chicago's great south side," according to the 1927 promotional brochure issued by the Kirkham–Hayes Corporation, the building's manager and selling agent. Supported by a limestone base and classically styled loggia entrance, the brick structure has elegant corbelling. A recreation room on the 16th floor sported windows "admitting ultra violet rays" for the benefit of residents' health.

The equity required for the 45 original apartments (five and six rooms, with two larger apartments on the 15th floor) totaled $410,000, besides the proportional shares of the extensive building mortgage. Thus initial prices of apartments ranged from $6,000 to $17,800, and the average monthly costs, for mortgage payments and operating expenses, were somewhere between $150 and $200. As in many other such developments, the architects and builders, Everett Quinn and R. C. Christiansen, were officers and directors of the building corporation, sharing in the sales profits. "Distinctly modern American in architecture," its promoters crowed, with permanent views of Jackson Park and its golf course, yacht harbor, and beaches.

In 1930, rental advertisements described it as "The Most Beautiful 15 Story Apartment Home in Chicago," and referred to its handball courts, billiard room, and banquet hall. Today 6700 South Crandon is a condominium, or, as it likes to call itself, a Crandominium.

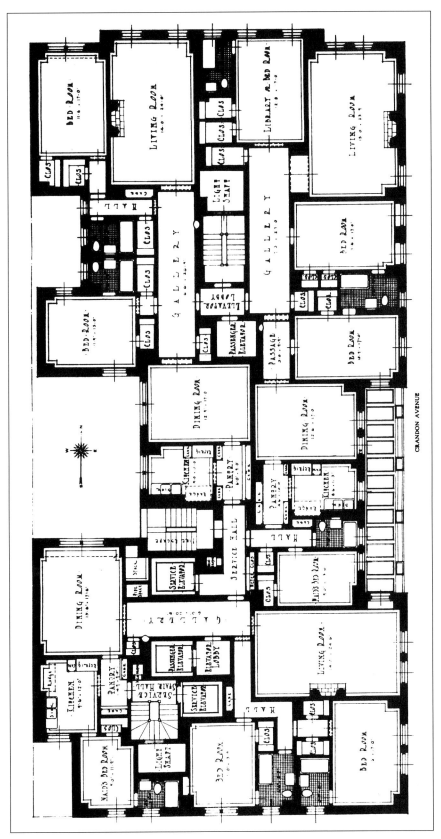

Plan, c. 1928. (*6700 Crandon,* brochure, courtesy Ryerson and Burnham Libraries, McNally and Quinn Collection, The Art Institute of Chicago. All rights reserved.)

6901 South Oglesby Avenue

Paul Frederick Olsen, Architect | A & E. Anderson Co., Builder | 1928–29

Exterior, c. 1985. (Courtesy Commission on Chicago Landmarks)

Paul Frederick Olsen, a prolific designer of Chicago apartment buildings, planned this for developer Harold C. Costello in an English Gothic style, complete with roofline turrets, three-sided, limestone-bordered window bays, gargoyles, and castellated battlements. Built as a 100% cooperative, its brochure emphasized "home-life," and freedom from "the clang and clamor...and fretful hubbub" of city life, along with convenient access to rapid transit, beaches, shops, and a golf course. A landscaped garden built over a 36-car garage, a roof garden, and a paneled lobby were among the amenities of a structure whose equity costs in 1929 ranged from $7,900 for a five-room, lower-floor apartment, to $12,200 for a seven-room apartment on the 11th, or top, floor. Kitchens sported pastel-colored appliances. The 30 apartments represented, in their capital stock of $422,800 and a first mortgage of $875,000, an investment of almost $1.3 million.

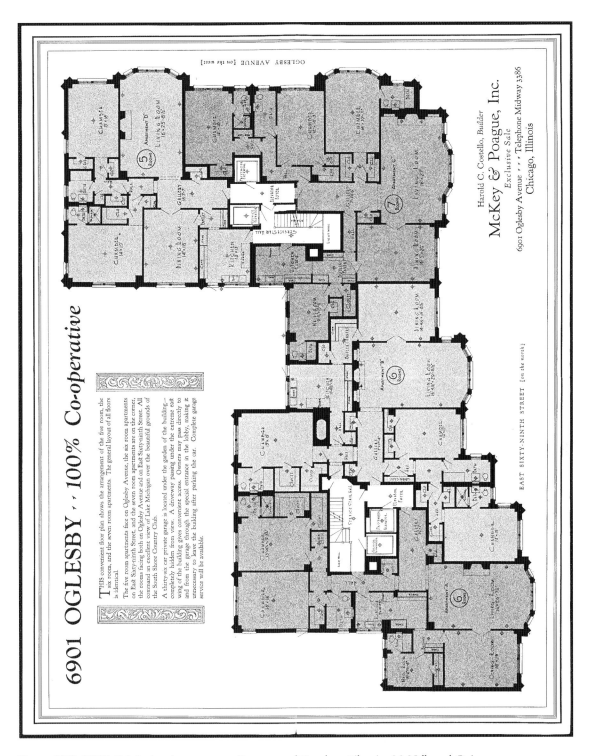

Plan, c. 1928. (*6901 Oglesby*, brochure, courtesy Ryerson and Burnham Libraries, McNally and Quinn Collection, The Art Institute of Chicago. All rights reserved.)

2666 East 73rd Street

THE COASTLAND

Charles Draper Faulkner, Architect, with Quinn & Christiansen | E. Edlund, Builder | 1927–28

ABOVE: Plan of bungalow.

LEFT: Exterior rendering, c. 1939.

BOTH: (Brochure, courtesy Ryerson and Burnham Libraries, McNally and Quinn Collection, The Art Institute of Chicago. All rights reserved.)

Charles Faulkner, a prolific designer of Christian Science churches, many of them in Georgian style, here produced one of his rare apartment houses, and in a Renaissance-revival mode. Faulkner also served as an officer of the building corporation. The Coastland occupies a site just a few feet from "the wild and rugged shores of old Lake Michigan," but it has a north–south orientation.

The 13-story brick building, with limestone and granite trim and two sets of bay windows, was divided into five- and six-room apartments; an eight-room penthouse occupied the top floor. Special features included circular breakfast nooks and a 14-car garage. In 1928, it all was valued at $725,525.33. The *Chicago Tribune* wondered about the 33 cents, but put it down to the pretensions of the "nationally known appraisers."

After enduring hard times in the Depression, the building was sold for $210,000 in 1939. In 1944 it returned to cooperative status, the first of a small group of South Shore apartment buildings to be so restored.

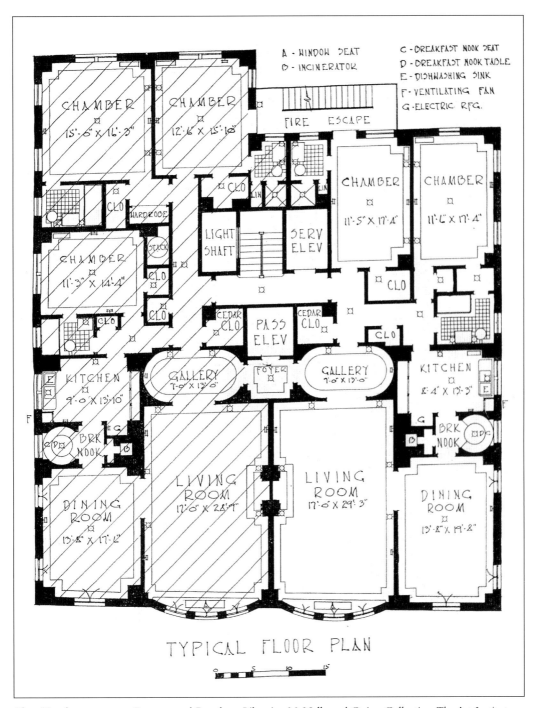

Plan. (Brochure, courtesy Ryerson and Burnham Libraries, McNally and Quinn Collection, The Art Institute of Chicago. All rights reserved.)

2231 East 67th Street

Shoreline Homes

Henry K. Holsman, Architect | Ralph Sollitt & Sons. Builder | 1926–28

LEFT: Exterior, 1927.
(*Illinois Society of Architects Handbook*)

ABOVE: Advertisement, 1926

This 16-story building just west of 6700 Crandon, and at first glance appearing as an integral part of it, also overlooks Jackson Park. It was planned for 50 apartments of six and seven rooms; a 10-room duplex on the 15th and 16th floors had two private gardens. "An Ideal Home for a man of wealth who must have the best," ran a 1930 ad for this rooftop bungalow. Designed by pioneering cooperative developer Henry K. Holsman, in what was described as an "adaptation of Spanish Gothic," the T-shaped structure of red-face brick, with a two-story base and trim of cast stone, has elaborate carvings and quatrefoils, along with a stone pergola. With its neighbor, it ranked among the tallest buildings in South Shore. The original lobby consumed two stories and according to one enthusiastic journalist resembled an "English baronial hall." It is a condominium today.

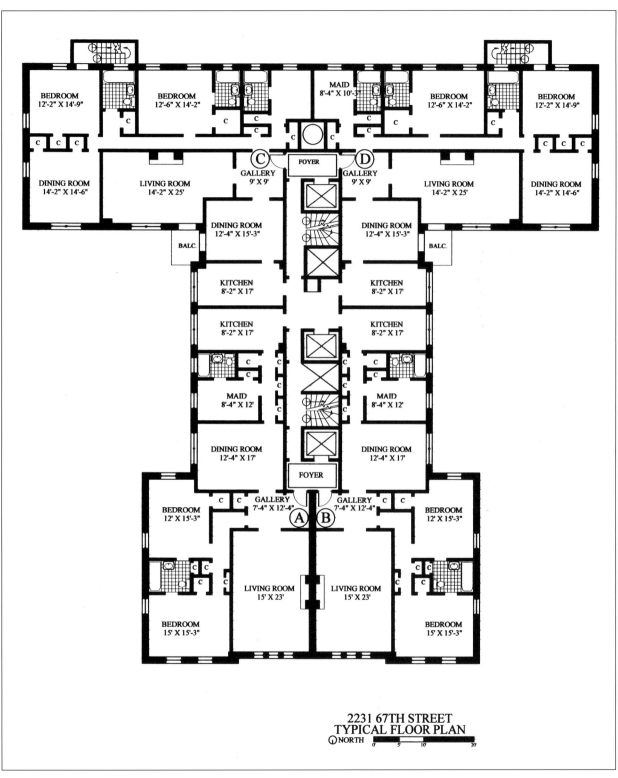

Plan.

7000 South Shore Drive

McNally & Quinn, Architects | H. Janisch, Builder | 1926–27

Exterior. (Brochure, courtesy Ryerson and Burnham Libraries, McNally and Quinn Collection, The Art Institute of Chicago. All rights reserved.)

When first built, this 16-story reinforced concrete building was an ambitious example of the partial cooperative. Divided into two separate units, the eastern portion contained just 31 tenant-owned apartments of six and eight rooms and was served by its own entrance, lobby, and elevators. The eight-room apartments featured circular entrance foyers. "This is said to be an innovation in this town," wrote Philip Hampson in the *Chicago Tribune*, "having been seen only by those having entree to the most select apartments of the Big Town in the East." The western unit contained 149 much smaller apartments, and it was to be leased, furnished, and managed as an apartment hotel by a management corporation. The "iron clad" lease assured building owners that they would not have to pay monthly assessments once they had purchased their apartments, which ranged from $16,000 to $31,000. The real estate taxes, insurance, and interest on the $1.5 million mortgage were to be met by the management corporation's lease on the apartment hotel.

Employing a limestone trim, its Italian Renaissance touches included pedimented windows, balconettes, and balustrades. A stone colonnade enclosed a large court with doorways opening into the two lobbies. The complex contained a dining room, some shops, and other hotel amenities, with "all the dignity and savoir faire that the smart Park Avenue district of New York can lend," declared Hampson, intent on further New York comparisons. Like most other partial cooperatives, the venture failed in the 1930s and is today a rental building.

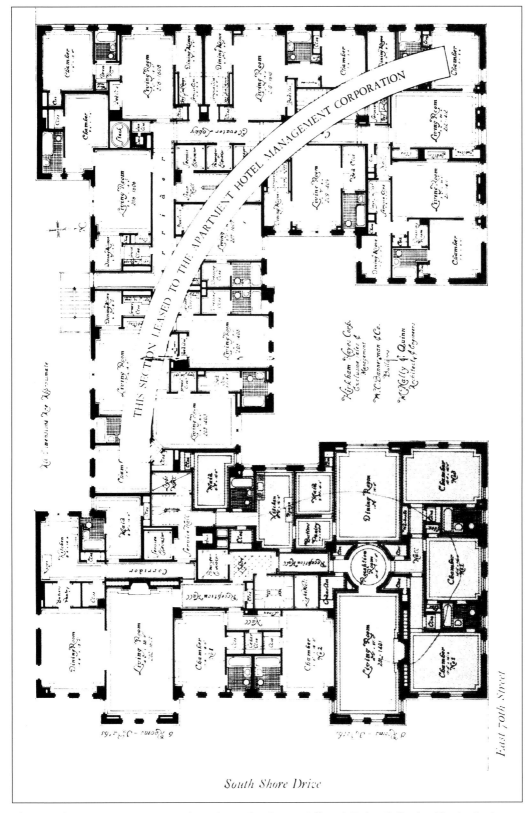

Plan. (Brochure, courtesy Ryerson and Burnham Libraries, McNally and Quinn Collection, The Art Institute of Chicago. All rights reserved.)

7321 South Shore Drive

Windsor Beach Apartments

Robert S. De Golyer, Architect | Lind Construction, Builder | 1927–28

Exterior. (Brochure, courtesy Ryerson and Burnham Libraries, McNally and Quinn Collection, The Art Institute of Chicago. All rights reserved.)

This unusually shaped and rather distinctive 13-story building takes the form of a Maltese cross. It was erected by the architect–developer team of Robert De Golyer and W. C. Bannerman, who were responsible for a series of such ventures. Earlier, another architect, Charles E. Fox, had been commissioned to design a 10-story, $600,000 apartment house for this site by its owner, Edward Carson Waller Jr., but De Golyer and Bannerman soon took over. Built as a cooperative, 7321 South Shore was converted to a rental after financial failure in the 1930s and was reconverted to a cooperative in 1950, which it remains. The 1950 estimates priced the apartments at one-quarter of their 1928 listings, averaging $2,000 a room. The 63 apartments of that day included 24 seven-room and nine eight-room units. The building possesses its own private beach and locker rooms. At one time there was a putting green, tennis courts, and a roof garden.

Evanston-born De Golyer, an M. I. T. graduate who had earlier worked for the celebrated local architect Benjamin Marshall, established his own practice in 1915 and moved through a range of eclectic vocabularies in his many apartment structures. Windsor Beach Apartments bears Northern Italian, or "Lombard," touches—a brochure suggested it be called the Lombardy—and is enhanced by a cloistered loggia entrance, patterned brickwork, and terra-cotta stringcourses and balconettes. An octagonal tower, outlined with special lights, gave the whole, according to the *Chicago Tribune,* something of a "lighthouse effect." To enable construction, the New Jersey Building—a relic of the 1893 Columbian Exposition, which had been towed to this site after the fair had closed and used as a residence—was destroyed.

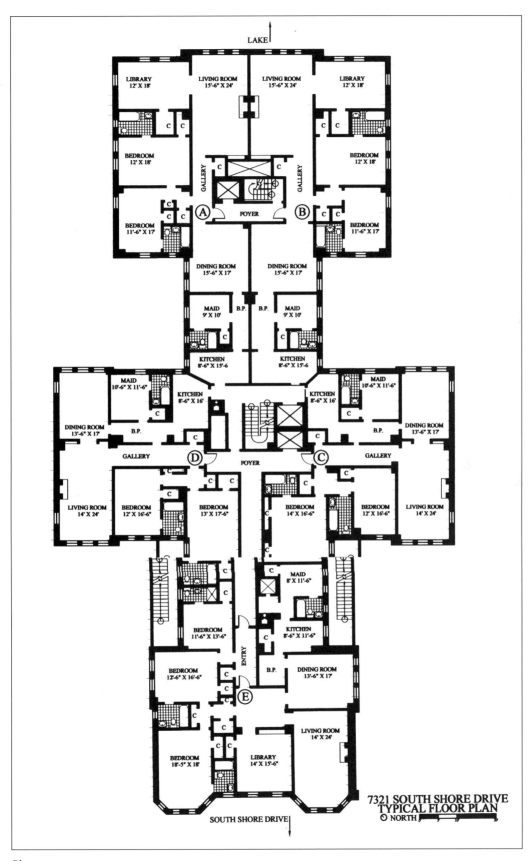

Plan.

HYDE PARK—KENWOOD

Hyde Park, Lake Shore Drive looking north, c. 1932. (Courtesy collection of David R. Phillips)

THESE TWO HISTORIC SOUTH SIDE NEIGHBORHOODS stretch from 47th Street to 59th Street, and from Lake Michigan to Washington Park, and are bound to the life of their most illustrious institution, the University of Chicago. The village of Hyde Park—which originally extended many miles south to what is now Pullman—contained almost rural, resort-like features for much of the 19th century. It voted to join the city of Chicago in 1889. Linked by excellent mass transit and the Illinois Central Railroad to the Loop some six or seven miles away, Hyde Park–Kenwood experienced a building boom just before the Columbian Exposition of 1893. Up to World War I, its housing mixed six-flat buildings, a number of spectacular mansions, and a few luxury hotels. In the 1920s, in the midst of a building boom of sometimes elegant three- and six-flat residences, groups of expensive high rises and elaborate residential hotels also began to dot the area. Dozens of smaller hotels were scattered about and extended south to Woodlawn, serving residents who preferred paying for extensive services over the rigors of housekeeping. Along with a group of luxurious apartment buildings, the most elaborate of these smaller hotels were concentrated east of the Illinois Central tracks, in a strip of land that would run from approximately East 50th Street to the Midway Plaisance. The southward extension on landfill of Lake Shore Drive eased commutation to the Loop, and the lake views and breezes were as satisfying as they were further north. The coming of the Great Depression abruptly cut short ambitious plans for still more luxury high rise buildings, particularly in the Chicago Beach area.

During the 1940s, 1950s, and 1960s, Hyde Park–Kenwood experienced a period of demographic change, physical decay, and urban renewal, which attracted national attention for its social, cultural, economic, and legal implications. East Hyde Park was affected somewhat less than most other areas of the community by these changes, but it did record some significant alterations. The condominium ordinance of 1963 came just in time to save some of its statelier old apartment buildings, as well as many smaller multi-family structures. Some massive apartment house complexes of 30 to 40 stories appeared at this time; while they offered impressive views and a wide array of modern services, they lacked the more lavish spaces of the 1920s.

5000 South Cornell Avenue

Conley and Carlson, Architects | William G. McNulty, Builder | 1929–30

Exterior, 1933. (Hedrich Blessing, courtesy Chicago Historical Society)

This 21-story, modified T-shaped brick structure was the fifth and final residential high rise completed for the Chicago Beach district by 1930. Many others were planned for the area that some 1920s optimists labeled Hyde Park's "Streeterville," a reference to the Near North Side's growing concentration of hotels and apartments. Right through 1931 various promoters floated ambitious visions for the area, with dozens of high rises scattered around 25 acres. With four apartments to a floor, no more than two to each elevator lobby, 5000 Cornell promised "luxurious living at modest cost," certainly more modest than its immediate, more expensive neighbors. Al Chase wrote approvingly in the *Chicago Tribune* that for the first time in the district, "the owner has broken away from the old fashioned precedent that every foot of the lot must be used." The building shape maximized air and light and views of the lake to the east. A "perambulator garage," a "tribute to the coming generation," was accompanied by a playroom on the first floor. Telephone niches, plug-in aerials, and built-in bookcases were among the "refinements which are useful and attractive without suggesting a Goldberg cartoon," wrote one journalist. Light-colored face brick covered all walls, relieved by the two tiers of window bays on its eastern facade.

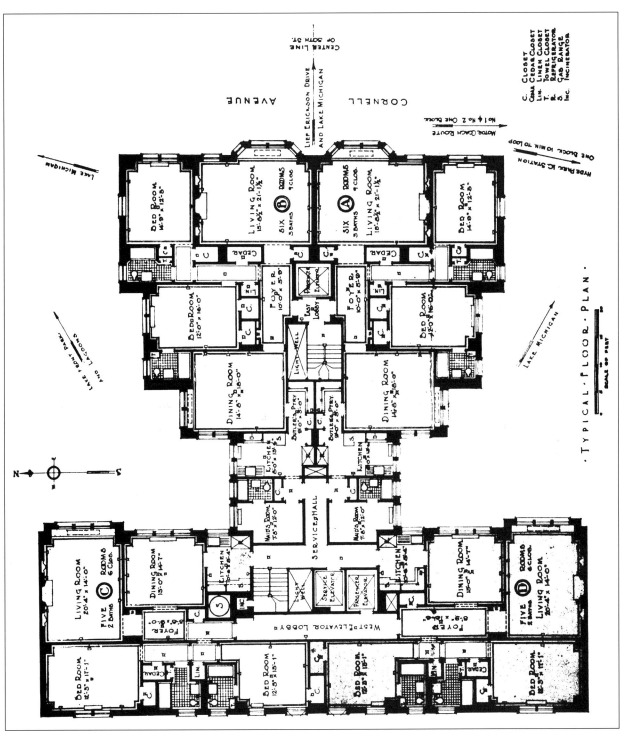

Plan, c. 1928. (*5000 Cornell,* brochure, courtesy Ryerson and Burnham Libraries, McNally and Quinn Collection, The Art Institute of Chicago. All rights reserved.)

5421 SOUTH CORNELL AVENUE

Reichert & Finck, Architects | Geo. L. Arquette, Builder | 1928

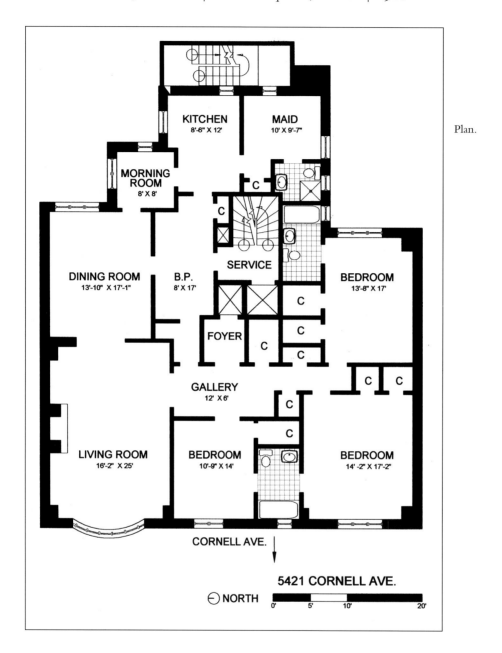

Plan.

These full-floor apartments, priced between $27,000 and $32,000 in 1928, represented a kind of building that could be seen in various parts of the city. Seventeen stories high, it offered tenant owners panoramic views west and east, while allowing a high degree of privacy. "A bungalow on each floor, each floor a bungalow," boasted the promotional brochure. Every apartment contained seven rooms, a breakfast nook, and "a sufficient number of bathrooms to keep family quarrels down to a minimum," noted the *Chicago Tribune*.

Rising "in the heart of a de luxe apartment section," its English Gothic facade of salmon-colored brick and limestone trim boasted roof line gables of oak, trimmed with plaster, an improbably stretched manor house transported to growing East Hyde Park. Viewed from the west, the picturesque roofline is particularly striking. Just two blocks away, the Flamingo Hotel on South Shore Drive shows the same firm's stylistic virtuosity. A mammoth luxury building, the Gotham, also designed by Reichert for the Chicago Beach district, was never built.

5421 SOUTH CORNELL AVENUE

Exterior rendering, 1928. (Brochure, courtesy Ryerson and Burnham Libraries, McNally and Quinn Collection, The Art Institute of Chicago. All rights reserved.)

5801–11 South Dorchester Avenue

THE CLOISTERS

Granger & Bollenbacher, Architects | E.P. Strandberg Co., Builder | 1927–28

Exterior, 1929.
(Architectural Record)

Built originally as an 84-apartment cooperative, the Cloisters was designed to service University of Chicago faculty members and has always been home to a substantial number of them. Meant to harmonize with the limestone gothic towers of the nearby university, the building's red brick, 13-story Romanesque exterior with limestone trim was further emphasized by a quartet of stone entrance arches. Similar in type and construction to "the co-operative apartment buildings which have been erected on Park Avenue, New York City, during the last few years," the Cloisters emphasized privacy with four separate elevator foyers placed around a landscaped courtyard whose cloister boundaries were flagged with slate. Originally a roof promenade was planned as well.

The apartments themselves range from four to seven rooms, each with its own carved stone fireplace. While a substantial number of apartments were quickly sold—the sculptor, Lorado Taft, was one early purchaser—the Cloisters is a rental building today, purchased by the University of Chicago for slightly more than $1 million in 1950. It is owned today by the Baptist Theological Union. Besides building another luxury high rise on North State Parkway, this architectural firm, consisting of two M.I.T. graduates, also built the downtown Chicago Club on Michigan Avenue and completed a series of commissions for colleges and universities.

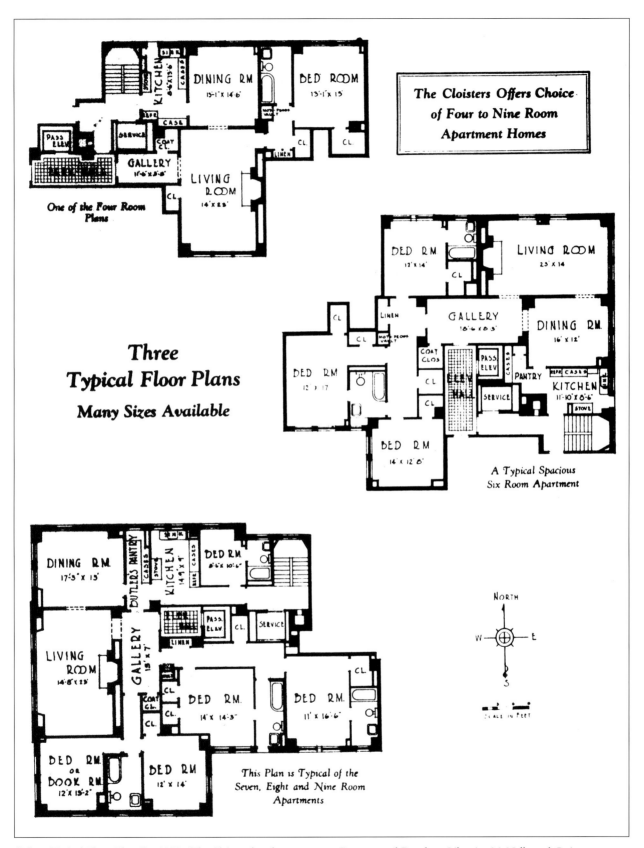

"Three Typical Floor Plans," c. 1928. (*The Cloisters,* brochure, courtesy Ryerson and Burnham Libraries, McNally and Quinn Collection, The Art Institute of Chicago. All rights reserved.)

5000 South East End Avenue

Robert S. De Golyer, Architect | Avery Brundage, Builder | 1927–28

Exterior, 1930. (Hedrich Blessing, courtesy Chicago Historical Society)

5000 East End Avenue was the first and largest of the building projects achieved for the Chicago Beach tract, a grandly ambitious enterprise slated to cost $25 million but that grew almost 10 fold, at least as a plan. Placed 300 feet north of the old Chicago Beach Hotel, some 28 stories high, the gray brick and terra-cotta building sits on a five-story stone base; its modified "Tudor Gothic" details are most notable at the roof line and entrances. With its 97 planned apartments, two entrances—only one is used today—and two duplex "bungalows" occupying the 26th and 27th floors, it stood as the tallest structure south of the Loop until well after World War II. At the time of its construction, the owners declared it Chicago's tallest apartment house. For a couple of decades it enjoyed an unobstructed view east to the lake. The engineering team of Smith, Clute, and Brown frequently worked with architect Robert De Golyer. Sales to prominent businessmen and professionals were brisk in 1928 and 1929. Built as a cooperative, 5000 East End remains one today.

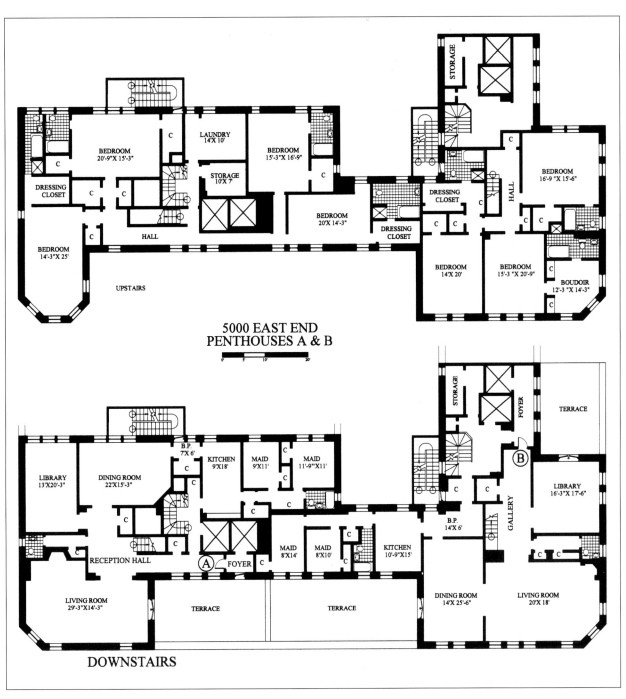

Plans of penthouses A and B.

5555 South Everett Avenue

JACKSON TOWERS

Walter Ahlschlager, Architect | Avery Brundage, Builder | 1924–26

Exterior of 5555 South Everett, seen from Museum of Science and Industry, 1951. (Margaret Mead, courtesy Chicago Historical Society)

Plans for this opulent structure facing Jackson Park were nurtured by an election decision to fund restoration of the 1893 Fine Arts Building—today's Museum of Science and Industry—just to its south. "One of the three greatest works of architecture to be found in the world," according to "some of our most famous artists," the rebuilt museum constituted part of the apartment building's scenic landscape. The land itself was part of a much larger parcel purchased from the Lehmann Estate in late 1923 for $469,000. Subdivided in 1924, this lot was sold for $211,000 to a syndicate headed by the owner of the Del Prado Hotel.

Jackson Towers, conceived in a late Spanish Renaissance style with an 18-story central tower and two 15-story wings—minus its missing 13th floor—boasts three passenger and three freight elevators for its 72 apartments. The L-shaped brick structure, festooned with elaborate terra-cotta decorations and stone trim, is reached through a massive porte cochere. Almost one quarter of the apartments are duplexes, some of them with stuccoed two-story living rooms and floor to ceiling fireplaces suggesting a Gloria Swanson movie set. Their tall, double-arched windows give a semi-ecclesiastical—a *Chicago Tribune* journalist suggested "cathedral"—aspect to the facade.

Architect Walter Ahlschlager was a noted hotel and theatre designer whose most celebrated commission was the fabled Roxy Theater in New York. An active investor and developer, Ahlschlager was also the architect for the Peabody Hotel in Memphis, Tennessee, the art deco Netherlands complex in Cincinnati, Ohio, the Medinah Club, today's Intercontinental Hotel in Chicago, and the unbuilt Crane Tower, which in 1929 would have been Chicago's tallest building. Announced as a partial cooperative, rentals from ordinary apartments were meant to supply income for the duplex owners. Jackson Towers later made all its apartments available for sale. The duplex purchase prices ran from $14,000 to $17,000 in the 1920s. Jackson Towers failed during the Depression, became a rental building—attracting, among others, baseball magnate Charles Comiskey—and was returned to tenant ownership through condominium conversion in the late 1960s.

5555 SOUTH EVERETT AVENUE

Exterior, c. 1926. (Courtesy collection of David R. Phillips)

Living room, W.J. Moore residence, 1926. (*Western Architect*)

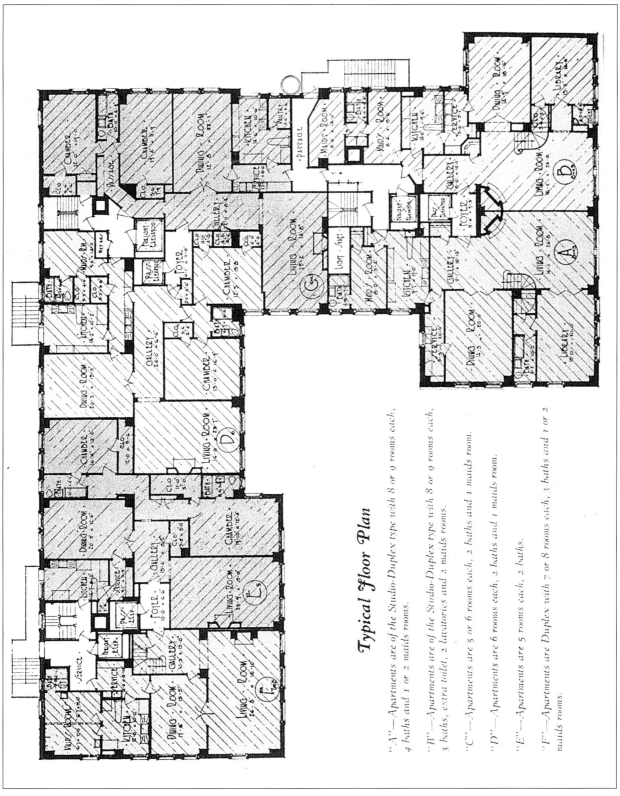

Plan, c. 1920. (Brochure, courtesy Ryerson and Burnham Libraries, McNally and Quinn Collection, The Art Institute of Chicago. All rights reserved.)

1640 East 50th Street

THE NARRAGANSETT

Leichenko & Esser, Architects | Charles B. Johnson & Son, Builder | 1928–30

The Narragansett (left) and the Powhatan (right), 1930. (Hedrich Blessing, courtesy Chicago Historical Society)

Financed and constructed by the same team that built the Powhatan, its near neighbor to the east, the Narragansett had different architects of record but shared the same decorating architect, Charles Morgan. Somewhat smaller and a bit less opulent than its neighbor, the Narragansett's limestone-based verticality and patterned terra-cotta spandrels complement the Powhatan, and the two buildings balance one another. Befitting its name, the Narragansett facade does contain some American Indian heads, and small, carved elephants add an unexpected touch of East Indian exoticism, which the *Chicago Tribune* found to symbolize strength. More traditional terra-cotta ornaments and zodiacal references round out the thoroughly eclectic mix. The elegant lobby mixes rich paneling and art deco era chandeliers, and when the Narragansett was first announced, a handball court and gymnasium were promised for the first floor. While originally each floor contained three two-bedroom apartments, a number of condominium owners have added rooms or combined apartments.

The architects, Peter M. Leichenko and Curt A. Esser, built smaller apartments throughout the city and in 1950 designed, on the corner of Rush and Ontario, the building that would contain Mies van der Rohe's famous Arts Club interior.

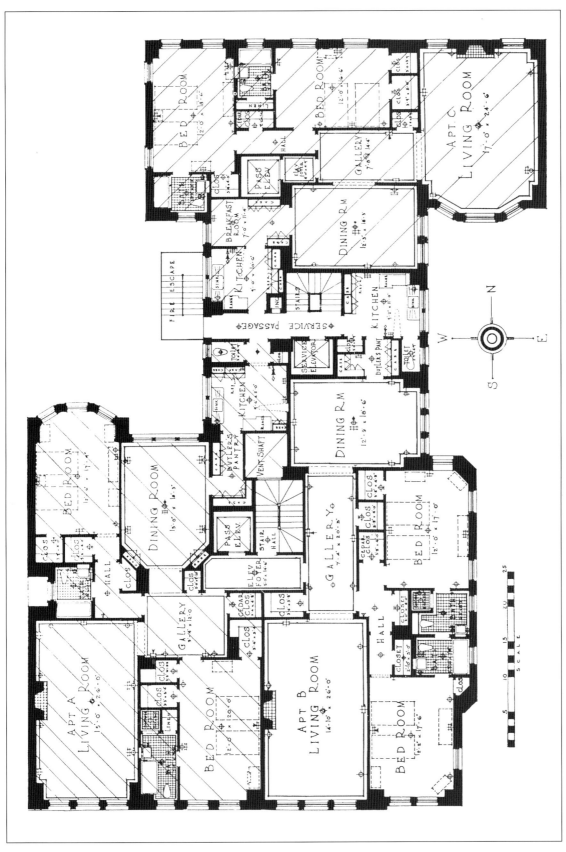

Plan. (Sexton, *American Apartment Houses*, 1929)

1648 E. 50th Street–
4950 South Chicago Beach Drive

THE POWHATAN

Robert S. De Golyer, Architect | Charles B. Johnson & Son, Builder | 1927–29

Lobby, 1930. (Hedrich Blessing, courtesy Chicago Historical Society)

The Powhatan, soaring 22 stories, is the most extravagant of the South Side's apartment high rises. It stands on properties developed in the late 1920s because of the Chicago Beach Hotel's surrender of its riparian rights and the extension of the Outer Drive. An art deco landmark inside and out, the limestone-faced Powhatan bears the influence of Eliel Saarinen's second place entry in the Chicago Tribune Tower Competition just a few years earlier, as well as the design ideals of Charles L. Morgan, the associate architect. Morgan was an active graphic artist, avowed modernist, and associate of Frank Lloyd Wright. He was responsible for the colorful mosaics and specially designed tiles lining the inner and outer lobbies as well as the elegant ballroom and the terra-cotta details on the exterior. A couple of mosaic panels in the swimming pool suggest the mural abstractions at Wright's Midway Gardens, where Morgan had worked; that complex was being demolished just as the Powhatan was nearing completion. Robert De Golyer handled the interior planning.

At various times intended for three apartments a floor, and then for two apartments of six and ten rooms, the final plan created two tiers, each served by its own elevator, of seven and nine room units. The attended elevators retain their original deco features and paneling and they open directly into many apartments. Bathrooms are numerous, and are primarily clad in the pastel colors 1920s plumbing specialists favored. The well-preserved ballroom sits atop the building, with terraces north and south. "All the luxuries of an ocean liner," marveled a contemporary Chicago journalist. American Indian references can be found throughout, from the entrance doors and light fixtures to the extraordinary spandrels, whose colorful abstractions were intended to evoke native themes and the waters of Lake Michigan. Built as a cooperative, at the cost of $2.35 million for land and building, the Powhatan, with its 40 apartments, remains a cooperative today.

1648 E. 50th Street – 4950 South Chicago Beach Drive

Exterior from the east, 1996. (Bob Thall, courtesy Commission on Chicago Landmarks)

Swimming pool, 1930. (Kenneth A. Hedrich/Hedrich Blessing, courtesy Chicago Historical Society)

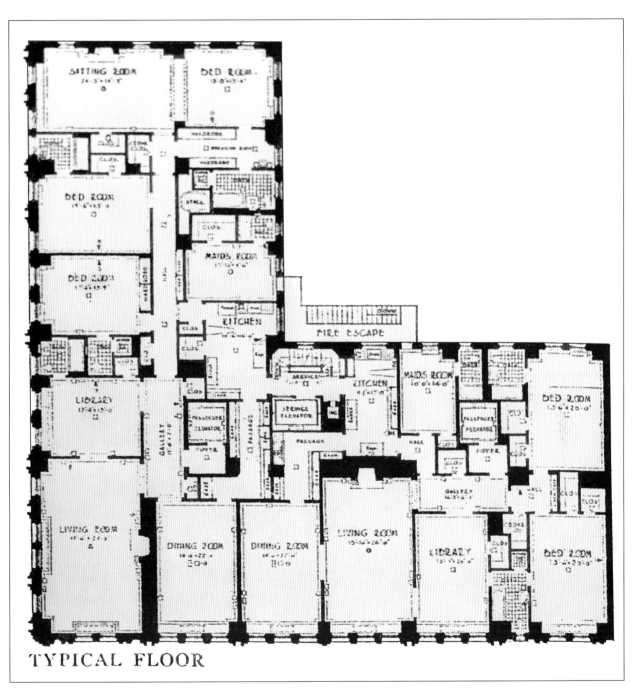

Plan, 1930. *(Architectural Forum)*

1648 E. 50th Street – 4950 South Chicago Beach Drive

Detail of doors, 2003.

1648 E. 50th Street – 4950 South Chicago Beach Drive

Mosaics in entry. Charles Morgan, designer, 1929.

1321 East 56th Street

TOWER HOMES

Henry K. Holsman, Architect | McNulty Construction, Builder | 1929

Exterior, 1931.
(Chicago Architectural
Photographing Company,
courtesy collection
of David R. Phillips)

Much further from Lake Michigan than almost any other building in this book, 1321 East 56th residents nonetheless enjoy fine views because it remains, at 14 stories, the only tall structure on its block. Henry Holsman, a crusader for modestly priced cooperative apartments, managed to keep land and building costs to $240,000. The 12 owners confronted total obligations of only $20,000 apiece for the seven room apartments, each with a wood-burning fireplace. The brick exterior walls change gradually in color as they rise, from "shades of purple brown," in the *Chicago Tribune* description, to a "pink buff." On top, near the battlemented roof line that hides elevator penthouses and acknowledges the gothic of the nearby University of Chicago, an elaborate rooftop recreation facility was planned, safe and child friendly. Thus the whole 50 by 50 foot site occupied by the building was "given back for outdoor use in a form better than the same area could be arranged on the ground," Holsman argued. 1321 remains a cooperative today.

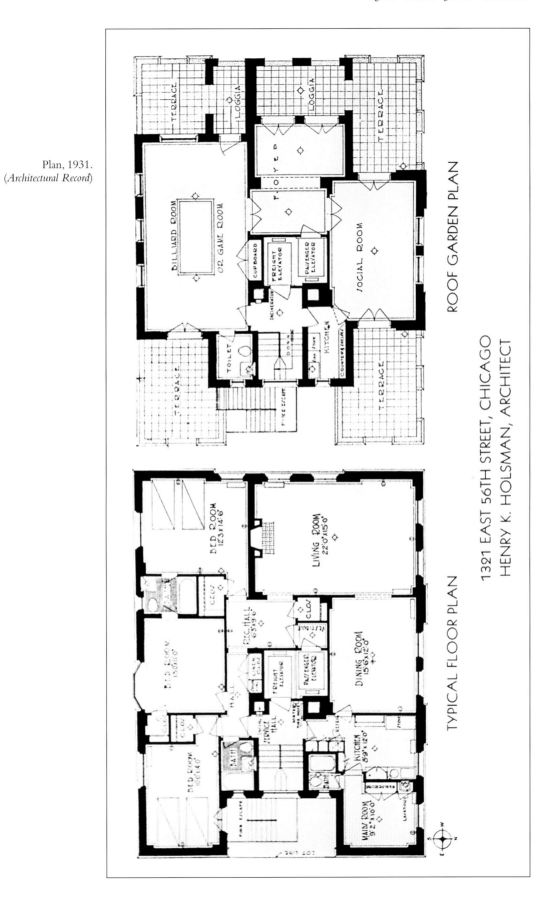

Plan, 1931.
(*Architectural Record*)

1644 East 56th Street

THE WINDERMERE

C.W. & George L. Rapp, Architects | Thompson Starrett, Builder | 1922–24

Exterior, c. 1930. (Courtesy collection of David R. Phillips)

Rapp & Rapp's plans were unveiled in 1917 and rumors about its construction went back to 1910. When it finally opened in 1924, the New Windermere Hotel was hailed as the "South Side's Greatest Hostelry" and the "most magnificent improvement" ever made in the area. The $3.6 million Windermere East as it was called is a C-shaped, classically detailed 12-story structure that faces Jackson Park and today's Museum of Science building. It stood just to the east of the famous old Windermere, which had been built for the 1893 World's Fair but is no longer extant. The two were connected by tunnels. The old Windermere had wired every room for a telephone, a novelty in 1893; the new version wired each of its rooms for radio as well. Six apartments on each floor out of 200 apartments in all had full kitchens, despite the hotel's ballroom and dining rooms; many of the other apartments had kitchenettes.

Designed primarily for long-term residents rather than transients, the Windermere's only real competition on the South Side was the Shoreland, and they split visiting celebrities between them. Clad in cream-colored brick and trimmed with terra-cotta, the building's elaborate vestibule—which bore a strong resemblance to the intricate ticket kiosks fronting Rapp & Rapp's extraordinary theaters—serviced both pedestrians and automobiles. Foreclosed during the Depression, in the 1970s it was purchased by the University of Chicago. In the 1980s, the Windermere was resold and renovated as a rental apartment building.

Porte cochere, 1938. (Hedrich Blessing, courtesy Chicago Historical Society)

1644 East 56th Street

Exterior, 1938. (Hedrich Blessing, courtesy Chicago Historical Society)

1644 East 56th Street

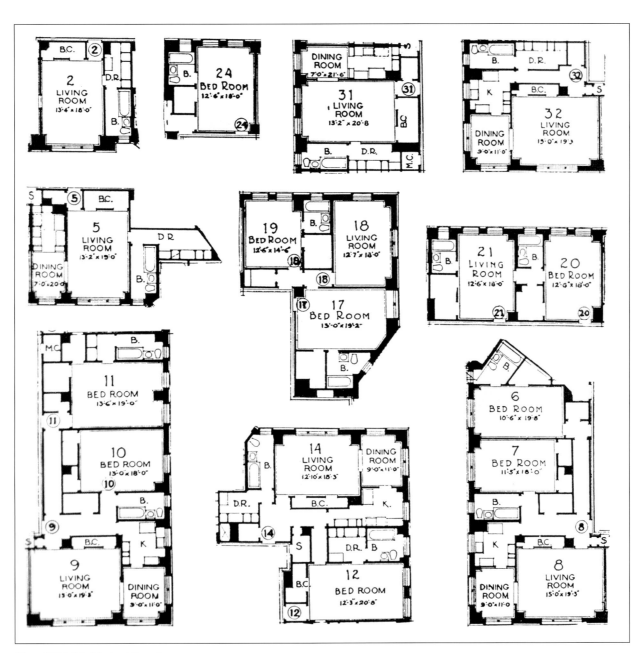

Plans, 1924. (*Architectural Forum*)

5454 South Shore Drive

The Shoreland

Meyer Fridstein & Co., Architect | G.H. Gottshalk & Co., Builder | 1925–26

5490 South Shore Drive (left) and the Shoreland (center), with landfill for Lake Shore Drive, looking west, 1926. (Courtesy collection of David R. Phillips)

Announced as an $8 million project in 1925, this was the South Side's largest residential hotel. It was intended not only to accommodate full-time residents who enjoyed the surrounding parks and nearly constructed Outer Drive connection with the Loop, but it was to serve as a hotel for transients who were expected to visit the restored 1893 Fine Arts Building, thought of for a time as a site for building trade conventions. Eleven stories high, with neoclassical, medieval, and baroque inspired details, the U-shaped structure's detailed ballroom and dining room made it a center for elaborate entertainments in the 1920s, 1930s, and 1940s, and it hosted many of the teams visiting the White Sox at Comiskey Park. Of pressed brick, terra-cotta, and Bedford limestone, its monumental scale, porte cochere, and dramatic outlines give it a powerful presence on the lakefront.

Like its great sister hotels on the North Side and the nearby Windermere, the Shoreland provided an extensive set of shops and services, including an indoor miniature golf course. "Built for homelovers," it advertised in 1926, some housekeeping suites ranged up to nine rooms and rentals of up to $1377 a month. The Shoreland furnished some of its permanent residents with their own silver, glass, china, and linens. As its glories waned in the 1970s the hotel was purchased by the University of Chicago and converted to an undergraduate dormitory. Its immediate future is now uncertain.

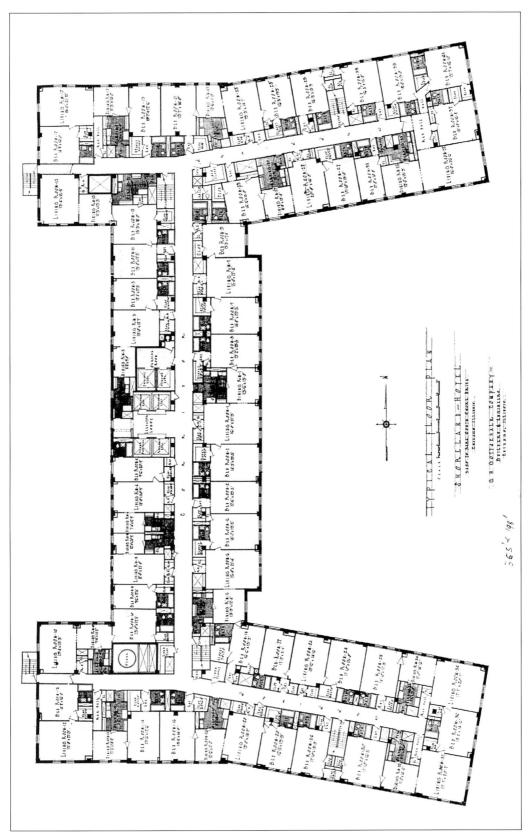

Plan, c. 1925. (Brochure, courtesy Ryerson and Burnham Libraries, McNally and Quinn Collection, The Art Institute of Chicago. All rights reserved.)

5454 South Shore Drive

Lobby, 1928. *(Advertisement, Illinois Society of Architects Handbook)*

5454 SOUTH SHORE DRIVE

Lobby redecoration, 1937. (Hedrich Blessing, courtesy Chicago Historical Society)

5490 South Shore Drive

Jackson Shore Apartments

C. W. & George L. Rapp, Architects | G.H. Gottshalk & Co., Builder | 1916–17

Exterior, 1945. (Hedrich Blessing, courtesy Chicago Historical Society)

The Rapp brothers were Chicago's most prominent cinema architects during the 1920s. Their many theaters included the Chicago and the Uptown. In this distinctive early addition to the southern lakefront created for Edward G. Carter, the Jackson Shore had the largest luxury apartments in any Hyde Park high rise. One of the Rapp brothers lived just a few blocks away.

The 12-story structure—its top floor meant to house extra servants—is of cream pressed brick and a ground-story Bedford stone base with classical details. It is most distinguished by its cylindrically shaped, six-windowed north and south corners. These contain the impressive sunrooms, or "orangeries" in the brochure floorplan, for each of the building's 20 apartments. Facing east, and originally just yards away from Lake Michigan, landfill and the coming Outer Drive would eventually distance the building from the shore while providing extensive neighboring park space. A small porte cochere serves the building's southeast corner; another entrance in the center is no longer used. Apartments were expected to rent between $350 to $500 a month, and the total cost was estimated to be more than $900,000.

Builder, and in time owner, G. H. Gottshalk was also the builder of the mammoth Shoreland, its immediate neighbor. Today, 5490 South Shore Drive is a cooperative.

5490 South Shore Drive

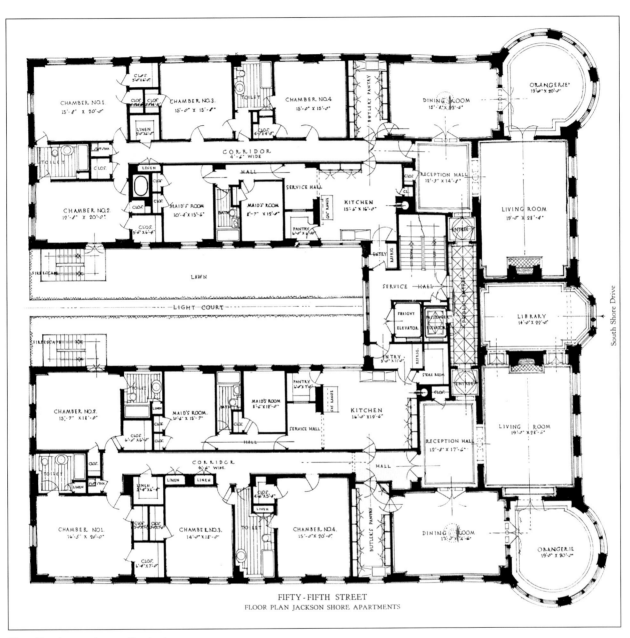

Plan. (Brochure, private collection)

Entry hall into living room, residence. Berta Shapiro, interior designer, 1995–1998. (Courtesy Hedrich Blessing and owner)

5490 South Shore Drive

Library, residence. Berta Shapiro, interior designer, 1995–1998. (Courtesy Hedrich Blessing and owner)

5530–32 South Shore Drive

THE PROMONTORY

Ludwig Mies van der Rohe and Pace Associates, Architects; Holsman & Holsman & Klekamp, Consulting Architects | Peter Hamlin Construction, Builder | 1947–49

Exterior from Lake Michigan, 1950. (Bill Hedrich / Hedrich Blessing, courtesy Chicago Historical Society)

This celebrated and much described building was Mies van der Rohe's first completed apartment house and was the prototype of the high rise slabs soon associated with his name. Twenty years earlier, John Eberson designed an elaborate 18-story beach and country club for the site, but it was never built. The Promontory's developer, Herbert Greenwald, Mies' most enthusiastic and most successful private American client, crusaded energetically on its behalf.

Twenty-two stories high and planned for approximately 120 separate apartments—a few would be combined—the double-T structure is divided into two distinct units sharing a common ground floor lobby. An exposed reinforced concrete frame forms the structure. Originally gray, the building has aged to a light brown. A parking lot just to its west, which originally was a landscaped area with a small parking strip, is reached by simple porte cocheres to the north and south. Administered by a somewhat unusual cooperative trust that still runs the building, the Promontory's modernity and comparatively modest pricing attracted immediate attention and forecast the democratizing trend of lakefront development for Chicago apartment houses. The luxurious spatial amenities of its predecessors were abandoned, but the geometries and rhythms of Mies' spare aesthetic possess their own drama.

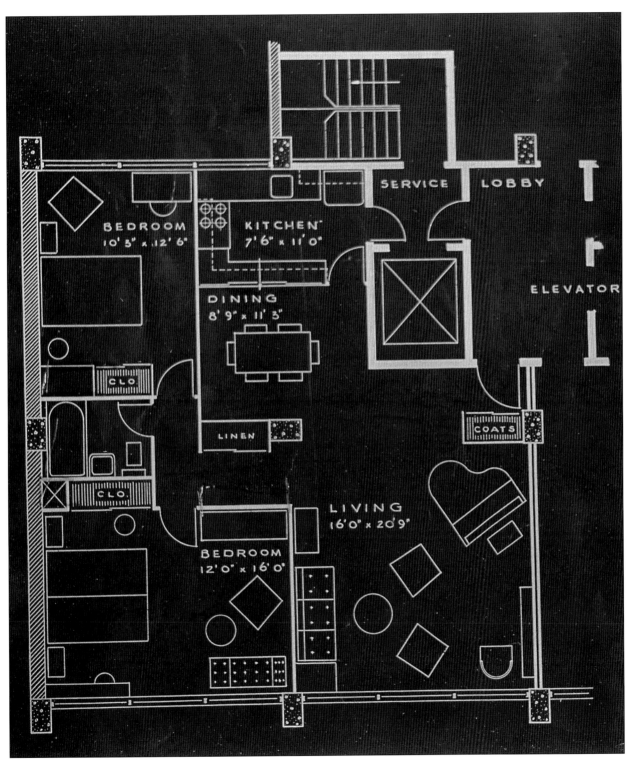

Plan, two-bedroom apartment. (Brochure)

5530–32 South Shore Drive

Interior. Eppenstein and Schwab, decorators, 1950. (Hedrich Blessing, courtesy Chicago Historical Society)

5530–32 South Shore Drive

Exterior. (Hedrich Blessing, courtesy Chicago Historical Society)

5830–44 South Stony Island Avenue

VISTA HOMES

Paul Frederick Olsen, Architect | Avery Brundage, Builder | 1925–27

Exterior, 1941. (Hedrich Blessing, courtesy Chicago Historical Society)

Vista Homes was the largest Chicago building developed by Albert W. Swayne, a prominent proponent of cooperative apartment living. Just a few years earlier, the same site had been projected to host a giant $10 million hotel. Seventeen stories high, with eight apartments on a typical floor, the building has four sets of passenger and freight elevators. "Towering high above the Midway, as picturesque as a Gothic castle and as efficient as the combined talent of the building field could make it," its promotional brochure claimed this was the largest cooperative building in the world. Its 120 apartments certainly entitled it to boasting rights. They ran from four rooms resembling "tiny suburban cottages" to "spacious 11-room apartments as pretentious as a town house." Enthusiasm for cooperative housing runs through its early tenant-owner newsletter, which treats the complex like a small village.

Constructed of red brick and Bedford stone trim, the pinnacled roof line, stone balconettes, and stained glass windows enliven the building's U-shaped profile. Alongside it just to the south, a huge athletic club was proposed and designed, but it was never built. In its place are a series of individual gardens maintained by the current tenant-owners. Connected to the building by tunnel is the "World's 1st Co-Op garage," two stories high with room for more than 100 cars, also designed by Olsen.

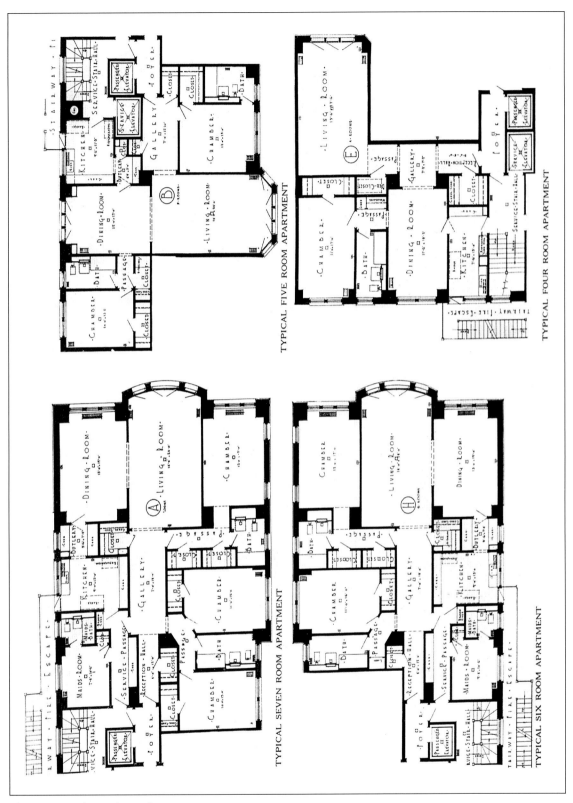

Plan, 1927. (*Architectural Record*)

NEAR NORTH SIDE

East Lake Shore Drive and beyond, 1940s. (Courtesy Commission on Chicago Landmarks)

WHILE SOME OF THE BUILDINGS IN THIS SECTION fall literally outside the boundaries of the Near North Side as Chicagoans understand it, extending as they do from the lake front to Dearborn Street and from just south of Randolph to North Avenue, they occupy what remains the most central, most concentrated, and, except for the Lincoln Park section, most expensive residential area of the city. More recent housing on the near west and near south sides has added impressive apartment complexes, but Streeterville and the Gold Coast have accounted for much of Chicago's most fashionable apartment housing for almost a century. Historians have followed the movement of wealthy, socially prominent families into this area during the late 19th century. They were drawn by individual establishments such as the elaborate Potter Palmer "castle" on Lake Shore Drive, the home of the city's society queen, encouraged by real estate developers—Potter Palmer among them—with the promise of elegant new apartment buildings. At the start of this movement many of them were only three or four stories high. In the years before World War I momentum, like building height, grew. The continuing improvements to Lake Shore Drive and the prestige of a lakefront address and view were permanent advantages, although neighboring streets—Astor, Scott, Dearborn and State Parkway—acquired their own cachet.

In the 1920s the elaborate town houses that had been erected in the 1880s and 1890s began to come down in some numbers, replaced by the high rise apartment buildings that are so prominent a part of these neighborhoods. Some town houses remain, projecting a distinct flavor to the area, but this process of replacement intensified after World War II. The newer buildings were higher and contained more units; they also offered, for the most part, smaller and more simply appointed apartments. The views and the location, with its proximity to beaches, hotels, promenades, restaurants, and shopping, remained attractive, and even gained in appeal. After filling out Lake Shore Drive and some contiguous streets, developers turned their attention to sections just north of the river and a bit further west. There, in the 1990s, on Erie, Huron, Superior, and Grand, came additional structures, offering prospective buyers larger and more idiosyncratic spaces than had previously been the norm. As this is written a number are being completed; others remain potential.

1200 North Astor Street

McConnell Apartments

Holabird & Roche, Architects | Pedgrift, Freeman & Co., builder | 1897

Exterior. (*Chicago Architectural Club Annual, 1896–99*. The Art Institute of Chicago. All rights reserved.)

This eight-story structure was built for John McConnell, who had recently purchased the northwest corner of Astor and Division Streets. When the building was sold in 1923 for $250,000, *The Economist* claimed it as the first modern fireproof apartment building in Chicago. This may be disputed, but the apartments themselves, originally two to a floor, were large and lavishly appointed, rented by socially prominent families. Servants' rooms took up the top floor. Massive in effect, even if small by today's standards, the red brick, limestone, and terra-cotta structure is supported by a steel frame, its corner bays evoking some of William Holabird and Martin Roche's celebrated commercial buildings in the Loop. Subsequently subdivided into smaller units, the McConnell Apartments is today a condominium.

1200 North Astor Street

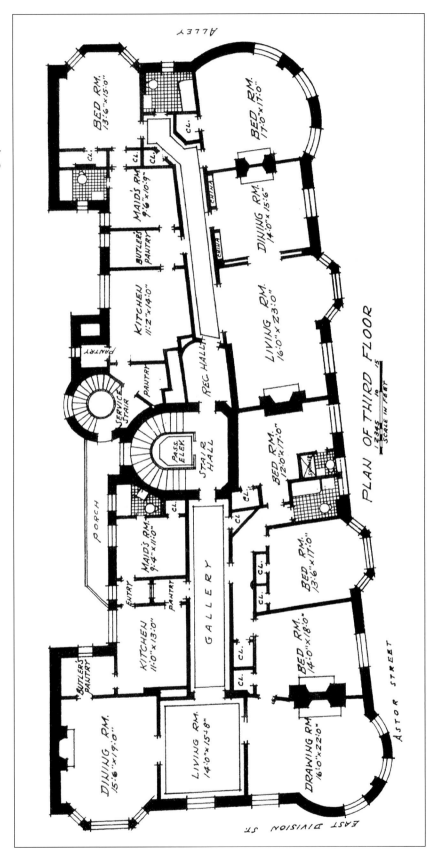

Plan c. 1897. (Courtesy Chicago Historical Society)

1209 North Astor Street

Alfred S. Alschuler, Architect | Hallbauer–La Bahn, Builder | 1926–27

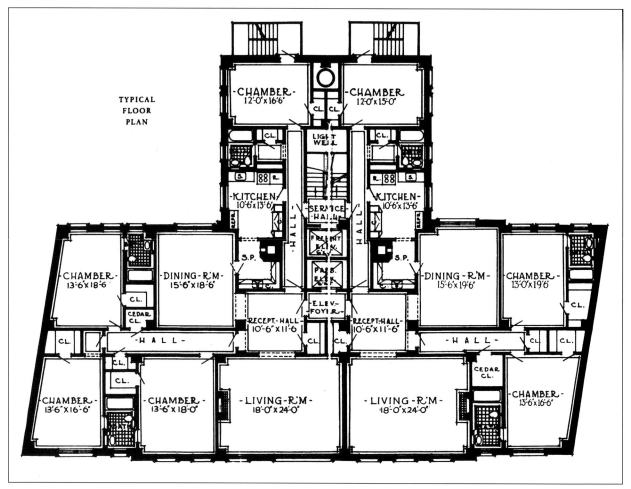

Plan, c. 1926. (*Twelve Nine Astor Street*, brochure, courtesy Ryerson and Burnham Libraries, McNally and Quinn Collection, The Art Institute of Chicago. All rights reserved.)

The first of a quartet of lavish cooperatives constructed on Astor Street in the 1920s, 1209, or Twelve Nine as its brochure announced, presented its 16 stories in a conservative, red brick and limestone trim facade, with Georgian details acknowledging the traditionalism of its immediate location. Alfred Alschuler, better known for his commercial structures, planned two apartments of six and seven rooms to a floor. Surprisingly they lacked any labeled servants' rooms, although the back bedrooms might have so served.

Astor Street "stands apart from distressing motor traffic—quiet, secluded, aristocratic" the building developers argued, emphasizing the investment security of the cooperative, adding that "the surrounding property is held by private owners in such manner as to eliminate any opportunity for encroachment of large buildings of objectionable nature." Subsequent building developments may certainly not have been objectionable, but they would just as surely be large.

Exterior, 1941. (Hedrich Blessing, courtesy Chicago Historical Society)

1260 NORTH ASTOR STREET

Philip B. Maher, Architect | Ouilmette Construction Co., Builder | 1930–31

Exterior, 1936.
(Hedrich Blessing, courtesy Chicago Historical Society)

This 16-story limestone clad building is, with its slightly older neighbor, 1301 North Astor, one of a pair of *moderne* cooperatives. In their relationship to one another, the two structures are unique in Chicago. Completed at a time when many Chicago cooperatives were starting to go bankrupt, 1260 Astor was saved by the wealth of its organizing syndicate, which included stockbroker Barrett Wendell, George Ranney, president of International Harvester, and Sterling Morton, of Morton Salt and the Teletype Corporation. These last two occupied customized duplex apartments on the building's four top floors, which were designed by Paul Schweikher, who worked in the Maher office. Philip Maher designed at least two other apartments as well. Other early residents included Potter Palmer III. As part of Maher's fee for the building, Potter Palmer paid for an apartment, meant as a wedding gift for his son. Robert Hall McCormick and Mr. and Mrs. Charles D. Stone also owned apartments. Mrs. Stone's family home was razed to prepare the building site.

Prospective owners of 1260 were given the option of creating their own spaces, although a set of early unsold apartments received a standardized floor plan. With its high ceilings, lavish appointments, prestigious address, domestic feel, and fashionably moderne exterior, the last of Chicago's great 1920s era apartment buildings remains a cooperative today.

1260 NORTH ASTOR STREET

Plans, Sterling Morton residence. 15th and 16th floor duplex, c. 1931.

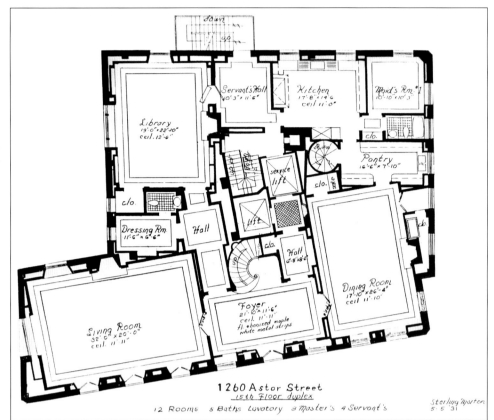

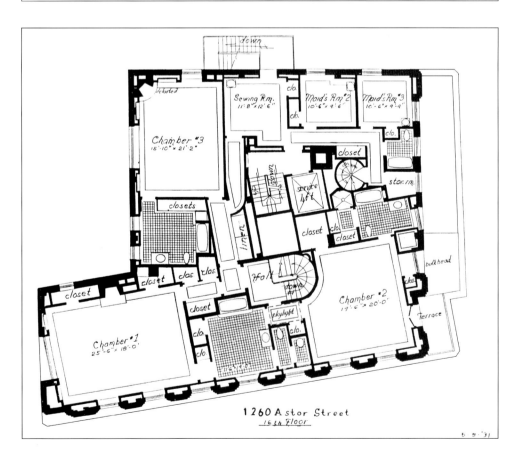

Terrace, George Ranney residence, 1935. (Private collection)

1260 North Astor Street

Hall, Robert Hall McCormick residence. Elsie Cobb Wilson, decorator. (Trowbridge, courtesy Chicago Historical Society)

Bathroom, Robert Hall McCormick residence. Elsie Cobb Wilson, decorator. (Trowbridge, courtesy Chicago Historical Society)

1260 NORTH ASTOR STREET

Bathroom, George Ranney residence, 1935. (Private collection)

1260 AND 1301 NORTH ASTOR STREET

Exteriors, 1260 N. Astor (left) and 1301 N. Astor (right), 1932. (Hedrich Blessing, courtesy Chicago Historical Society)

1301 North Astor Street

Philip B. Maher, Architect | E.P. Strandberg Co., Builder | 1928–30

Proposed exterior rendering, c. 1927. (*Hugh McLennan Announce 1301 Astor*, brochure, courtesy Ryerson and Burnham Libraries, McNally and Quinn Collection, The Art Institute of Chicago. All rights reserved.)

As with 1260 Astor built shortly thereafter, this limestone-finished *moderne* high rise was financed by wealthy Chicagoans who, according to the *Architectural Forum*, "wanted all of the convenience and space of town houses without the attendant expense." Philip Maher recalled every floor being sold within 24 hours of a cocktail party for prospective buyers. Erected on the site of the Frederic Norcross home—Norcross moved into the new building—its clean vertical lines and *moderne* setbacks distinguished it from its Astor Street neighbors, until 1260 came along. Early owners included philanthropist Robert H. Allerton, fellow Art Institute trustees Frederic Clay Bartlett and Potter Palmer, and architect John Root, Jr.

The most celebrated architectural delineator in America, Hugh Ferriss of New York, produced a rendering of Maher's finished design that was quite different from the traditional Mansard-roofed sketch that accompanied a preliminary announcement, one much resembling 1530 North State. The building offered complete customizing possibilities, including ceiling height, and Maher interviewed each buyer. The 10 owners occupied what would have been 16 floors of normal height. Lower floors contained 3500 square foot simplexes, with duplexes above them and a triplex for Potter Palmer, who vacated the famous castle on Lake Shore Drive. The celebrated country house architect, David Adler, designed several 1301 North Astor interiors.

1301 North Astor Street

Exterior portico, 1930. (Hedrich Blessing, courtesy Chicago Historical Society)

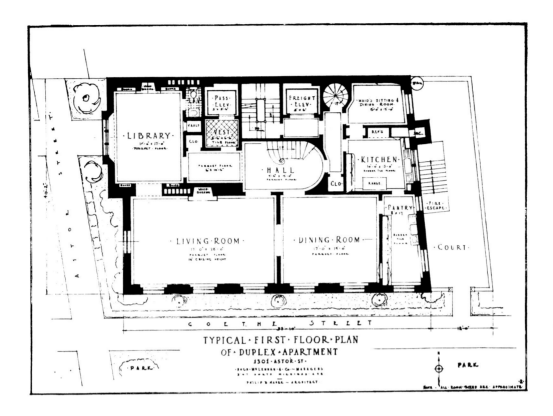

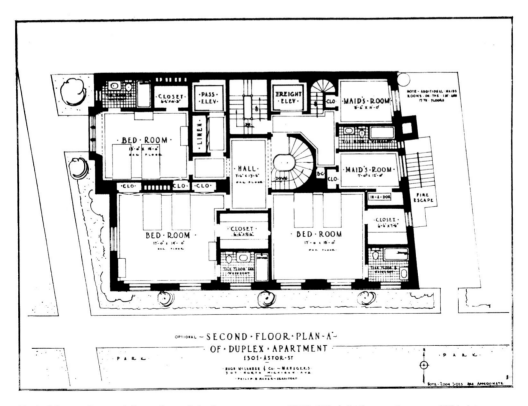

Typical first and second floor plans of duplex apartment, c.1928. (*Hugh McLennan Announce 1301 Astor*, brochure, courtesy Ryerson and Burnham Libraries, McNally and Quinn Collection, The Art Institute of Chicago. All rights reserved.)

Dining room, Ely residence, 1929. David Adler, architect; Frances Elkins, decorator. (Trowbridge, courtesy Chicago Historical Society)

Library, Ely residence, 1929. David Adler, architect; Frances Elkins, decorator. (Trowbridge, courtesy Chicago Historical Society)

Hall, Philip Maher residence, 1930. (Hedrich Blessing, courtesy Chicago Historical Society)

Dining nook, John Root residence, 1933. (Hedrich Blessing, courtesy Chicago Historical Society)

1325 NORTH ASTOR STREET

Rebori, Dewey, and Wentworth, Architects | Dahl–Stedman Co., Builder | 1928–29

Exterior.
(Hedrich Blessing,
courtesy Chicago
Historical Society)

A traditional 14-story red-brick and limestone building with classical references and details, 1325 North Astor featured a two-story, 18-room house on its top. The apartments below, of 11 rooms and 4 baths, were lavish even by the standards of the day. The 30-foot living room contained one of each unit's two wood-burning fireplaces. Frederick Stock, conductor of the Chicago Symphony, purchased one apartment, and his daughter another, wooed perhaps by the extensive soundproofing promises of the designers. The plans were so opulent they provoked Al Chase of the *Chicago Tribune* to unusually sardonic prose. 1325 had water purifiers "for we could hardly expect our Gold Coasters to drink or dine on chlorine flavored lake water." Chase also decided that the circular marble entry room on Astor was meant to "assure visitors that they're not entering a common vegetable variety of flat building." Given the building's scale and finish, any such misconception was hardly likely.

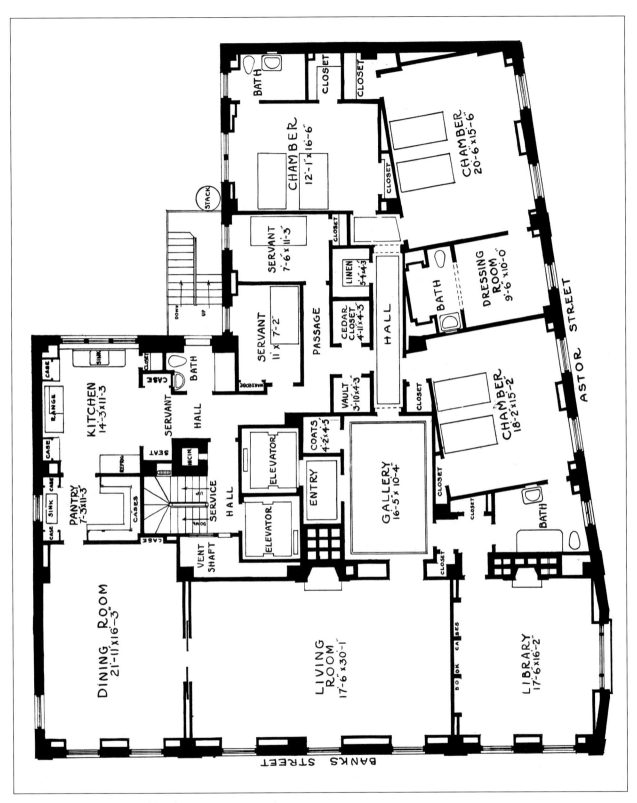

Plan. (Baird and Warner, *Portfolio of Fine Apartment Homes*)

1325 North Astor Street

Kitchen, duplex penthouse. Booth Hansen, architects, 1998. (Courtesy Booth Hansen)

Living room and fireplace, Perry I. Newton triplex. Cornelia Conger, decorator, 1920s or 1930s. (Trowbridge, courtesy Chicago Historical Society)

Dining room, Samuel A. Marx residence, 1941. Samuel A. Marx, architect. (Hedrich Blessing, courtesy Chicago Historical Society)

Hallway, Samuel A. Marx residence, 1941. Samuel A. Marx, architect. (Hedrich Blessing, courtesy Chicago Historical Society)

20 East Cedar Street

BRADLEY APARTMENTS

Fugard & Knapp, Architects | McLennan Construction Company, Builder | 1924–25

Living room with stairway, 1962. (Hedrich Blessing, courtesy Chicago Historical Society)

Both the property and the building have complicated pasts. In 1920, the *Chicago Tribune* described plans for an elaborate structure to be built on this site. Designed by William D. Mann, it was to have double-decker living rooms, blending functions of the great halls of English country houses and modern artists' studios. With rentals of $4,200 a year, no artists were expected to apply, but it was hinted that a special wing might accommodate actual practitioners. The following year, patent attorney Charles A. Brown announced that he was selling his home at 20 East Cedar, a site earlier occupied by the Brand Brewery. Charles F. Henry, a well-known developer, bought the site in exchange for an elaborate bungalow for Brown that would top a $500,000 seven-story apartment house. Roy France was to be the architect. In June, 1922, Marshall & Fox were supposedly building a studio building here. By the summer of 1923 Harold Bradley, a prominent local realtor and pioneer developer of luxury cooperatives, had taken over the project, and announced two possibilities: a 60-flat rental building, or "the most luxurious cooperative apartment building in the country": 40 duplex flats of eight to 14 rooms.

What emerged from architects John Reed Fugard and George Knapp was an elaborate brick and terra-cotta building, with trefoil tracery on double windows, pointed arches, and many gothic details. In an uncanny bow to the earlier Mann plan, several of the large apartments were duplexes, with two-story living rooms and massive fireplaces. But Bradley over-extended himself, building what newspapers called his "masterpiece," and in early 1924 he fled Chicago for parts unknown, leaving his debts and considerable reputation far behind. Weeks elapsed while newspapers reported on supposed sightings of the fugitive realtor in his black Packard roadster. His office closed and employees joined rival firms, but 20 East Cedar was completed. In 1926, it won honorable mention in a contest sponsored by the Lake Shore Trust and Savings Bank for the most beautiful building in the north central district. Second place was not ignominious, for the winner was another gothic adaptation—Raymond Hood's Tribune Tower.

Exterior, Bradley Apartments, 1925. (Courtesy collection of David R. Phillips)

20 East Cedar Street

Mrs. Frederick Mandel residence. TOP: Living room. BOTTOM: View of library to living room. (Trowbridge, courtesy Chicago Historical Society)

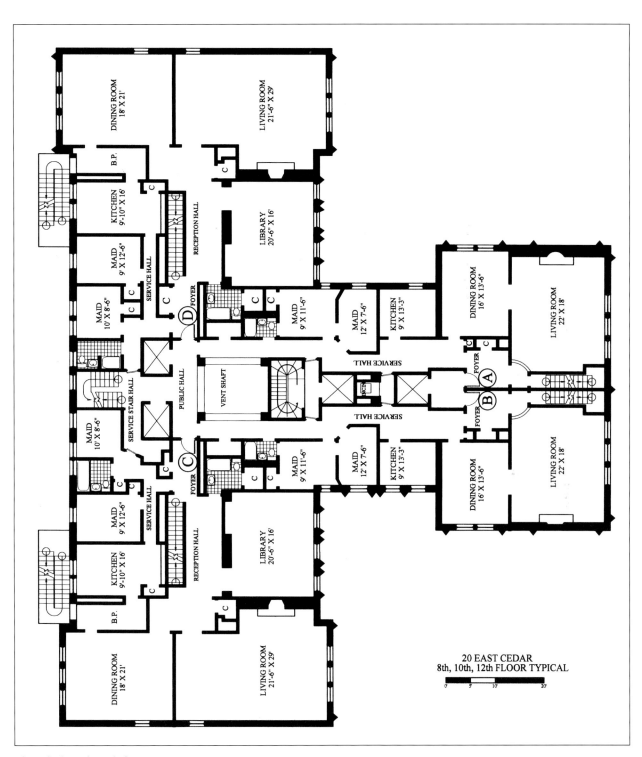

Plan of 8th, 10th, 12th floors.

70 East Cedar Street

McNally & Quinn, Architects | H. Janisch, Builder | 1926–27

Exterior, 1949.
(Hedrich Blessing,
courtesy Chicago
Historical Society)

The property on which 70 East Cedar stands was bought in 1926 from the Potter Palmer estate, whose property holdings dominated much of the Gold Coast. A sober, traditional brick building, it rests on a three-story limestone, Italian Renaissance base, complete with keystones, scrolls and rustication. 70 East Cedar offers somewhat less dramatic interiors than its neighbor to the west, but it is topped by four penthouse duplexes above the 13th floor. Setbacks on the 14th and 16th floors make terraces possible, and the garage has an elegant stone-arched entry that harmonizes with the facade exterior.

"Just off the Drive" was the promoter's motto, suggesting the virtues of relatively quiet Cedar Street. Built as a 28-unit cooperative with the architects being among the principal stockholders, the building was forced by its bondholders to reorganize as a rental in the 1930s. In 1949, it was reconverted to cooperative ownership by a group of tenants for a $750,000 payment, some of which included stock and leases on remaining unsold apartments.

70 East Cedar Street

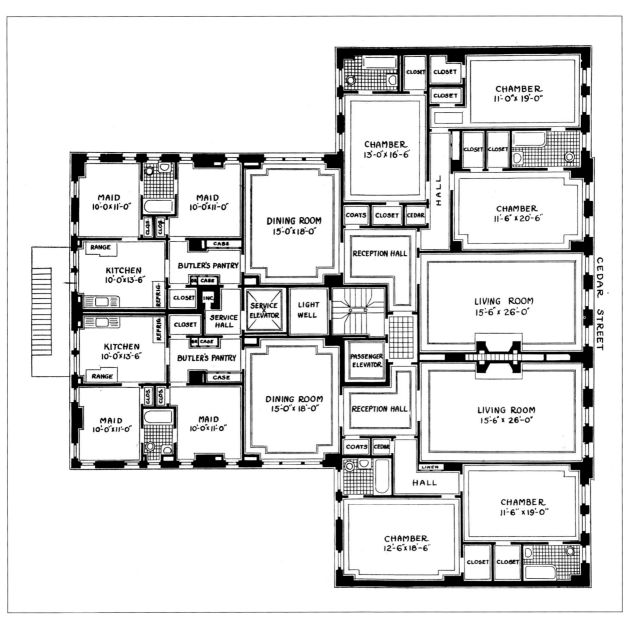

Plan. (Baird and Warner, *Portfolio of Fine Apartment Homes*)

40–50 East Chicago Avenue

HOTEL ST. BENEDICT FLATS

James J. Egan, Architect | 1882–83

Exterior, postcard. (Courtesy Commission on Chicago Landmarks)

The oldest building in this book, the Hotel St. Benedict Flats, on the northeast corner of Chicago and Wabash Avenues, were built during a flurry of apartment construction in the period following the Great Fire of 1871. One estimate had more than 1,000 flat buildings constructed in 1883. The fanciest, like the Hotel St. Benedict, took their inspiration from France. The hotel title was a response to Illinois legislation of 1872 forbidding incorporation of groups solely for buying and improving land; a hotel corporation, even if it was actually an apartment house, avoided the prohibition.

Although the present building contains smaller apartments resulting from a 1930s subdivision, the warmly picturesque combination of red brick, limestone, and a black slate tile mansard roof, with steep gables, is much the same as it was 120 years ago. The four separate entrances, including three on Chicago Avenue, increase the sense of privacy and reinforce the domestic, town house-like character of the larger complex. Designed by one Irish immigrant and owned by another, Patrick J. Sexton, the flats recall an era now barely visible in this part of the city.

40–50 East Chicago Avenue

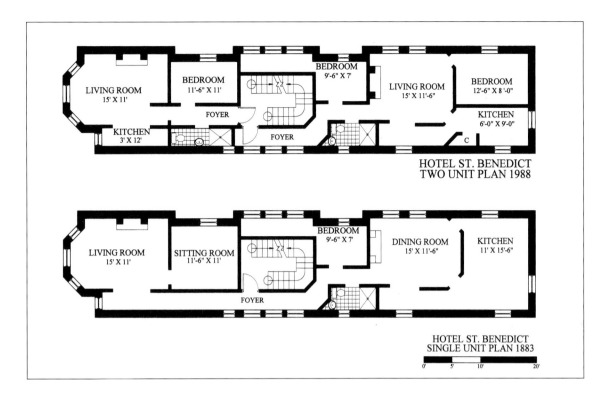

TOP: Plans approximating 1988 and 1883 layouts. BOTTOM: Exterior. (Bob Thall, courtesy Commission on Chicago Landmarks)

161 East Chicago Avenue

OLYMPIA CENTRE

Skidmore, Owings & Merrill, Architects | Paschen Contractors; Gust. K. Newberg Construction | 1978–86

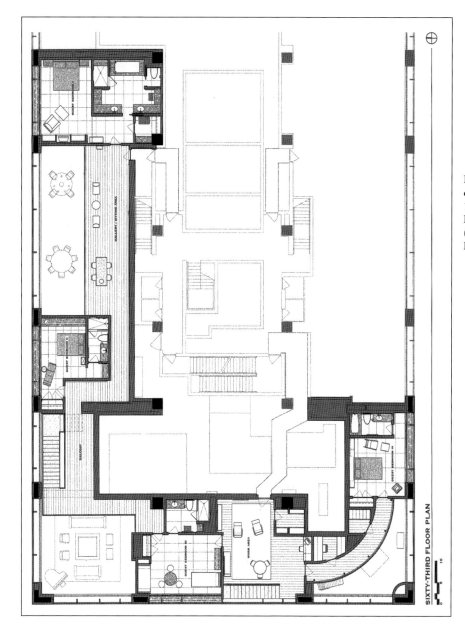

Plan for floor one of duplex penthouse, 1998-2002. Vinci Hamp, architects. (Courtesy Vinci Hamp Architects)

One of the mammoth, multi-use high rises completed in Chicago during the 1970s and 1980s, the 63-floor Olympia Centre contains some 640,000 square feet of residential space and a little more than half as much for offices. It is attached to a single anchor tenant, Neiman-Marcus, which has entrances both on Michigan and Chicago Avenues.

A dramatically sloping concrete structure with a varied fenestration pattern reflecting its mixed use, Olympia Centre's residences are condominiums and vary considerably in size and height. There are a number of duplexes, some relatively small, and at least two quite large; as in other buildings of its type and era, an elaborate athletic complex on an upper floor serves the residents.

161 East Chicago Avenue

Exterior with Water Tower (left), 1986. (Bob Shimer/Hedrich Blessing, courtesy Hedrich Blessing)

Balcony looking into living room, 1998-2002. Vinci Hamp, architects. (Courtesy Jon Miller/Hedrich Blessing and Vinci Hamp Architects)

161 East Chicago Avenue

Balcony, duplex penthouse, 1987. Krueck & Sexton, architects. (Courtesy Krueck & Sexton Architects)

1366 North Dearborn Parkway

DEARBORN SCHILLER

McNally & Quinn, Architects | Fitzgerald Construction, Builder | 1926–28

Exterior, 1936.
(Hedrich Blessing,
courtesy Chicago
Historical Society)

Fourteen stories high, built originally with two six-room and one four-room apartment units to a floor, the Dearborn Schiller's tapestry brick and cut-stone exterior invokes Italian Renaissance palazzo features, particularly its three-story stone base and rooftop balustrade. The original brochure emphasized its fashionable location, accessibility to clubs and recreational facilities, and a building "highly restricted" to "fastidious people." An elaborate lobby, "which means marble, walnut, ornamental plaster, and other background for the wealthy section of our population," was comment-ed upon by the *Chicago Tribune*, which also noted that "family rows will be quite all right in these apartments for the dividing walls…will be of double thickness with felt deadening…"

Despite the fact that apartments could be combined into units as large as nine rooms, no one took advantage of the opportunity, at least up to the 1980 conversion of the building into condominiums. Prices for the 39 apartments ranged in 1980 from $83,000 to $198,500 for the highest two bedroom, although once again developers offered larger combinations.

Typical floor plan, c. 1926. (*The Dearborn Schiller*, brochure, courtesy Ryerson and Burnham Libraries, McNally and Quinn Collection, The Art Institute of Chicago. All rights reserved.)

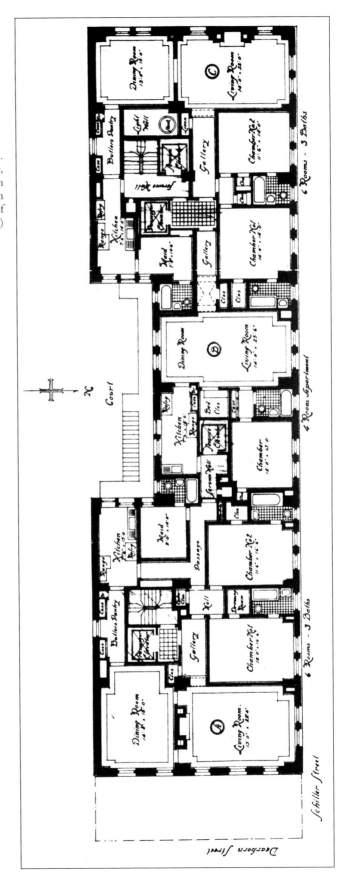

132 East Delaware Place – 900 North Michigan Avenue

Kohn Pedersen Fox, Architects | Kelley Steel Erectors, Builder | 1987–89

Exterior, 1989.

A steel and concrete framed, limestone and granite sheathed structure, this combination shopping mall, hotel, office tower, garage, and residential high-rise bears a series of postmodern touches, including the four lanterns at each corner of its rooftop. Entered on East Delaware Place, the condominium apartments have the services of a Four Seasons hotel below, and occupy floors 49 to 62 of this enormous building. The New York architectural firm of Kohn Pedersen Fox was responsible for a set of huge Chicago buildings in the 1980s, although this was their only entry with residential use. Building this complex required the razing of two historic and much mourned apartment structures, 900 North Michigan and the still older Raymond Apartments at 910.

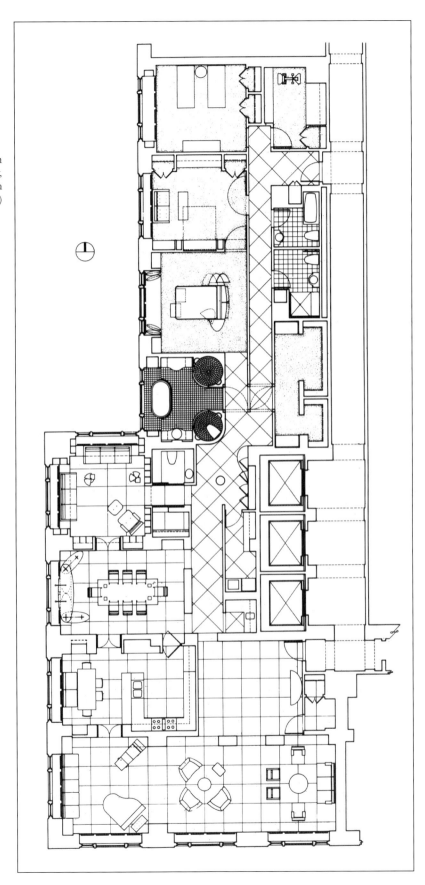

Plan, 1996. Stanley Tigerman and Margaret McCurry, architects. (Courtesy Tigerman McCurry Architects)

Kitchen, 1998. Margaret McCurry, architect. (Courtesy Steve Hall/Hedrich Blessing and Tigerman McCurry Architects)

Living Room, 1996. Stanley Tigerman and Margaret McCurry, architects. (Courtesy Steve Hall/Hedrich Blessing and Tigerman McCurry Architects)

132 East Delaware Place–900 North Michigan Avenue

View of 132 (left) and 175 (center) East Delaware Place, 1989. (Marco Lorenzetti/Hedrich Blessing, courtesy Hedrich Blessing)

175 East Delaware Place

John Hancock Center

Skidmore, Owings & Merrill, Architects | Tishman Construction, Builder | 1965–70

Exterior, with East Lake Shore Drive in foreground, 1969. (Hedrich Blessing, courtesy Chicago Historical Society)

The Hancock Center's great height, tapered shape, and distinctive braced frame have made it a Chicago landmark from the day of its completion. Even while under construction, a scale model toured the Soviet Union under the auspices of the United States Information Agency. Its complex construction challenges clouded the fortunes of its original developer, Jerry Wolman, who had to sell it before its completion to the John Hancock Life Insurance Company.

The joint product of architect Bruce Graham and engineer Fazlur Khan, who devised his ingenious braces and tubular construction for the building, the Hancock Center contains the world's highest residences. The 44th floor lobby and swimming pool begin a set of apartments that continue through the 92nd floor. It originally housed 711 apartments, but some have been combined. The building also contains 29 stories of offices, an observatory, restaurants, stores—including its own grocery store—and other facilities.

While multi-use on a large scale had been pioneered by Marina City a few years earlier, the Hancock popularized the concept, particularly for Michigan Avenue, and helped propel the immediate area on its course of immensely profitable commercial and residential development. Residents of many apartments—rental in the beginning, condominium since 1973—look out on their spectacular views through windows partially obscured by the diagonal bracing that remains one of the building's most memorable features.

175 East Delaware Place

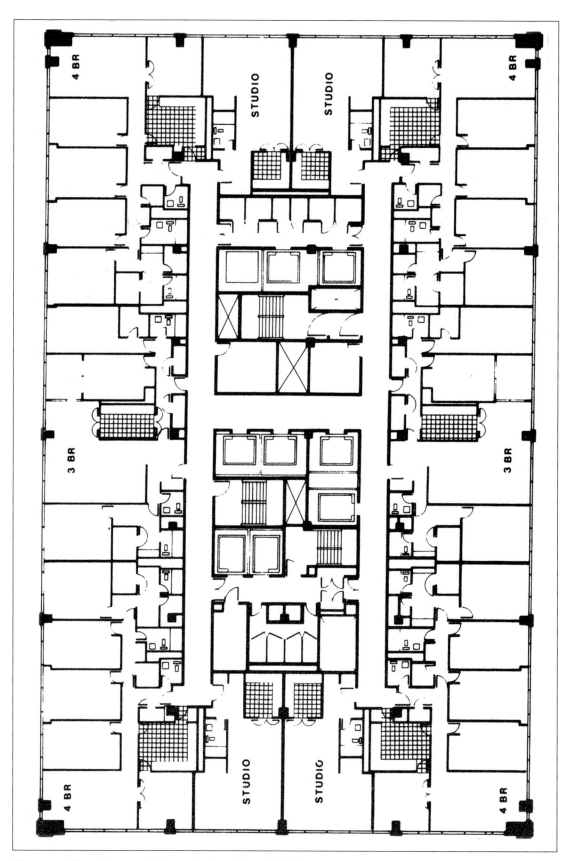

Plan, typical floor. (Courtesy Skidmore Owings & Merrill LLP)

Exterior, 1972. (Hedrich Blessing, courtesy Chicago Historical Society)

Living area, model apartment, 1968. (Hedrich Blessing, courtesy Chicago Historical Society)

Foyer, model apartment, 1968. (William C. Hedrich/Hedrich Blessing, courtesy Chicago Historical Society)

257 East Delaware Place

John A. Nyden, Architect | Axel H. Johnson, Builder | 1917

Exterior.
(Baird and Warner, *Portfolio of Fine Apartment Homes*)

A 10-story masonry structure, with nine full-floor apartments, 257 East Delaware reflects the standards of pre-1920s high-rise luxury. Its brick, stone, and terra-cotta facade adopted a Renaissance revival vocabulary that was married to delicate 18th-century style details, a combination that would soon be widely imitated by other apartment house planners. Balustrades above the second, eighth, and tenth floors accent the stone-fronted base and highly decorated upper floors.

The Swedish born architect, John A. Nyden, lived in Evanston and designed a number of hotels, banks, office buildings, and churches in Chicago. He also served on the boards of some of these institutions. Rentals in 1917 were expected to hover in the $4,000 to $5,000 per year range, reflecting the building's prime location, amenities, and interior plan. Its estimated 1917 cost was $225,000. In 1940, the building was put up for sale with an asking price of $175,000. 257 East Delaware is a condominium today.

257 East Delaware Place

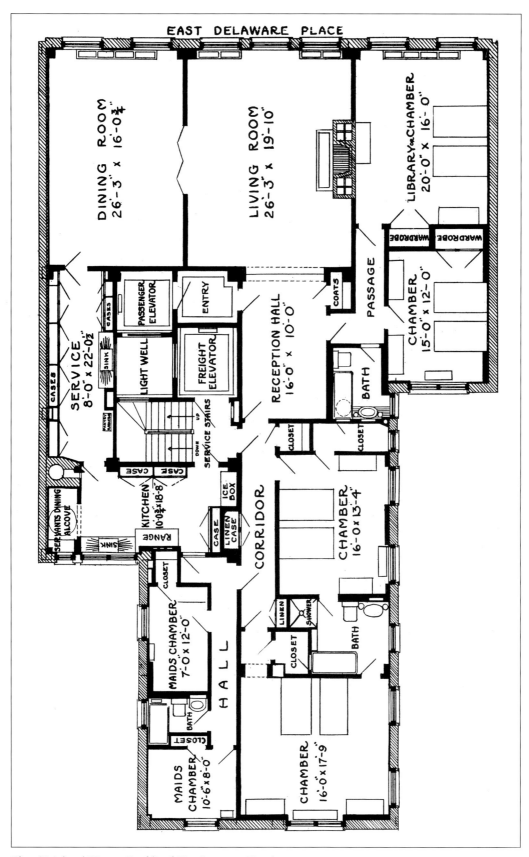

Plan. (Baird and Warner, *Portfolio of Fine Apartment Homes*)

55 East Erie Street

Fujikawa Johnson & Associates, Architects | Searl & Associates, Interior Architects
Walsh Construction, Builder | 2001–03

Exterior rendering, 2003. (Building prospectus)

Recently completed 55 East Erie captures a set of trends in luxury Chicago apartment house design: great height, open terraces, and floor plan diversity. With 56 stories of reinforced concrete holding more than 200 apartments, the building stands atop an 11-story garage in a River North area exploding with new, extremely tall condominium developments.

Much too high to be absorbed by pedestrians, the building's street impact comes primarily from its limestone and granite base and the concrete and glass garage floors it supports. Upper floors contain larger apartments, while penthouses and Sky Houses (with dedicated elevators) service an even higher-end clientele. In effect the building is zoned within: its amenities increase with the expansiveness of its views. The stated price range of apartments during construction—$638,000 to $4.35 million—suggests the variation.

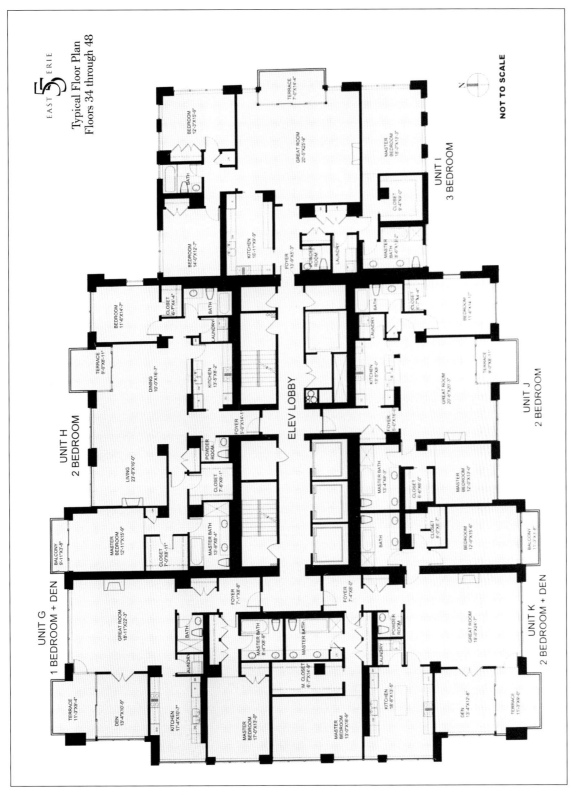

Typical floor plan, floors 34–48. (Building prospectus)

65 East Goethe Street

Lucien Lagrange, Architect | E.W. Corrigan, Builder | 1999–2003

Exterior. Lucien Lagrange, architect, 2003. (Courtesy Lucien Lagrange Architects)

Clear evidence of the new luxury in apartment design of the 1990s, 65 East Goethe was first presented by its developer in 1996 as a 32-story condominium building. Responding to protests from neighbors, the size was lowered to 24, then 18, then 12, and finally 8 stories. Both the architect, Lucien Lagrange, and the developer, the Fordham Company, have been involved in a series of upscale apartment projects, but this Parisian-inspired limestone-clad building with its bay windows, turrets, balconies, and zinc mansard roof may be the quintessential symbol of 1990s ambitions and prosperity.

Planned for six town houses or maisonettes on the lowest two floors and another 16 or 18 apartments above, both size and price impressed locals. The town houses ran to 8,500 square feet, and prices for smaller units began at $2.5 million. The raw space cost neared $700 per square foot. High ceilings, multiple fireplaces, rooftop garden terraces, a resident concierge, underground parking, and huge rooms were meant to invoke the most lavish of the 1920s apartment buildings in an area of the city where they had flourished—and continue to do so.

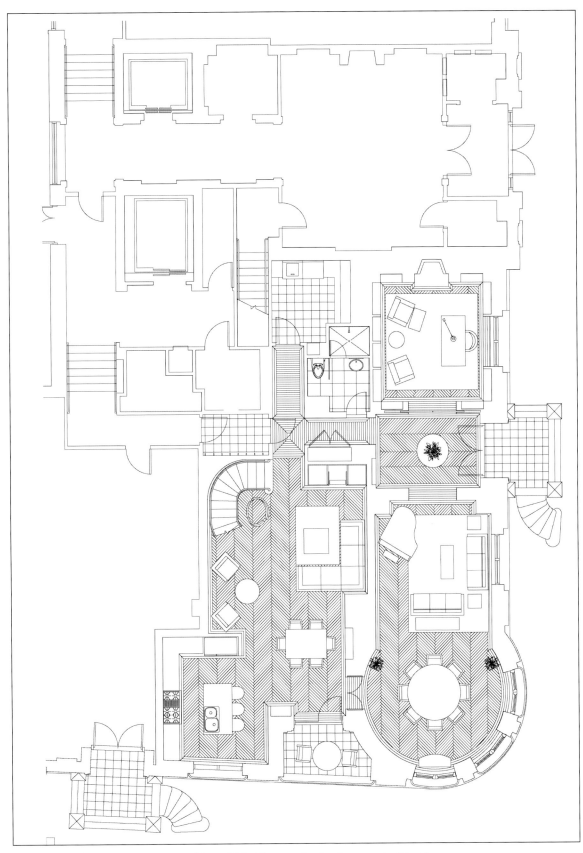

Typical floor plan. Lucien Lagrange, architect, 2000. (Courtesy Lucien Lagrange Architects)

179 East Lake Shore Drive

DRAKE TOWER

Benjamin H. Marshall, Architect | Benjamin H. Marshall, Builder | 1928–31

View looking south on Lake Shore Drive towards the Drake Hotel (right) and apartment buildings on East Lake Shore Drive, 1943. (Courtesy Chicago Historical Society)

The Drake Tower formed the newest and tallest entry in that wall of hotels and apartment houses defining East Lake Shore Drive, a short but very expensive strip of residential real estate. While North Lake Shore Drive apartment houses look east and generally occupy narrower lots, these eight structures face north with unencumbered access to lake and shoreline views. Benjamin Marshall's buildings have a prominent place here: his Drake Hotel stands just to the west of the Drake Tower, and Tower residents have access to its services.

The Drake Tower gives a somewhat stripped-down architectural impression, at least as compared to Marshall's other buildings, and it may reflect his growing sympathy for modernism. Its appearance has changed somewhat since 1931 because of new fenestration and a penthouse expansion. The 30 floors were divided into three- and four-room apartments on the lower levels, and seven- to nine-room suites on the upper stories. Today it contains 66 units, including the penthouses. Like several other East Lake Shore Drive structures, it has its own garage and, more than that, an automobile turntable.

179 EAST LAKE SHORE DRIVE

Exterior, c.1986.
(Bob Thall,
courtesy Commission
on Chicago Landmarks)

179 East Lake Shore Drive

Living room, Claire Zeisler residence, 1956. (Hedrich Blessing, courtesy Chicago Historical Society)

179 East Lake Shore Drive

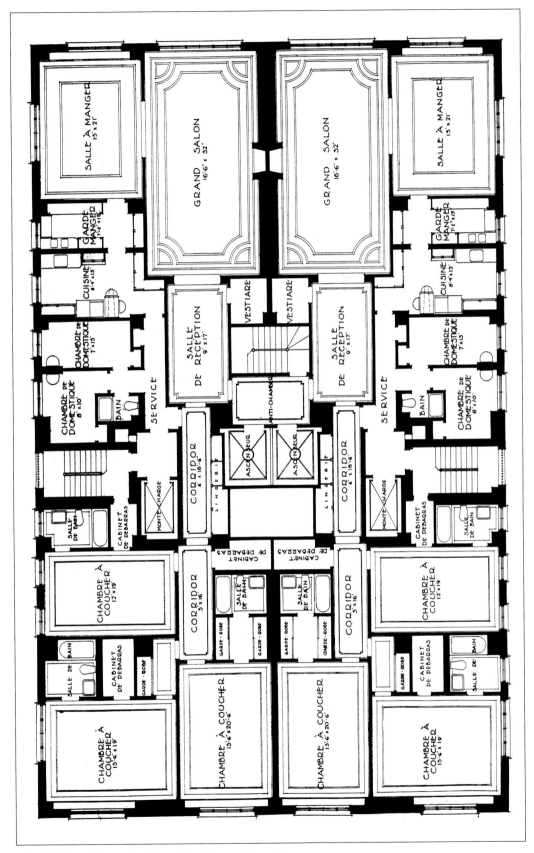

Plan. (Baird and Warner, *Portfolio of Fine Apartment Homes*)

199 East Lake Shore Drive

THE BREAKERS

Marshall & Fox, Architects | 1911–13; 1915–16

999 (left) and 199 (right, before addition) East Lake Shore Drive, c. 1913. (Courtesy Commission on Chicago Landmarks)

This pre-World War I apartment house remains one of the more elegantly conceived residences in the city. An 11-story red brick and white-glazed terra-cotta building, its distinctive classical details and central row of bay windows are matched by an urbane variation several doors east at 999 Lake Shore Drive, also by Marshall & Fox. The two stood in 1913 as lonely pioneers.

The main building was erected as an investment by architect Benjamin Marshall four years before he added the annex just to the west. Most main building apartments are one to a floor, but the annex contains a series of duplexes. There are 13 apartments in all. Each is divided into public, private, and service sectors—or living, sleeping, and servants' quarters as its self-description put it—revealing Marshall's careful planning and sensitivity to his wealthy clients. "Every modern convenience obtainable in present day life is included in the equipment," the developers promised, and in this case it was no overstatement. A rental building for many years, 199 East Lake Shore was converted to a cooperative in 1995.

199 East Lake Shore Drive

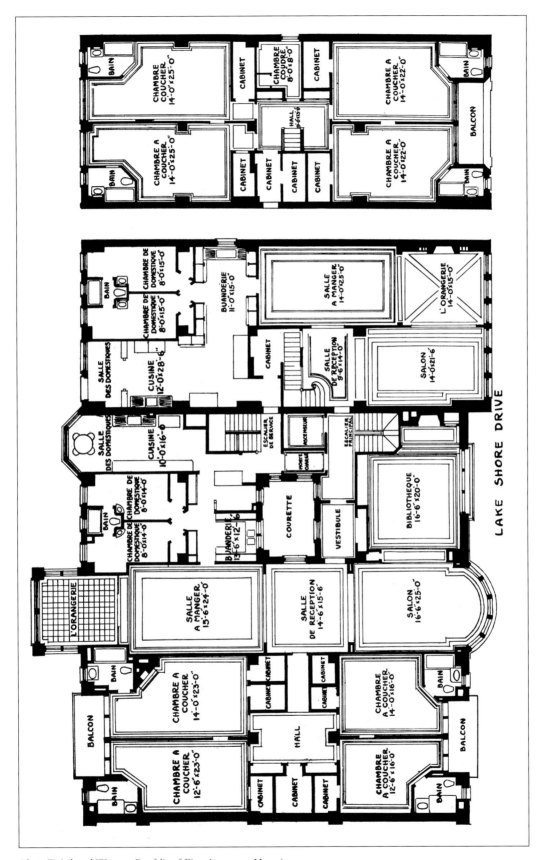

Plan. (Baird and Warner, *Portfolio of Fine Apartment Homes*)

199 East Lake Shore Drive

Exterior. (Baird and Warner, *Portfolio of Fine Apartment Homes*)

199 East Lake Shore Drive

Living room, duplex residence. Booth Hansen, architects, 2001. (Courtesy Booth Hansen)

209 East Lake Shore Drive

Benjamin H. Marshall, Architect | Benjamin H. Marshall, Builder | 1924–25

Exterior. (Baird and Warner, *Portfolio of Fine Apartment Homes*)

An 18-story brick and limestone building by Benjamin Marshall, 209 East Lake Shore contains two 6,500 square foot apartments on a typical floor. Each offers the possibility of a 60-foot long en suite vista facing the lake. Italian Renaissance in inspiration, the four-story rusticated base is punctuated by three large archways, two of which are designed for automobile access to and from its garage. Carl Condit called this the "most sober" of all the East Lake Shore Drive facades; whether true or not, it may well be the most elegant.

Since its construction, it has been among Chicago's most expensive apartment structures. The 1925 bond issue appraised the building and property at more than $4 million. An earlier Marshall design, with its gabled roof and still more elaborately pillared entry way, was more Italianate than the final version. In an effort to humanize this imposing structure, one advertisement for the building noted that Mrs. Ogden McClurg, an original owner, had established a kindergarten with a trained teacher on the 18th floor for some local children.

209 EAST LAKE SHORE DRIVE

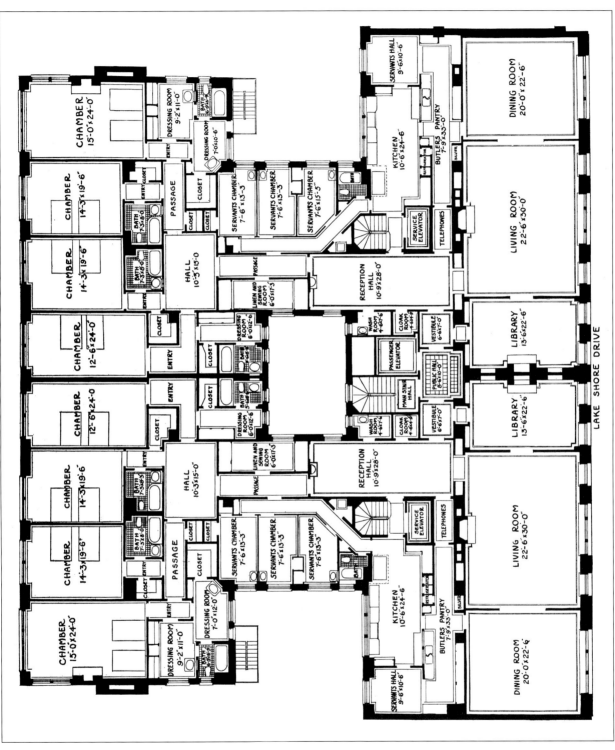

Plan. (Baird and Warner, *Portfolio of Fine Apartment Homes*)

Detail of door, 1986. (Bob Thall, courtesy Commission on Chicago Landmarks)

Living room, 1997. Booth Hansen, architects. (Kate Roth, courtesy Booth Hansen)

219 East Lake Shore Drive

Fugard & Knapp, Architects; Horace Colby Ingram, Associate Architect
McLennan Construction, Builder | 1921–1922

Exterior, 1941.
(Hedrich Blessing,
courtesy Chicago
Historical Society)

With its 12 stories and originally 44 apartments, 219 East Lake Shore is slightly less imposing than many of its neighbors, but its dignified and restrained facade harmonizes well with them. It was built for Hugh McLennan, who also served as the construction contractor. "Quietly aristocratic," ran the phrase of one publicist in the 1920s.

A brick Georgian design over a limestone-clad base, 219 features a series of classical ornaments, including a scrolled, broken pediment over its entrance with a terra-cotta balconette. The original interior, with four apartments to a floor, was a bit less spacious than others on its block, although the reduced scale was welcomed by some. "A Bit O'Cheer For The Poor Rich Newlyweds," ran the *Chicago Tribune* story line. "...one especially depressing feature has always been overlooked. No mention has ever been made about the unfortunate millionaire newlyweds who, despite their unwieldy bank balance can't find a small, cozy Lake Shore Drive flat with a rental exorbitant enough to be interesting." Some of today's condominium owners have combined apartments.

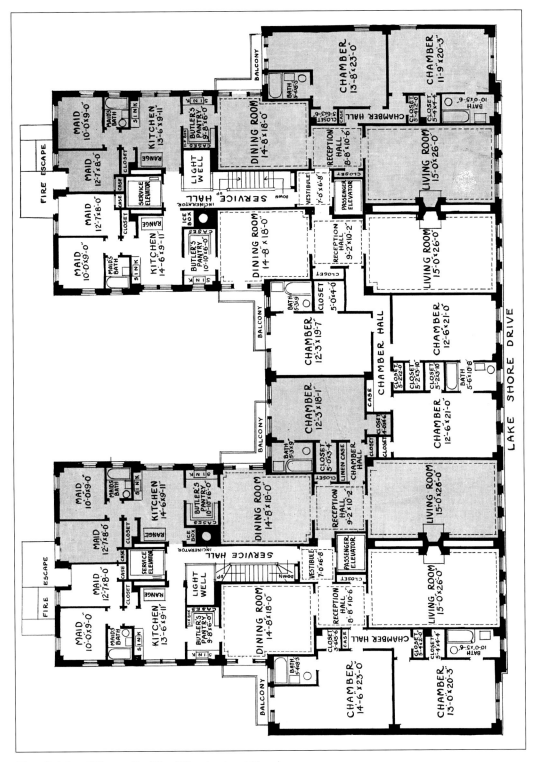

Plan. (Baird and Warner, *Portfolio of Fine Apartment Homes*)

229 East Lake Shore Drive

THE SHORELAND APARTMENTS

Fugard & Knapp, Architects | Melemore Construction, Builder | 1918–19

Exterior, 1986. (Bob Thall, courtesy Commission on Chicago Landmarks)

Compared with 219 East Lake Shore, the grander scale of the earlier 229 is revealed by the fact that while the two cornice lines of both are nearly at the same height, 229 East Lake Shore contains one less story. Although this slightly older building invokes more of the literalism of a Renaissance palazzo, its gray limestone front projects much of the simplicity and restraint of 219, befitting the fact that John Fugard designed both. Most of the units have 12 rooms divided clearly into three functional zones. The master bedroom fireplaces make for an especially luxurious touch.

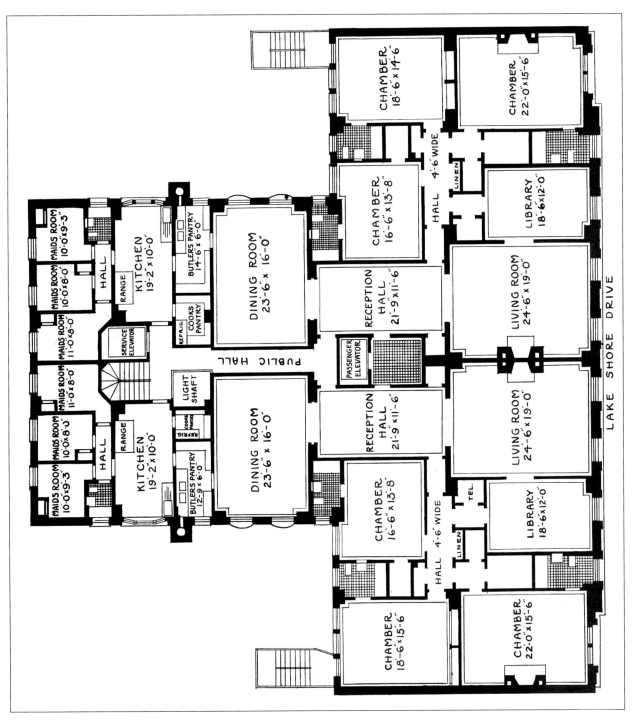

Plan. (Baird and Warner, *Portfolio of Fine Apartment Homes*)

505 North Lake Shore Drive

LAKE POINT TOWER

Schiporeit–Heinrich, Architects | Crane Construction, Builder | 1965–68

Exterior, 1969. (Hedrich Blessing, courtesy Chicago Historical Society)

Architects George Schipporeit and John Heinrich once worked with Mies van der Rohe, and they adapted a Miesian design created almost 50 years earlier to produce this striking structure. A notable landmark, it is the only apartment building east of North Lake Shore Drive. The 69-story, Y-shaped, curtain-walled structure sits atop a podium, which contains the garage and various support facilities. A small garden with pools and playground gives the building its own landscaped setting.

Once fairly isolated, the renovation and development of Navy Pier have brought more activity to its immediate neighborhood. The curvilinear shape and tripartite organization of the building allow relatively short public corridors leading to the many apartments on each floor, an adaptation of a technique Benjamin Marshall used in the Edgewater Beach Apartments. Originally a rental with a string of one-bedroom and efficiency apartments complementing larger units, Lake Point Tower is now a condominium with quite a few units that have been combined.

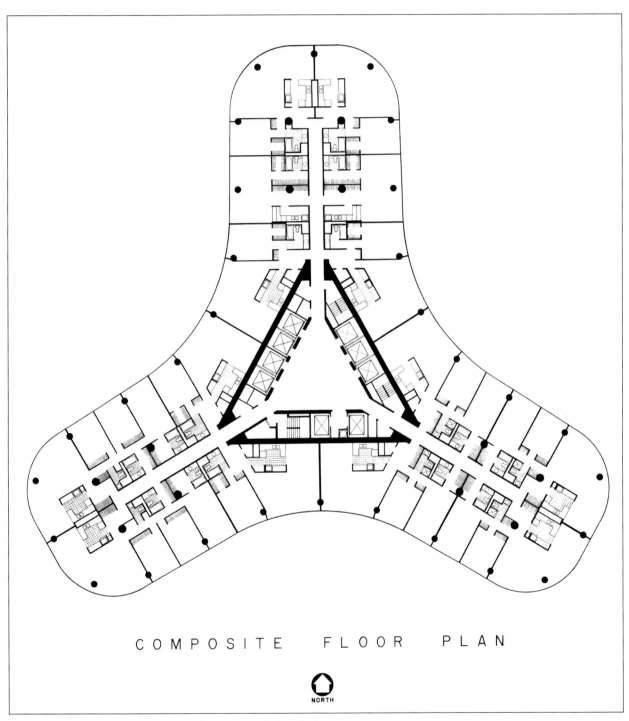

Plan, 1965. (Hedrich Blessing, courtesy Chicago Historical Society)

Living room–dining room, 1965. (Hedrich Blessing, courtesy Chicago Historical Society)

505 North Lake Shore Drive

Living room–dining room, 1968–69. (Hedrich Blessing, courtesy Chicago Historical Society)

167

680 North Lake Shore Drive

American Furniture Mart

Henry Raeder, Architect; George C. Nimmons and N. Max Dunning, Associate Architects; Conversion, Lohan Associates | Wells Brothers, Builder | 1923–26; converted 1979–84

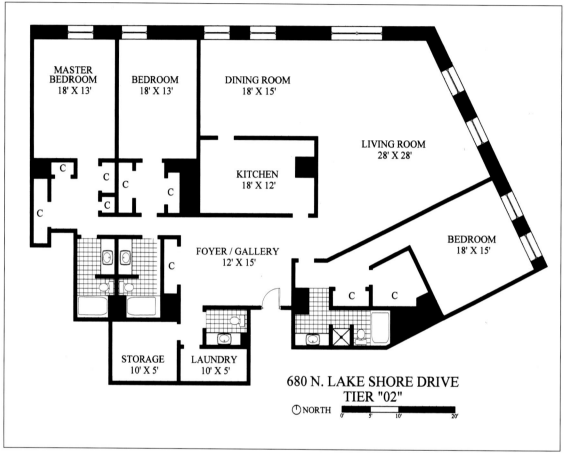

Plan, Tier 02.

As 666 Lake Shore Drive—the address change reflects concerns about charges of Satanist symbolism—this was the American Furniture Mart, whose original builders hailed it as the largest building in the world. Thirty-four acres of space served the exhibition needs of the American furniture industry and allowed for an exposition palace as well. Two years after opening, a western addition with a 30-story tower added to the capacity of the complex.

Described as "English Renaissance" in style, with groined vaults, marble floors, and decorated ceilings, the lavish detailing and sumptuous interiors reflected the importance of furniture making. The 472-foot blue and gold tower in the western, steel-framed addition was modeled on London's Houses of Parliament and briefly claimed the height record for a building outside of New York City.

Remodeling in the 1980s made this an early example of a conversion from commercial to residential status. Given the scale and character of the building, a large number of unusually shaped apartments were created, with space left over for parking and commercial services as well. A foreclosure in the mid-1980s, which reflected a soft condominium market of the time, led to a change of management and ownership. For a time, many of the new apartments were rented. Today three separate condominium associations operate the more than 400 residential units within the vast structure. There is extensive office and retailing space as well.

Exterior, (Hedrich Blessing, courtesy Chicago Historical Society)

860–880 NORTH LAKE SHORE DRIVE

Mies van der Rohe, Architect; Holsman, Holsman, Klekamp, and Pace Associates, Associate Architects | 1949–51 Architects | 1949–51

Lobby, 1950–69. (Hedrich Blessing, courtesy Chicago Historical Society)

These two 26-story towers, the Glass Houses as they have long been known, are among Chicago's most photographed buildings and probably constitute the most celebrated apartment houses of the 20th century. Almost at once, 860–880 North Lake Shore Drive received international recognition and won an impressive set of awards. Mies van der Rohe's design, brought to fruition because of developer Herbert Greenwald's energy and confidence, helped move Chicago and much of America down the road toward modern steel and glass buildings as the basic prototype for high-rise office and residential structures alike. Few if any of these later buildings matched the formal elegance of the $6 million Glass Houses, whose refinement rested not simply on the functionalist ethos Mies proclaimed, but on a formalist aesthetic which required use of some of the structural materials as ornament. The floor plans went through a series of changes; developer Greenwald persuaded Mies to make them tighter and less open, thus more appealing to American tastes.

The two buildings contain more than 200 units; 860 was planned for 90 three-bedroom apartments, and 880 for 158 one-bedroom apartments. Many owners have created their own spaces by combining units. Modest in scale and simple in layout, the apartments enjoyed views enhanced by the glass walls. This, and the opportunity of living in an extraordinary design, compensated the first occupants for any technical shortcomings, such as long elevator delays.

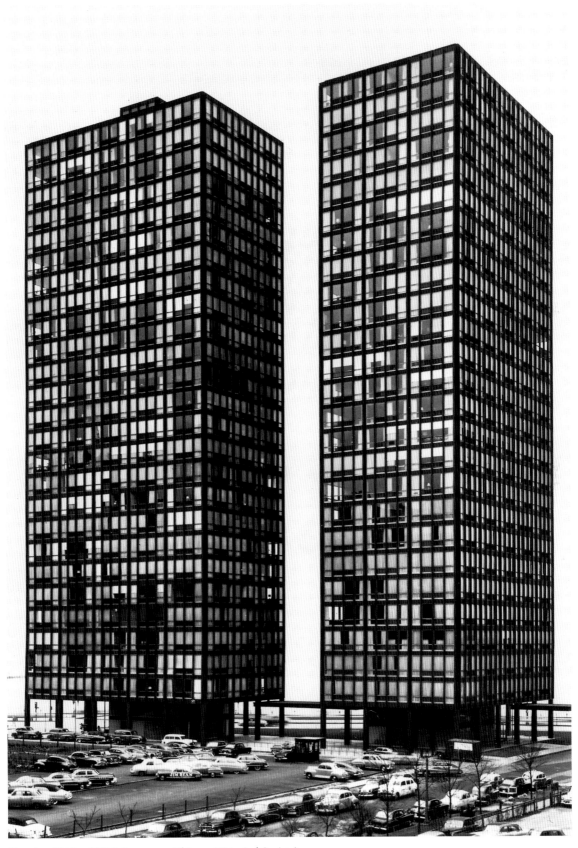

Exterior. (Richard Nickel, courtesy Chicago Historical Society)

Detail. (Hedrich Blessing, courtesy Chicago Historical Society)

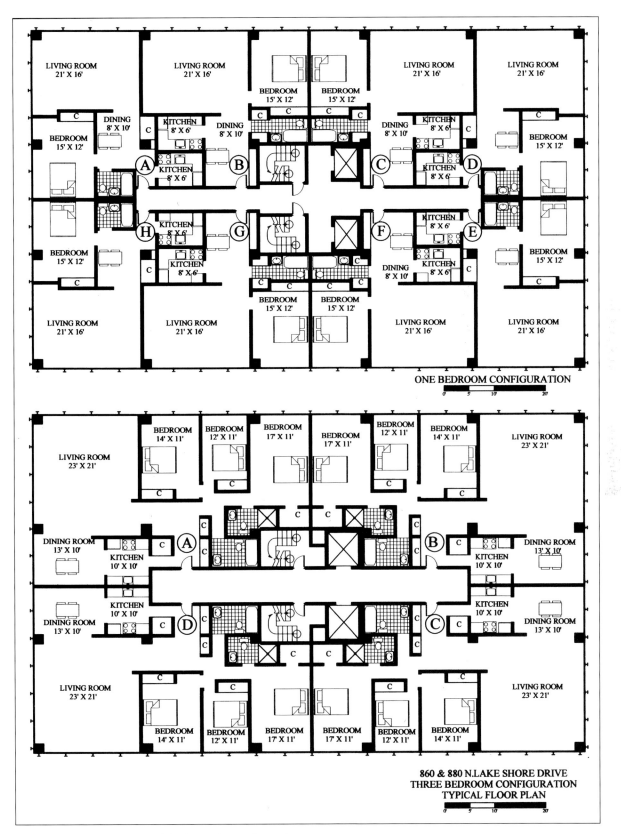

Plan, 1950. (Based on plans published in *Architectural Forum*)

Room with TV, 1952. (Hedrich Blessing, courtesy Chicago Historical Society)

Dining room, 1953. Eppenstein, decorator. (Hedrich Blessing, courtesy Chicago Historical Society)

Balcony., duplex penthouse, 1992. Krueck & Sexton, architects. (Courtesy Krueck & Sexton Architects)

Dining room, duplex penthouse, 1992. Krueck & Sexton, architects. (Courtesy Krueck & Sexton Architects)

936 North Lake Shore Drive

William Ernest Walker, Architect | Melemore Construction, Builder; McLennan Construction | 1912–13

936, 942, 999 Lake Shore Drive (left to right), 1965. (F.G. Dauwalter, courtesy Chicago Historical Society)

Demolished in the late 1960s to make room for new apartment building construction, 936 and its next door neighbor 942 N. Lake Shore Drive suggested the spatial luxury reached by some Chicago apartments before World War I. With 14 rooms and 45 windows to each apartment, a 60-foot sweep of dining room, reception hall, and living room, and a separate windowed laundry for every unit, 936 North Lake Shore enjoyed a further distinction in having what was probably Lake Shore Drive's first penthouse, a $40,000 bungalow built on its roof for architect William Walker. The 45 by 90 foot bungalow was surrounded by a terrace, which allowed the owner and his family to discover that "the air was not only better at this height (the 9th floor), but cooler by several degrees in summer than at the street level." According to a 1917 article, in the *Architectural Record*, Walker was even able to dispense with window screens "since the site of the bungalow is above the fly belt, the mosquito line, and even above the realm of that occasional summer pest, the sand fly."

In 1917, Walker prepared plans for an unprecedented 16 story apartment house near the site of the present 209 East Lake Shore Drive, but it was never constructed. Remodeled in 1941 by Skidmore Owings Merrill into 36 apartments plus the bungalow penthouse, the building brought $425,000 when sold in 1967.

936 North Lake Shore Drive

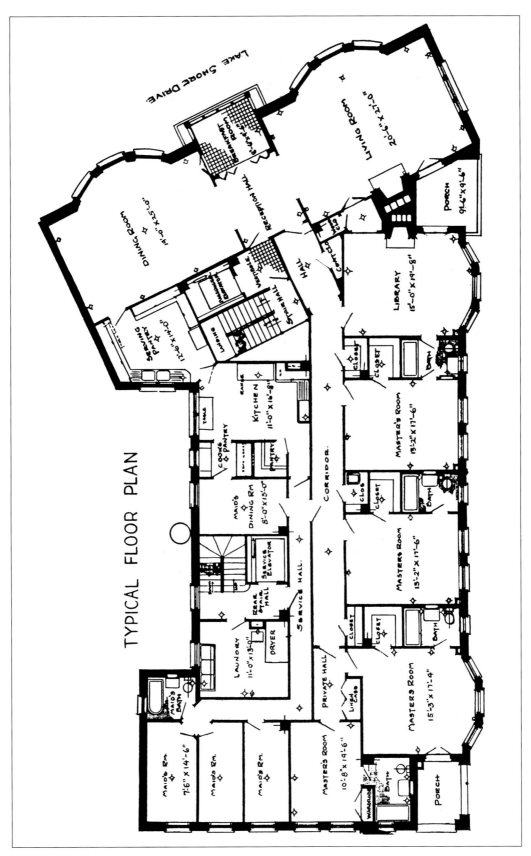

Plan. (Baird and Warner, *Portfolio of Fine Apartment Homes*)

936 North Lake Shore Drive

Exterior. (Baird and Warner, *Portfolio of Fine Apartment Homes*)

936 North Lake Shore Drive

TOP: Pergola, 1917. BOTTOM: Bungalow on roof, 1917. *(Architectural Record)*

181

999 North Lake Shore Drive

LAKE SHORE APARTMENTS

Marshall & Fox, Architects | 1911–1912

Exterior, 1981. (Bob Thall, courtesy Commission on Chicago Landmarks)

This red brick and mansard-roofed 10-story structure, built for Stuart G. Shepard and Ogden McClurg, commands one of Chicago's most desirable corners, the short bend of Lake Shore Drive, granting the building unencumbered views both east and north. The three apartments on each floor have different plans, but each exploits the generous bow windows on the Second Empire front. All bedrooms originally had balconies. The facade, with its swells and recesses, bows and balconies, limestone framed porte cochere and contrasting colors, is one of the liveliest and most energetic on this strip of extraordinary luxury buildings.

Units were expected to rent in 1912 for $3600 annually, but in 1920 a number of tenants purchased shares in the building's equity, making it one of the city's early luxury cooperatives. After failing as a cooperative during hard times, it reincorporated in 1950. Later tenant owners included design patron Walter Paepcke, chief of the Container Corporation of America, and industrialist Preston Tucker, who was forced to sell when his ambitious but ill-fated automobile company collapsed.

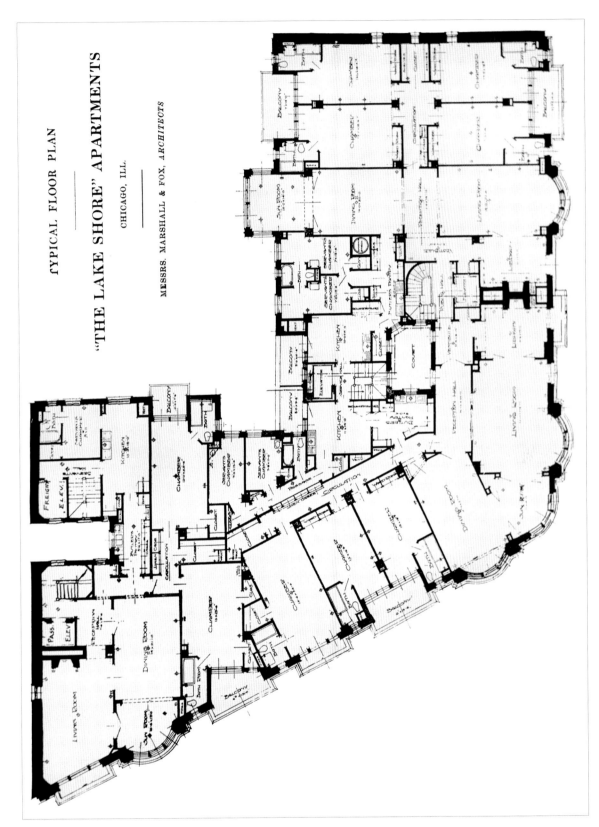

Plan, 1914. (*American Architect*)

1040 North Lake Shore Drive

THE CARLYLE

Hirschfeld, Pawlan and Reinheimer, Architects | Robin Construction Co., Builder | 1964–67

Exterior, 2003.

The 36-story, $11 million Carlyle is considered Chicago's first luxury high-rise condominium, planned shortly after the Illinois legislature produced the enabling legislation. For it the financing agent Dovenmuehle issued its first condominium loan.

Far more generous in square footage than other apartment buildings of the period, the Carlyle's layout and services still reflected important changes from luxury buildings constructed before the Depression. Room dimensions and the number of servants' rooms had shrunk, although, unlike its contemporaries, the Carlyle featured formal dining rooms. There were conveniences that soon would be available in many new lakefront buildings: balconies for every apartment, a swimming pool, and a health club. Apartments were as large as five bedrooms and up to 5,300 square feet. A typical floor was divided into two tiers, each with its own set of elevators, containing four somewhat smaller units.

To sell the more than 100 apartments, the "Little Carlyle," a furnished residence on nearby Cedar Street, displayed sample layouts. The Carlyle remains a condominium today.

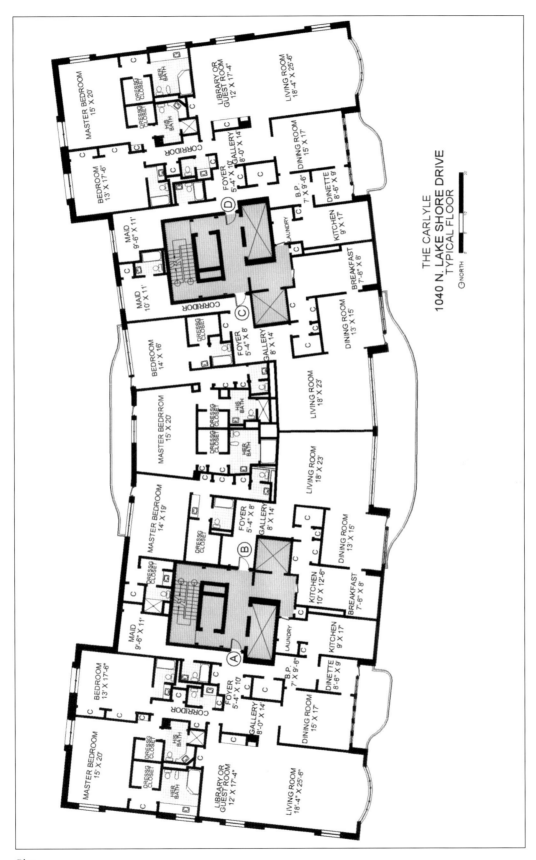

Plan.

1100 North Lake Shore Drive

Marshall Apartments

Marshall & Fox, Architects | 1905

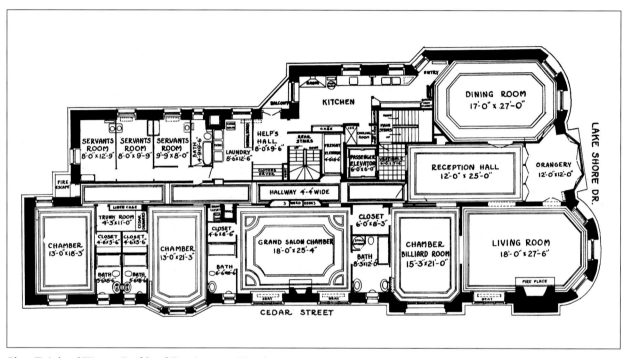

Plan. (Baird and Warner, *Portfolio of Fine Apartment Homes*)

According to historian Carroll William Westfall, this apartment house was designed by Benjamin Marshall for his father, who had purchased the property for $45,000. The red brick building, with its shuttered windows and white trim, suggested a domesticated 18th-century English ideal come to early 20th-century Chicago. An orangery, or sun porch, occupied the center of the Lake Shore Drive facade; bow-fronted living and dining rooms, both of ample dimensions, flanked it. With five baths, three servants' rooms and a servants' hall, and ample closets, these apartments, while understated on their exterior, provided comfortable space and nicely separated rooms for entertainment and service.

Indeed, the building pulled wealthy residents from south side homes on Prairie Avenue to the new Gold Coast, and even in the 1920s socially prominent families, like the Arthur Meekers, were drawn from their private houses. The four bedrooms of each apartment faced south on quieter Cedar Street, avoiding Lake Shore Drive distraction. The eight apartments rented initially for $4,200 a year. A rental for many years—tenants included utilities magnate Samuel Insull—1100 was turned into a cooperative just as the Depression was beginning.

In the 1970s, 1100 was torn down to make way for a 40-story apartment building that bears the same address.

1100 NORTH LAKE SHORE DRIVE

Exterior, 1966. (Sigmund J. Osty, courtesy Chicago Historical Society)

1120 North Lake Shore Drive

Robert S. De Golyer, Architect | Walter Stockton, Associate Architect | 1924–25

Exterior, c. 1925. (Trowbridge, courtesy Chicago Historical Society)

Built for the realty company Baird & Warner, 1120 North Lake Shore Drive marked a revolution in scale for both apartment buildings and for the Drive. At 18 stories, in 1925 it was Chicago's tallest co-op, although the title would not last long. Fifteen years earlier, a nine-story apartment house was planned for the same corner, but it was never erected.

The site was purchased for $225,000, having been owned by the architects William Holabird and Martin Roche; for a time it held a small and lively "studio" used by their successors, John Holabird and John Root. This was De Golyer's first building on the Drive, and the first to have its shape defined by the new zoning code of 1923. Its pinnacled rooftop and gothic details projected a romantic if somewhat forbidding quality, intensified by its temporary isolation from other tall buildings and by dramatic renderings done at the time. 100% cooperative, taking advantage of recent legal changes, the five, six, and seven-room units included one tier of duplexes; according to legend, the duplexes resulted from an inability to expand the plot further westward, as was originally hoped. Today the building is home to 40 apartments, although 58 were originally planned.

Financial capacity was "only a minor consideration" in the "searching scrutiny" to greet prospective purchasers. Apartment prices began at $12,800. Wood burning fireplaces and a garage awaited those fortunate enough to survive the ordeal intact.

1120 North Lake Shore Drive

Plan. (*Western Architect*)

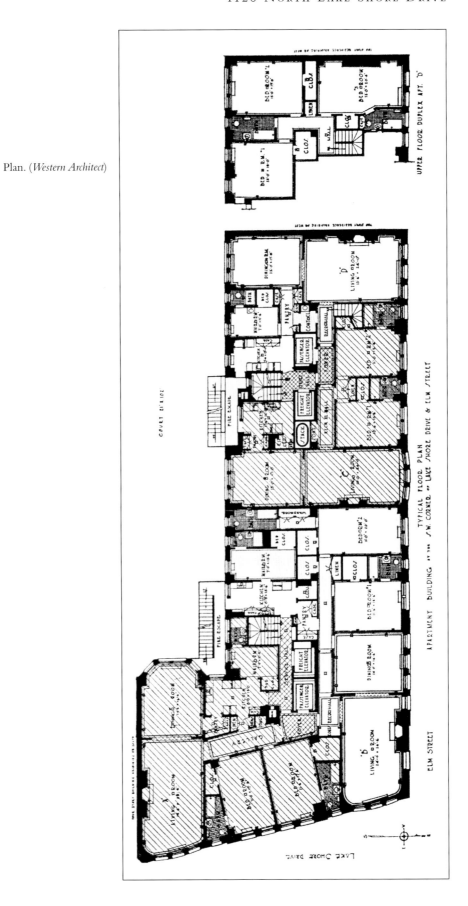

1130 North Lake Shore Drive

Howard Van Doren Shaw, Architect | Lanquist & Co., Builder | 1910

Exterior, 1916.
(*House Beautiful*)

Howard Van Doren Shaw is best known for his city and country houses, dozens of which are scattered across Chicago's south side and its northern suburbs. Shaw, a prominent civic leader and trustee of The Art Institute of Chicago, also designed several apartment houses, and he lived in two of them.

The *Chicago Tribune* considered 1130 North Lake Shore Drive to be the city's first luxury cooperative apartment building. The site was purchased from La Verne Noyes for $60,000; the following year eight tenant–owners each paid between $35,000 and $55,000 for their full-floor apartments. In 1918, Shaw was among the first to sell his unit, which went to Mrs. George A. Thorne. A brick and stone building of nine stories with Tudor Gothic references and bay window arrangements, 1130 North Lake Shore was broken up in later years into smaller units. A number of today's owners have reassembled the apartments. Today its entrance on Elm Street faces its southern neighbor 1120 Lake Shore Drive.

House Beautiful in 1916 approvingly endorsed the rigid separation of "service and masters" parts of the apartments and the convenient placing of stairs and elevators. "Grounds and gardens do not exist" for most urbanites, so it is up to the designer to create "those elements which create for the occupants of an apartment the illusion of privacy." The first occupants included several of Shaw's wealthy clients. Shaw's own top floor apartment, with its wood panelling and vaulted ceiling, obeyed the logic of the exterior, "Gothic in feeling, but unique and free in design."

1130 North Lake Shore Drive

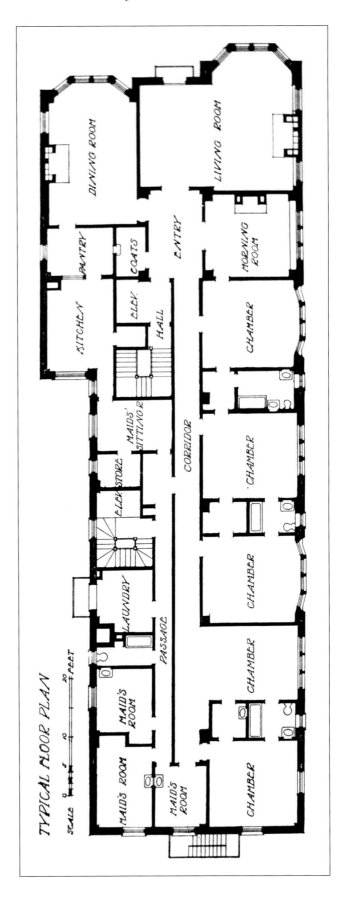

Plan, 1912. *(The Brickbuilder)*

Entrance hall, Howard Van Doren Shaw residence, 1916. (*House Beautiful*)

Hallway into dining room, 1993. Vinci Hamp, architects. (Courtesy Judith Bromley Photography and Vinci Hamp Architects)

1200 North Lake Shore Drive

STEWART APARTMENTS

Marshall and Fox, Architects | 1912

Exterior. (Baird and Warner, *Portfolio of Fine Apartment Homes*)

The 12-story apartment house Benjamin Marshall designed for owner John K. Stewart is an elegant exercise in neoclassical design, resembling in some respects the larger, but only slightly more luxurious, structure Marshall put up at 1550 North State. Of gray stone and yellow brick, it originally had accomodations for 10 families, the first two floors being used for servants, and the 13th for playrooms and extra maids' rooms—all this despite the presence of five servants' rooms in each apartment.

Swags placed in the spandrels between the first and second floors, a row of bay windows facing the lake, rosettes, urns, and foliated ornament all reveal the architect's impressive mastery of this traditional vocabulary. The apartment plan, labeled in French, demonstrated the building's ambition. The building still stands but it has been cut up into much smaller units.

1200 North Lake Shore Drive

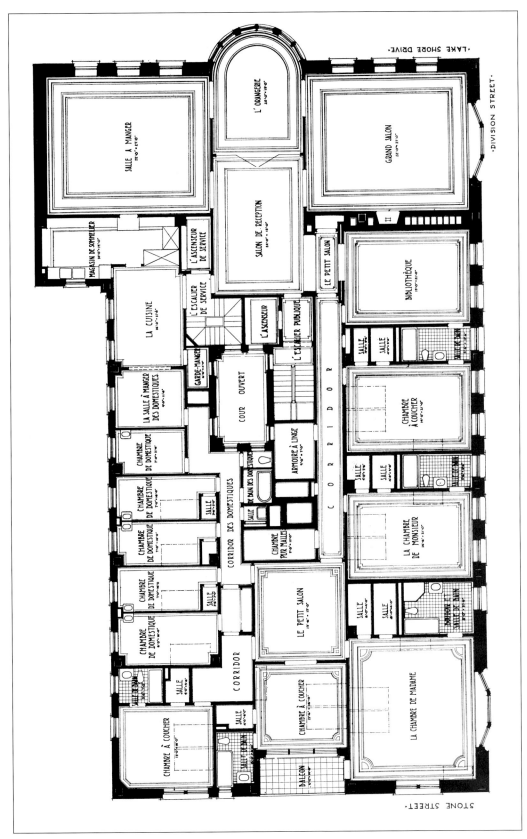

Plan. (Baird and Warner, *Portfolio of Fine Apartment Homes*)

1242 North Lake Shore Drive

Robert S. De Golyer, Architect | Turner Construction, Builder | 1928–30

Dining room, Morse residence, 1930. (Hedrich Blessing, courtesy Chicago Historical Society)

A syndicate of prominent Chicagoans, including Samuel Insull and Sterling Morton, financed construction of this planned 100% cooperative building on the site of the George High mansion. Actually the site contained two houses designed by Henry Ives Cobb. One was owned by High's mother-in-law who presented her daughter with the other. The land cost the investors $250,000, and the buildings another $1.5 million.

Twenty-eight stories high, of steel construction but with a Tudor and Gothic limestone lakefront facade and 242 weight reducing aluminum spandrels, 1242 North Lake Shore Drive was planned for 35 apartments, including six 8-room duplex units, and seven 11-room duplexes. Despite extensive advertising, only one-quarter of the apartments sold, and Turner Construction rented out the remaining units. Thus, there was more standardization to the apartment plans than had been expected earlier. Nonetheless, a 5300 square foot duplex penthouse sits atop the building, and was once occupied by Ray Kroc of McDonald's fame.

On some floors, special elevators enabled maids to travel to and from their laundry rooms. Turner Construction listed Rosario Candela of New York as associate architect on the project, although Candela is generally given credit for working on only one Chicago building, 1500 Lake Shore Drive. Reorganized as a cooperative in 1946, the total cost of $900,000 was significantly less than site and construction costs had consumed just 16 years earlier.

Exterior rendering. Advertisement for Turner Construction, 1929. (*Illinois Society of Architects Handbook*)

1242 NORTH LAKE SHORE DRIVE

Exterior, 1986.
(Courtesy Commission on Chicago Landmarks)

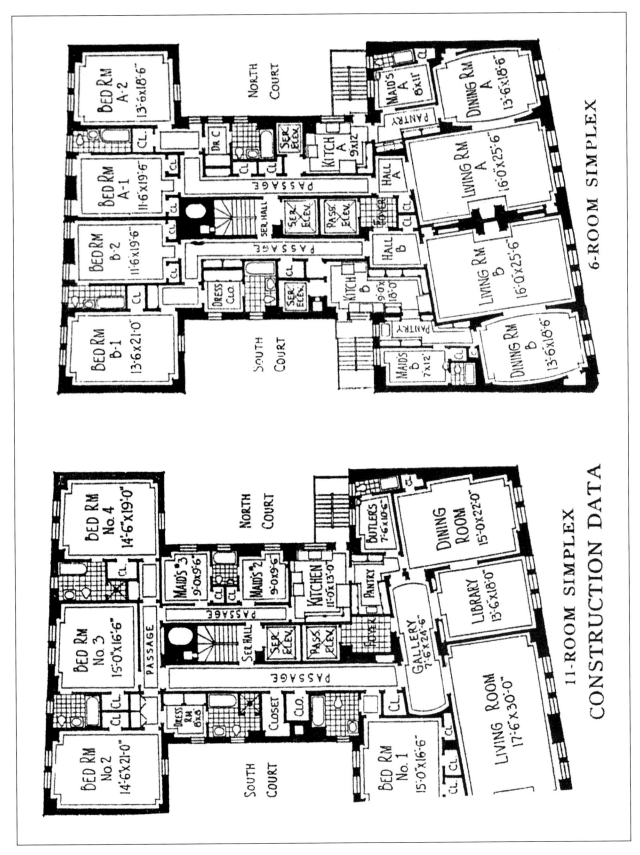

Plans, 1930. *(Architectural Forum)*

1418 North Lake Shore Drive

Solomon Cordwell Buenz, Architects | Mayfair Construction | 1980–83

Exterior, 2003.
(Courtesy Hedrich Blessing and Solomon Cordwell Buenz & Associates)

Only 44 feet wide, 1418 North Lake Shore Drive continued a tradition of whole floor lakefront apartments, sometimes on very tight sites, begun by the architects Benjamin Marshall and William Ernest Walker some 80 year earlier. According to *Inland Architect*, 1418 North Lake Shore was the first multi-family structure with one residence per floor to be constructed in Chicago since 1929. Built as a condominium, the 28-story building contains 27 apartments. Three tiers of angled and cantilevered windows permit the tenant–owners to catch glimpses of the wall of apartments to the north and south, as well as the lake itself. They also salvage some neighbors' views. Structural columns run through the apartment living rooms the full height of the building. Prices for these 3,100 square foot units in 1984 ran from $544,000 to $678,000.

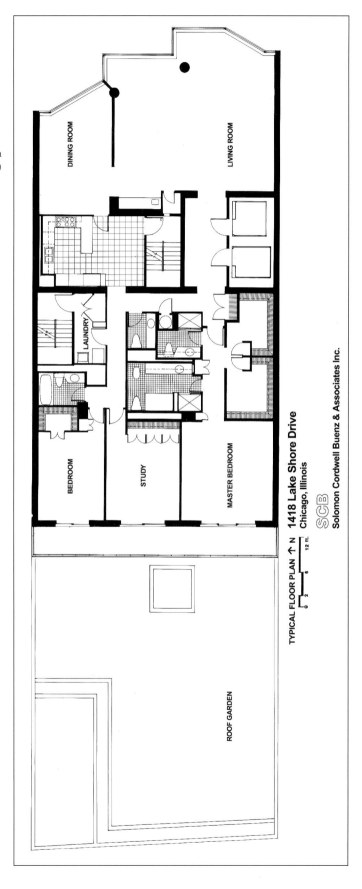

Plan, 1984. (Courtesy Solomon Cordwell Buenz & Associates)

1420 North Lake Shore Drive

Hooper & Janusch with David Saul Klafter, Architects |
Nelson Construction Co., Builder | 1928–30

Detail of exterior, 1933. (Hedrich Blessing, courtesy Chicago Historical Society)

1420 North Lake Shore Drive was constructed on the site of the Archibald Freer mansion, razed for this purpose. Another English Tudor adaptation with a steeply sloping roof, gable, oriel windows, and two chimneys topped with clay pots, the undulating facade with its window bays gives it depth and drama. The 19-story building was planned for 35 apartments, one of them a duplex at the top with open terraces, "helping to form a miniature country estate within sight of the Loop," wrote Philip Hampson in the *Chicago Tribune*. The manorial tradition was emphasized further by the presence of wood storage rooms and paneled libraries in a number of the apartments. The *Tribune* noted that the servants' quarters, in an effort to make the domestic staff "more contented," were a bit more pleasant than in comparable buildings.

Both Cincinnati-born David Klafter, who had worked for Daniel Burnham and Jarvis Hunt before setting up independent practice, and William T. Hooper and Fred Janusch, were responsible for a series of apartment buildings throughout Chicago.

1420 North Lake Shore Drive

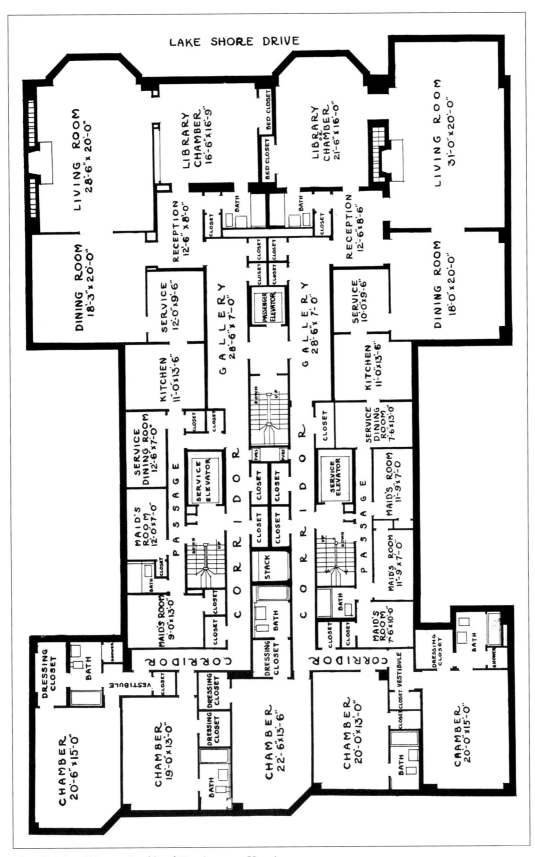

Plan. (Baird and Warner, *Portfolio of Fine Apartment Homes*)

1420 North Lake Shore Drive

Exterior, 1992.
(Courtesy Commission
on Chicago Landmarks)

Residence of Ike Sewell, 1968. (Hedrich Blessing, courtesy Chicago Historical Society)

1430 North Lake Shore Drive

Robert S. De Golyer, Architect | Lind Construction, Builder | 1927–28

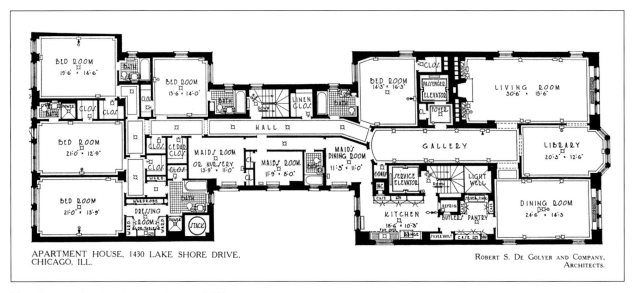

Plan. (Sexton, *American Apartment Houses*, 1929)

Developer William C. Bannerman, a frequent De Golyer partner, bought the site for this 25-story building from the James Deering estate and wrecked the existing mansion. Only 45 feet wide, the building was so "skinny" it swayed in the wind, according to Walter Stockton, who worked for De Golyer and did much of his designing. One year later, a new neighboring building braced it up.

The Indiana limestone front in English Gothic was topped by a false gable. 1430 North Lake Shore Drive was planned for only one apartment to a floor. The number of rooms varied because the apartments were partitioned differently; from the 2nd to the 13th floor the flats were to have had 12 rooms and six baths; above that level, 11 rooms. The *Chicago Tribune* declared the building to be the last word in luxury, with its wood burning fireplaces, linen rooms, silver vaults, cedar closets, "and other little conveniences which make being a millionaire such a pleasant sort of occupation."

1430 Lake Shore was more expensive to build than its investors anticipated. Bannerman, who erected dozens of impressive luxury buildings in a brief but intense career, turned out to be a swindler. In Miles Berger's study of Chicago developers, Bannerman was shown to have set up reams of dummy corporations to disguise his staggering debt levels, inflated costs, kickbacks, and an assignment of shares he did not actually pay for. Some time before the Depression began he was declared insolvent. Angry 1430 shareholders sued, and Bannerman was ordered to pay the corporation more than $200,000, or two-thirds the par value of the shares. His stock was sold below its face value, and the other shareholders never fully recovered their money. Bannerman fled the city, but 1430 survived. Today it remains impressive testimony to the De Golyer firm's excellent planning.

1430 NORTH LAKE SHORE DRIVE

Exterior. (Sexton, *American Apartment Houses*, 1929)

1448 North Lake Shore Drive

Childs & Smith, Architects | Avery Brundage, Builder | 1926–27

Exterior.
(Baird and Warner,
*Portfolio of Fine
Apartment Homes*)

Architects Frank A. Childs and William Jones Smith, producers of a series of Midwestern school buildings, had also worked on Northwestern University's recently built Chicago campus before designing 1448 North Lake Shore Drive; they claimed as inspiration the Chateau at Blois, whose features had become familiar some years earlier to members of the American Expeditionary Force.

Steel framed but faced in Bedford stone and brick, the building's typical floors were divided into three apartments of six, seven, and eight rooms, these last having a separate elevator lobby. Larger apartments were also available for purchase. The spectacular lobby, in faience tile and oak paneling, and the 10-foot ceilings in many apartments, made for particularly impressive features. The *Chicago Tribune* commented that "if there is a convenience left out of the building it will only be because it hasn't been invented." A battlemented balustrade with "Gothic pinnacles" finished the building at the top.

Built as a 100% cooperative, it remains so today. Handling the original sales, Baird & Warner erected a two-story cottage on the site, and proceeded to feed newspapers the names of a series of initial purchasers, a strategy designed to encourage further activity.

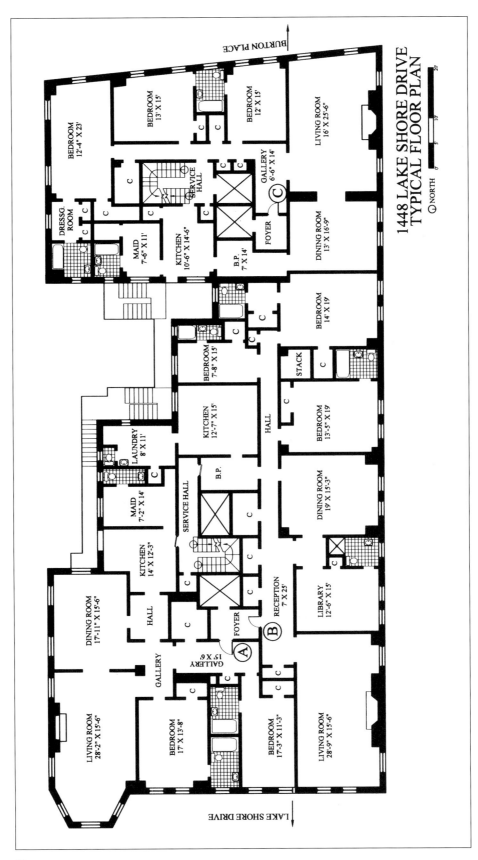

Plan.

1500 North Lake Shore Drive

McNally & Quinn Architects; Rosario Candela, Associate Architect | Turner Construction, Builder | 1927–29

Exterior with chimneys and pool. Woodruff penthouse duplex, 1930. McNally & Quinn, architects. (Hedrich Blessing, courtesy Chicago Historical Society)

1500 North Lake Shore Drive occupies the site where the great Chicago newspaper publisher Victor Lawson had built his million dollar, built-to-last mansion. Portions of the house were, in fact, inserted into some apartments of the new building. At 25 stories high, of limestone and brick in French Renaissance style, 1500 presented itself as a different kind of cooperative from the start. "Olympus is more beautiful," Ruth Bergman wrote in the *Chicagoan*, "but the gods have never chilled their nectar in such magnificent ice boxes." For one thing, there was its expense, estimates running at $5 million for land and building. For another, there was the New York participation of architect Rosario Candela, real estate advisor Douglas Elliman & Co., and Turner Construction. "Manhattan seems to figure excessively in this project," Al Chase reflected in the *Chicago Tribune*. Finally, the 57 apartments, most of which were sold before the building had been completed, offered purchasers the opportunity of being individually designed. Their only common features, noted one journalist, were silver vaults and wood-burning fireplaces. A series of architects created interior spaces for individual clients, although Turner Construction completely finished the building's interiors to the architects' specifications.

The basic plan had three tiers of apartments: one of 11 rooms to the south; 9 rooms in the center; and 10 rooms to the north. There were two maisonette apartments and a rooftop 18-room bungalow, with its own reflecting pool and set of gardens. But purchasers undertook major variations in layout throughout, including the shifting of bathrooms and kitchens, and the planning of several duplexes. The fact that work essentially was completed in 22 months, between December 1927 and October 1929, became a major boast for the contractors, who pointed out that architects and engineers prepared some 850 descriptive drawings and that ultimately 50,000 blue prints were distributed. Some of the apartments, however, were not finished until several years later. Peter F. Reynolds, the head of the building syndicate, lived in 1500 alongside a string of prominent Chicago business figures including William Wrigley, Jr., Chauncey Blair, and banker George Woodruff, who moved into the elaborately decorated penthouse. A large garage and an ample porte cochere serviced the automobile-blessed ownership. Despite the bad economic timing of its completion, 1500 has remained a 100% cooperative building since opening.

Exterior, 1936. (Hedrich Blessing, Hogan and Farwell series, courtesy Chicago Historical Society).

1500 North Lake Shore Drive

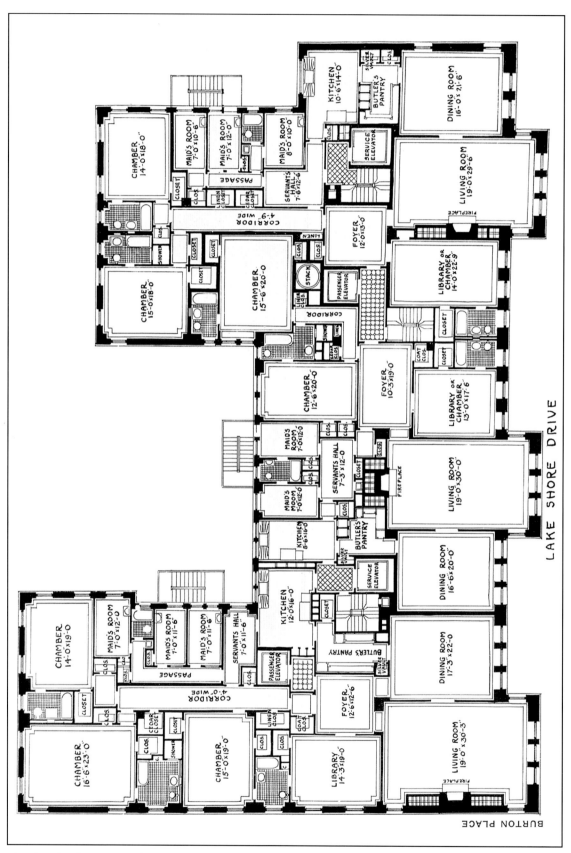

Plan. (Baird and Warner, *Portfolio of Fine Apartment Homes*)

Hallway, Woodruff penthouse duplex, 1930. McNally and Quinn, architects; A.C. Rindskopf, decorators and furniture. (Hedrich Blessing, courtesy Chicago Historical Society)

Dining room, Woodruff penthouse duplex, 1930. McNally and Quinn, architects; A.C. Rindskopf, decorators and furniture. (Hedrich Blessing, courtesy Chicago Historical Society)

Stairway, Woodruff penthouse duplex, 1930. McNally and Quinn, architects; A.C. Rindskopf, decorators and furniture. (Hedrich Blessing, courtesy Chicago Historical Society)

Bathroom of Mrs. Woodruff in Italian Renaissance style, Woodruff penthouse duplex, 1930. McNally and Quinn, architects; A.C. Rindskopf, decorators and furniture. (Courtesy, Ryerson and Burnham Libraries, The Art Institute of Chicago. All rights reserved.)

Bathroom of Mr. Woodruff in Pompeian style, Woodruff penthouse duplex, 1930. McNally and Quinn, architects; A.C. Rindskopf, decorators and furniture. (Hedrich Blessing, courtesy Chicago Historical Society)

Living room, William Wrigley residence, 1927. (Trowbridge, courtesy Chicago Historical Society)

Foyer, William Wrigley residence, 1927. (Trowbridge, Courtesy Ryerson and Burnham Libraries, Edwin Clark Collection, The Art Institute of Chicago. All rights reserved.)

1540 North Lake Shore Drive

Huszagh & Hill, Architects | Avery Brundage, Builder | 1925–26

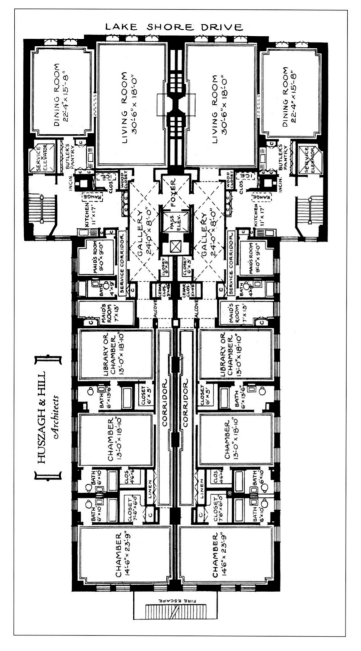

Plan. (Baird and Warner, *Portfolio of Fine Apartment Homes*)

The site for 1540 North Lake Shore Drive was an empty lot purchased by developer Milton Plotke from Chauncey Keep for $168,000, or $2,250 a front foot, as newspapers pointed out. At the time the R.T. Crane home stood just to its north, and the Victor Lawson mansion was a few doors to its south. This was the northernmost advance of the Lake Shore Drive phalanx of apartment buildings, as they marched inexorably toward North Avenue and Lincoln Park in the 1920s. While the 17-story red brick and stone-trimmed cooperative was replete with classical details, including a three-story rusticated limestone base suggesting the Adam style, its steep slate roof and circular stone towers evoked a French chateau. Typical floors contained two 8-room apartments, although there were variations.

Like many other cooperatives, 1540 Lake Shore went into receivership during the Depression. In 1947, 90% of its 30 resident families combined to return the building to cooperative status, which it remains today.

Exterior. (Trowbridge, courtesy Chicago Historical Society)

Lobby, 1950. (Hedrich Blessing, courtesy Chicago Historical Society)

Library, Hirshfield residence, 1950. (Hedrich Blessing, courtesy Chicago Historical Society)

Dining room, Ethel and Mortimer Harris residence, c. 1940s. Samuel A. Marx, architect. (Private collection)

Pantry, Ethel and Mortimer Harris residence, c. 1940s. Samuel A. Marx, architect. (Private Collection)

2130 North Lincoln Park West

Oman & Lilienthal, Architects | Lilienthal, Builder | 1926–27

Exterior rendering, c. 1926. (*Twenty-one Thirty Lincoln Park West*, brochure, courtesy Ryerson and Burnham Libraries, McNally and Quinn Collection, The Art Institute of Chicago. All rights reserved.)

"Beautiful originality rises above mobs," declared the brochure promoting this cooperative, "not with the freak who strives for attractive shams, but with the personality of refined genuineness." Such promotional rhetoric may have been intended to justify the unusual rooftop profile of this classically inspired but relatively austere brick and stone building. Perhaps it meant to emphasize the dweller's privacy as well. Though there were only two apartments per floor, each enjoyed its own private elevator landing. Special sound deadening between the apartments was accomplished through hollow tile partitions, or "Flaxinuum," and layers of felt. *The Economist* reported that many new owners planned distinctive features ranging from imported paneling to replicas of celebrated Italian mantels.

Mr. and Mrs. Howard Willett occupied the 18th-floor bungalow. Mrs. Willett was president of the Drama League of Chicago, and the rooftop gardens included a moonlit stage for private performances. Special lighting capacities and varying floor levels added to the bungalow's character. Neighbors added stained glass window decorations, marble fountains, and, for the president of the Indiana Limestone Company, limestone mantels. Apartment prices ranged from $14,400 to $37,100 for the 13-room full-floor apartment on the 17th floor.

2130 North Lincoln Park West

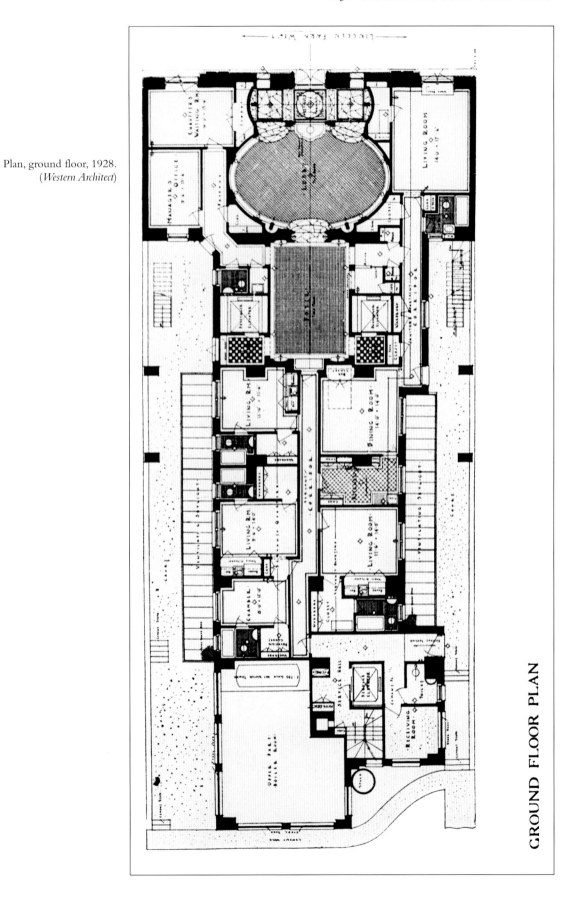

Plan, ground floor, 1928. (*Western Architect*)

GROUND FLOOR PLAN

2130 NORTH LINCOLN PARK WEST

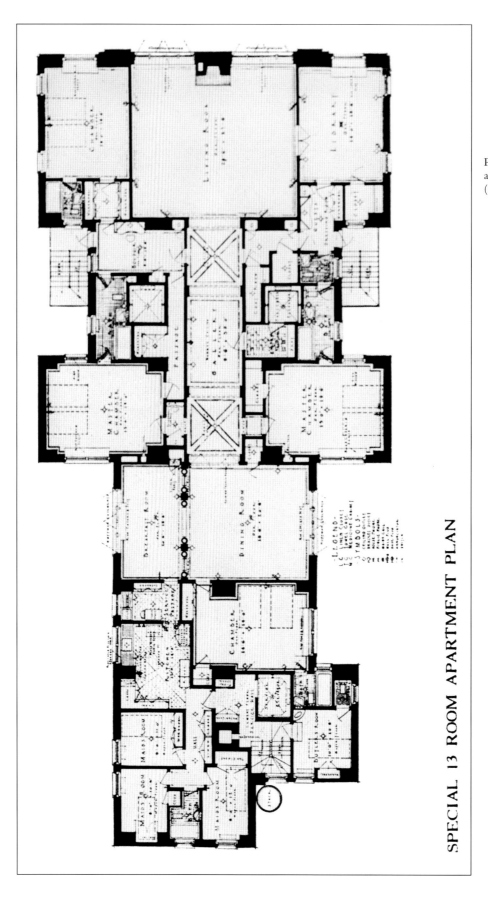

Plan, 13-room apartment, 1928. (*Western Architect*)

2130 North Lincoln Park West

TOP: Lobby; BOTTOM: Living room. 1928. *(Western Architect)*

2300 North Lincoln Park West

BELDEN—STRATFORD HOTEL

Meyer Fridstein & Co., Architect | G.H. Gottshalk, Builder | 1922–23

Exterior, 1939. (Hedrich Blessing, courtesy Chicago Historical Society)

The Belden Hotel, as it was originally called, was put up by the same team that would build the Shoreland Hotel on the south side just a couple of years later. The $4 million, 650-room building was announced by the Lott Hotel Company, the owners of the Parkway and Webster Hotels. Clad in light colored brick, with neoclassical French detailing and a striking, terra-cotta mansard roof, the Belden was a colorful addition to the area.

The Fridstein firm at various times served as architect, engineer, and contractor. Meyer Fridstein, who worked briefly for Marshall and Fox, built theaters and commercial structures as well as hotels. The Belden-Stratford's exterior exuberance reflects these varied commissions. It offered a variety of apartment layouts ranging from single rooms to two-bedroom suites. Many of them had their own kitchenettes, but, given the hotel services, lacked maids' rooms. Auctioned in 1954, it has recently been remodeled into condominium apartments, although its lavish lobby and dining rooms remind visitors of the opulence of a 1920s apartment hotel.

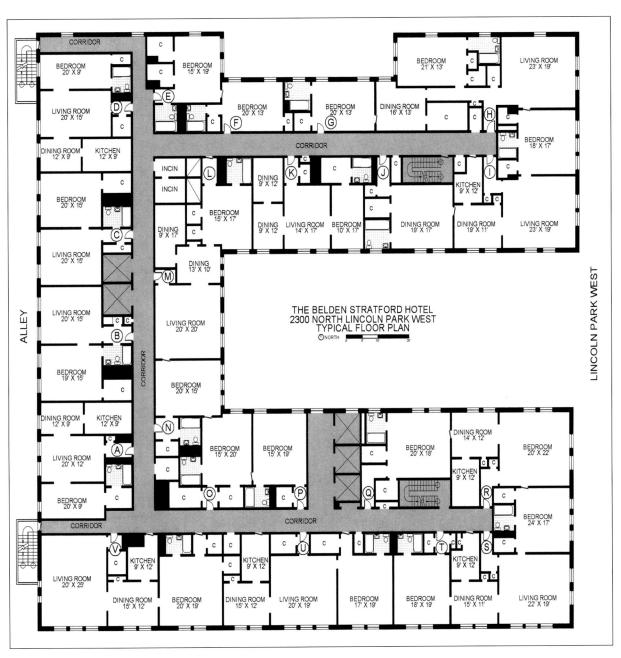

Plan.

6 North Michigan Avenue

MONTGOMERY WARD TOWER BUILDING

Richard Schmidt; addition Holabird & Roche; remodeled Loebl, Schlossman & Bennett | 1899; 1923; 1955; 2002–04

Exterior. (Bob Thall, courtesy Commission on Chicago Landmarks)

This was the downtown headquarters of the great mail order house Montgomery Ward. Architectural historians ascribe the design to Hugh M. G. Garden, then a Schmidt employee. At the turn of the century, the building was topped by a tower, pyramid, tempietto, and a gilded weather vane. The tower was later taken down and four floors were added. The elegant rusticated base was also covered over and shops placed within its first floor.

An office building for the century that followed its construction, the Tower Building has recently undergone conversion to condominium apartments, one of a series of signature structures in the central city so converted. Portions of the tower have been rebuilt; the basic fenestration has been retained, the exterior cleaned, and in places reclad. Office buildings of this type, with ceilings of 9 feet or more, have proven hospitable to apartment conversion, and while most of the apartments are smaller than 2,000 square feet, the 17th, 18th, and 19th floors offer large units, some with private terraces.

6 North Michigan Avenue

Michigan Avenue looking north from Adams Street showing Ward Tower (far right) after 1914. (Kaufmann & Fabry, courtesy Chicago Historical Society)

6 North Michigan Avenue

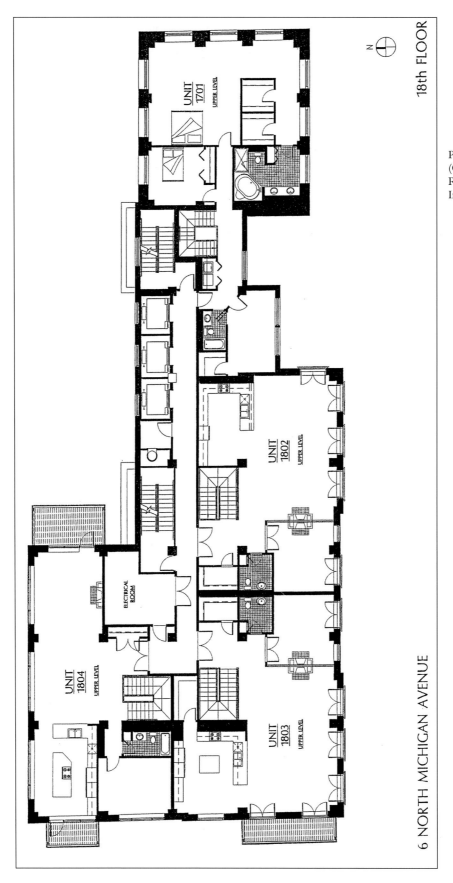

Plan, 2002. (Courtesy Globus Real Estate Investments)

6 North Michigan Avenue

Michigan Avenue looking south from Washington Street, 1924. (Courtesy Chicago Historical Society)

800 North Michigan Avenue

PARK TOWER

Lucien Lagrange, Architect | James McHugh Construction, Builder | 1998–2001

Exterior, 2000. Lucien Lagrange, architect. (Courtesy Anthony May, photographer and Lucien Lagrange Architects)

The architect Lucien Lagrange has designed a series of luxury apartment buildings while converting a number of older structures into residences. His Park Tower design combines the functions of hotel and condominium residences. As with a number of other recent nearby buildings, saleable floor space is maximized by shifting athletic and recreational facilities to the hotel.

Park Tower stands on the site of an earlier Hyatt Hotel. Its height, prominent location, and distinctive copper roof brought the Park Tower local attention, but more than that, the prices commanded by the raw space being sold—or more accurately, resold by speculative investors—pierced existing barriers in the Chicago market, and encouraged development of other high rise condominiums in the city. Many purchasers brought their own architects to design and finish their units. The apartment units on typical floors enjoy impressive views and recall prewar apartment dimensions, but they lack service entries and easy access to freight elevators, a common feature in comparable 1920s buildings.

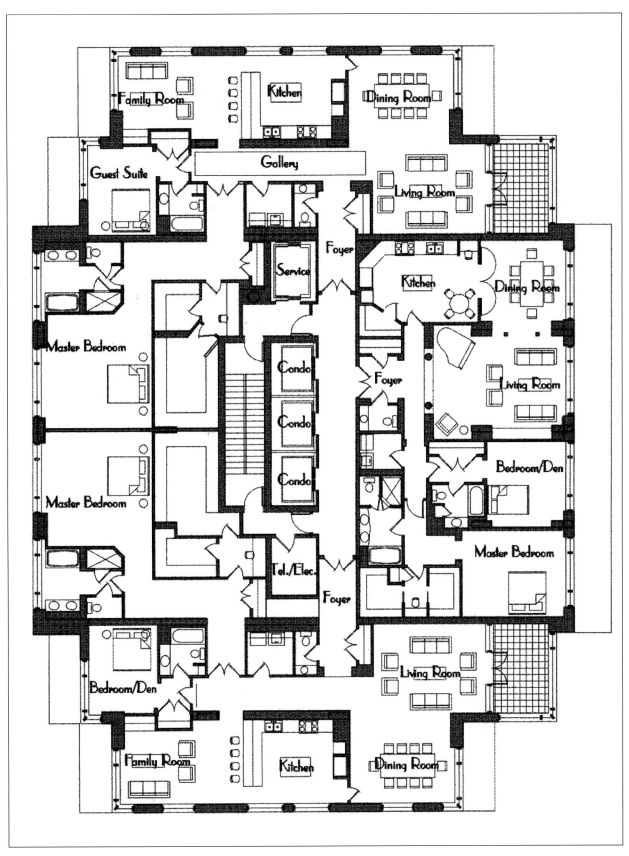

Typical floor plan. Lucien Lagrange, architect, 1996. (Courtesy Lucien Lagrange Architects)

900 North Michigan Avenue

Jarvis Hunt, Architect | J.B. French, Builder | 1925–27

Exterior, c. 1950. (Courtesy Ryerson and Burnham Libraries, The Art Institute of Chicago, Jarvis Hunt papers)

This building, razed in 1984 to make way for a huge multi-use complex, was an unusual early multi-use effort in itself, and still evokes nostalgic memories among some older Chicagoans. The ground floor housed a string of fashionable shops and an open landscaped courtyard with fountain held a popular restaurant, Jacques. U-shaped, with a four-story limestone base and six levels of brick above it, 900 North Michigan Avenue—or, as it was called for a time, 900 Michigan North—was a simple and relatively undecorated building, save for some balconettes and a balustrade separating the two wings. Inside, however, dozens of the syndicate's socially prominent investors, led by Cyrus McCormick, Jr., installed elaborate interiors with as many as 14 rooms. Some duplexes had 21-foot high living rooms. The building's lower floors held smaller rental apartments. *The Economist* and the *Chicago Tribune* announced that its foundations permitted a much taller building—the *Tribune* declared that 21 stories would have been possible.

Jarvis Hunt, nephew of the more famous architect Richard Morris Hunt, came to Chicago to design the Vermont Building for the 1893 World's Fair, and he stayed for more than three decades. Hunt proposed important elements of the Burnham Plan of 1906 and designed, among other things, Union Stations for Kansas City and Dallas, and the Lake Shore Athletic Club in Chicago. Hunt was himself an investor in 900 North Michigan.

When Jerrold Wexler and a syndicate purchased the building in 1960, the new owners proposed adding 6 to 10 additional stories. After the old structure was taken down in 1984, its much larger replacement became 132 East Delaware–900 North Michigan, covered elsewhere in this book.

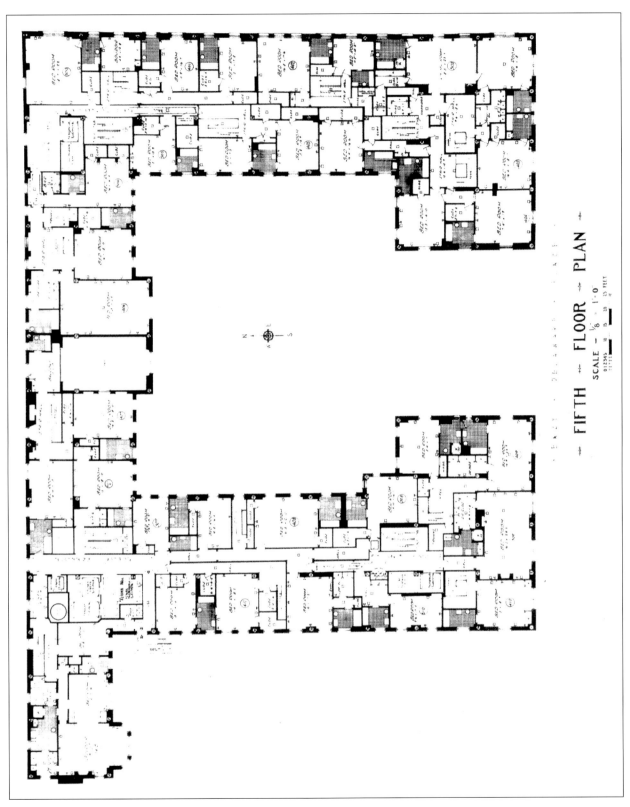

Plan, fifth floor. (Courtesy Ryerson and Burnham Libraries, The Art Institute of Chicago, Jarvis Hunt papers)

Interior of an apartment, 1943. (Hedrich Blessing, courtesy Chicago Historical Society)

900 NORTH MICHIGAN AVENUE

Living room. Cyrus McCormick, Jr., residence. Walcott and Work, architects, c. 1930s.
(Trowbridge, courtesy Chicago Historical Society)

919 North Michigan Avenue

PALMOLIVE BUILDING

Holabird & Root, Architects | Booth Hansen, redesign | Hegemann–Harris Co., Builders | 1927–29; 2002–04

Lightning over Palmolive Building and Lake Shore Drive East, 1937. (Hedrich Blessing, courtesy Chicago Historical Society)

The Palmolive Building was Chicago's most distinctive art deco monument. Its elegant setbacks, carved elevator door panels, nickel metal mail boxes, walnut and marble lobby, etched glass lighting, revolving Lindbergh Beacon, and sleek profile summed up the spirit of 1920s moderne. After Colgate–Palmolive moved out in 1934, the building was sold a number of times, and served for some years as the headquarters for Playboy Enterprises. Most recently the building was sold to be developed, as with some other Chicago icons, into a luxury condominium building.

"The highest levels of design and construction went into the Palmolive," Carl Condit noted. Its architects constituted "the front rank" of Chicago skyscraper design. The office ceiling heights, the 12 elevator shafts, along with the six setbacks, allow for unusual layouts and sophisticated technical support systems. As the presence in the 1930s of the Bror Dahlberg apartment on the Palmolive's 32nd floor indicates, residential living is not a wholly new idea for this building. Dahlberg was president of the Celotex Company and maintained a residence at 999 North Lake Shore Drive; this may well have been a demonstration unit to show off his product.

Exterior, 1950s. (Hedrich Blessing, courtesy Chicago Historical Society)

Vestibule. Bror C. Dahlberg residence on the 32nd floor. (*Townsfolk*, 1930. Courtesy Chicago Historical Society)

Lounge and vestibule. Bror C. Dahlberg residence on the 32nd floor. (*Townsfolk*, 1930. Courtesy Chicago Historical Society)

919 North Michigan Avenue

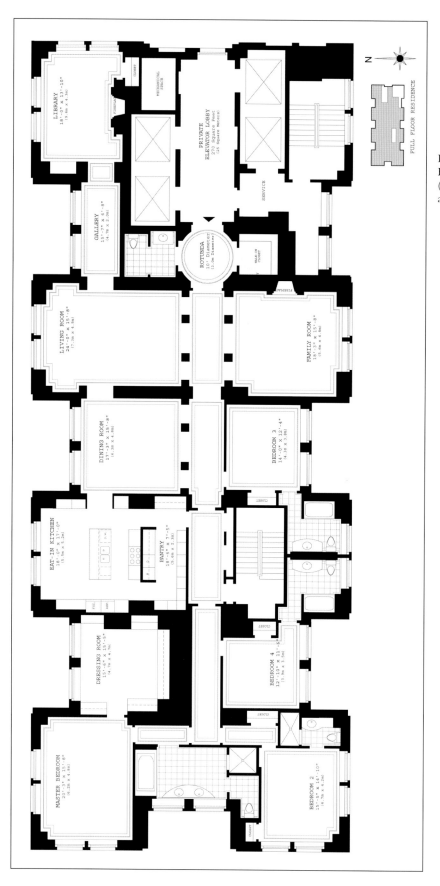

Plan, floors 23–32. Booth Hansen, architects, 2003. (Courtesy Draper and Kramer and Booth Hansen)

919 North Michigan Avenue

Designs on elevator doors, 1929. (Courtesy Chicago Historical Society and Commission on Chicago Landmarks)

940–980 NORTH MICHIGAN AVENUE

ONE MAGNIFICENT MILE

Skidmore, Owings & Merrill, Architect | Schal Associates, Builder | 1978–83

Exterior.
(Courtesy Hedrich Blessing and Skidmore, Owings & Merrill LLP)

A combination of three floors of commercial spaces, 18 floors of offices, and 36 condominium floors, One Magnificent Mile—along with the Drake Hotel just opposite—is the northern terminus of Michigan Avenue. Skidmore partner Bruce Graham supervised the design, which incorporates an innovative system of several reinforced concrete bundled tubes, exploiting a technology that the same firm had developed for Chicago's tallest building, the Sears Tower. The pink color of the granite, the sloping rooflines, and the unusual shape give it a strong presence on Chicago's skyline. The almost 200 apartments have, as a result, uncommon shapes, and there are a number of terraced penthouses.

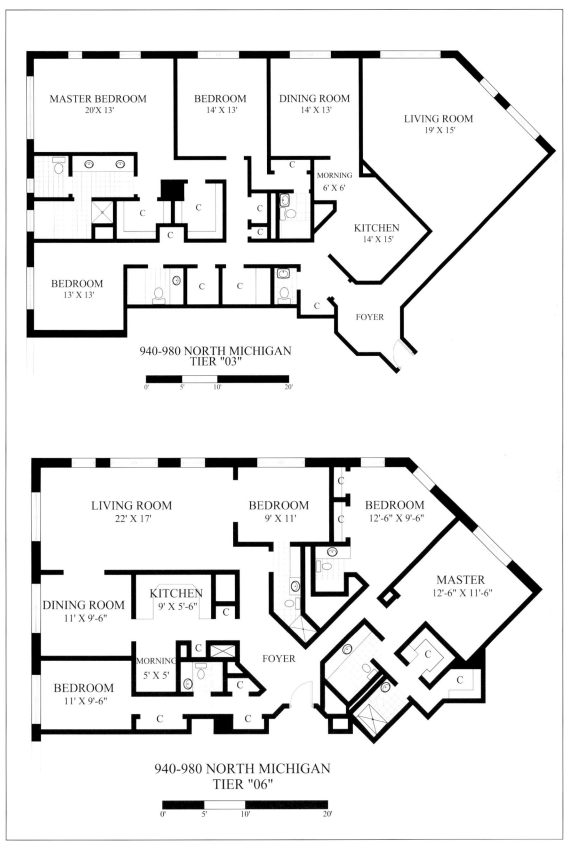

Plans.

180 East Pearson Street

Water Tower Place

Loebl, Schlossman, Dart & Hackl, Architects | Inland–Robbins Co., Builder | 1972–76

Exterior, 1975.

This complex, consisting of an eight-level atrium mall, hotel, and condominium apartments, made a significant contribution to North Michigan Avenue's explosive growth, and set some important patterns for future developments nationally as well. A megaplex, with 640 underground parking spaces and 74 floors, it contained one of the country's first vertical malls, and it would be followed by quite a number of others, several of them just a few blocks away. Hotel facilities, from dining to swimming, were made available to the condominium residents, another model that would be repeated in subsequent years.

The apartments, some duplex, others with saunas, and all with nine-foot ceilings, were somewhat larger in size than those that met the luxury standard of the 1960s and early 1970s. Stretching from the 33rd to the 72nd floors, there are more than 250 units.

The building complex itself, with the large, marble, windowless shopping mall block facing Michigan Avenue, its hotel and apartment tower placed further east along Pearson Street, received distinctly mixed reviews on opening.

180 EAST PEARSON STREET

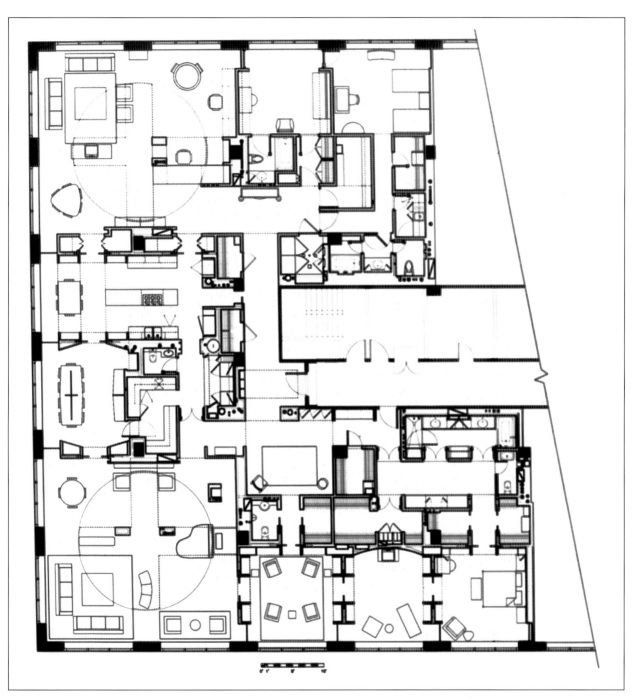

Plan, c. 1976. (*The Condominium Residences at Water Tower Place*, brochure, courtesy Ryerson and Burnham Libraries, McNally and Quinn Collection, The Art Institute of Chicago. All rights reserved.)

Living Room. Stanley Tigerman and Margaret McCurry, architects, 2001. (Courtesy Chris Barrett/Hedrich Blessing and Tigerman McCurry Architects)

180 East Pearson Street

Office. Stanley Tigerman and Margaret McCurry, architects, 2001. (Courtesy Chris Barrett/Hedrich Blessing and Tigerman McCurry Architects)

200 East Pearson Street

CAMPBELL APARTMENTS

Robert S. De Golyer, Architect | Nelson Bedgbo, Builder | 1916–17

Exterior elevation from the southwest, c. 1925. (Trowbridge, courtesy Chicago Historical Society)

An Italian palazzo transferred to the streets of Chicago, this six-story, 10-apartment residence bears Renaissance-inspired details that have variously been linked to the Palazzo Strozzi in Florence and the Palazzo Farnese in Rome. The corner quoins and the rusticated entrance arch are particularly noteworthy. Completed in 1917 for George Campbell at an estimated cost of $136,000, this was one of De Golyer's earliest commissions as an independent architect. The brown brick building, with cast concrete and metal trim, is locally celebrated as the home of Mies van der Rohe, who continued living there after completing and apparently briefly contemplating moving to his Lake Shore Drive Glass Houses a few blocks away. Whatever the reasons for his decision, the obvious ironies have served critics of modernism as a metaphorical label for its shortcomings.

200 East Pearson Street

Plan. (Pardridge and Bradley, *Directory of Apartments*)

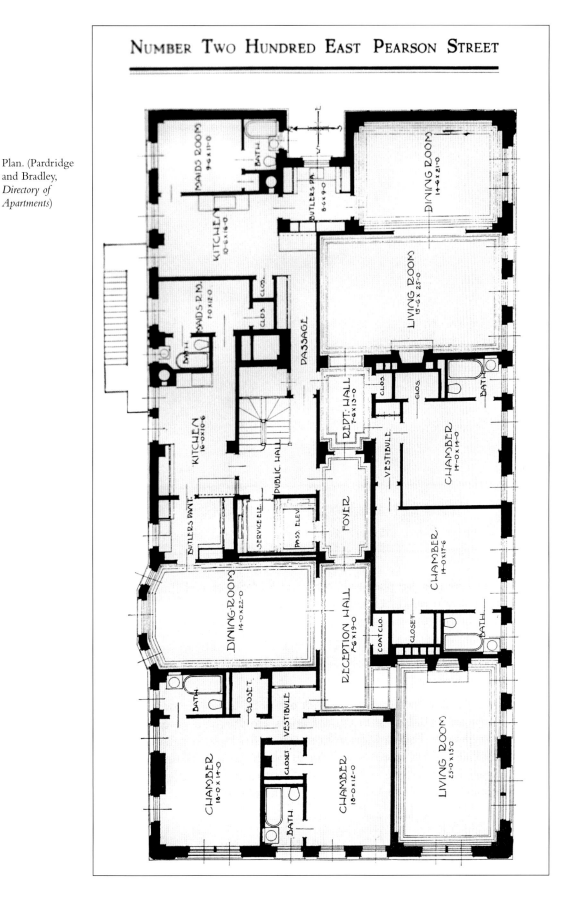

400 East Randolph Street

Outer Drive East

Hirschfeld, Pawlan and Reinheimer, Architects | Crane Construction, Builder | 1963

Exterior with Lake Point Tower under construction, 1963. (Hedrich Blessing, courtesy Chicago Historical Society)

One of the first truly mammoth middle-class apartment structures to go up after World War II, Outer Drive East still stands out for its size, cost, and location. Its $20 million mortgage was the largest issued in Illinois at the time. With more than 900 units, the building's construction caused a bitter legal battle over the air and riparian rights of the Illinois Central Railroad, resolved only through the aggressive development skills of Jerrold Wexler. Forty stories high, with an attended garage housing 850 cars, the giant T-shaped structure was a lonely pioneer. It was sold in 1973 for purposes of conversion to condominiums and now stands amid a number of other large apartment buildings.

Brand new, its huge white and black balconied facade crowned by an undulating penthouse hiding mechanical equipment, Outer Drive East seemed the epitome of modern comfort. Linked to a glass-domed, kidney-shaped swimming pool, there was "no need to dash off to Florida or southern France to escape the wintry weather," promised the brochure. It also contained, on its top floor, a popular restaurant, La Tour. Today it sums up a distinctly late-1950s design sensibility.

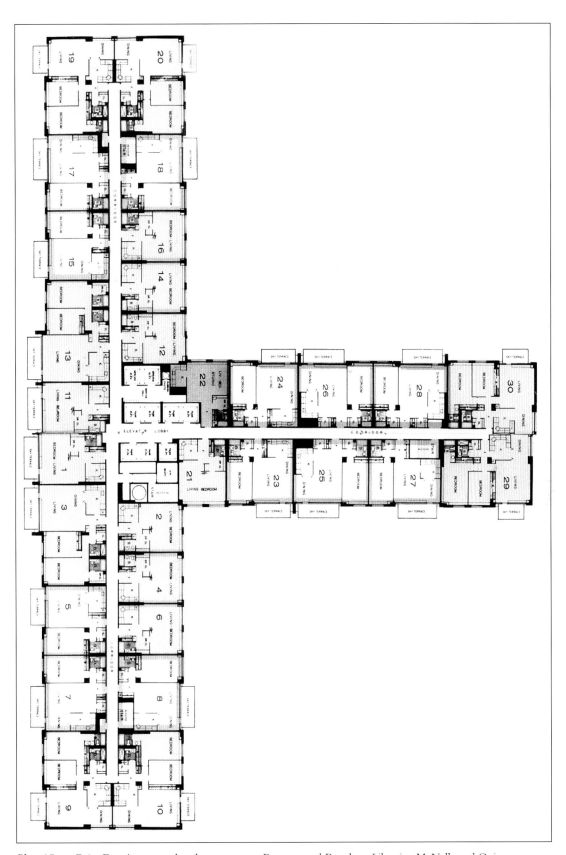

Plan. (*Outer Drive East Apartments,* brochure, courtesy Ryerson and Burnham Libraries, McNally and Quinn Collection, The Art Institute of Chicago. All rights reserved.)

Chicago, showing Outer Drive East alone by the lake (far right), c. 1971. (Courtesy collection of David R. Phillips)

Living room, Adelaide Radcliffe residence, 1964. (Hedrich Blessing, courtesy Chicago Historical Society)

60–70 East Scott Street

Fugard & Knapp, Architects | McLennan Construction, Builders | 1917–18

Exterior, 1968.
(Hedrich Blessing,
courtesy Chicago
Historical Society)

According to Zurich Esposito, a student of the architectural firm of Fugard & Knapp, this was John Fugard's first luxury apartment house, preceding his series of East Lake Shore Drive structures by several years. Nine stories tall, with neoclassical details, the brick building has a central courtyard fronted by an elaborately rusticated Italian Renaissance gate. The project of developers Harold Bradley and A. J. Pardridge, who also co-authored a directory of "apartments of the better class," the 16-flat building was built for a group of tenant-owners who rented out portions of it—probably the westernmost section, whose dining rooms lacked the generous bays of the eastern units. At least one unit was a duplex of 18 rooms with seven bathrooms.

The *Chicago Tribune* described it in 1920 as the first of the city's semi-cooperatives, reporting that the building was owned by five of its tenants. Several members of Chicago's meat packing families lived in these commodious apartments for some years. The three fireplaces and large master bedrooms must have exerted some appeal. One flat was being offered at $650 per month in 1925. The apartments have since been divided.

60–70 East Scott Street

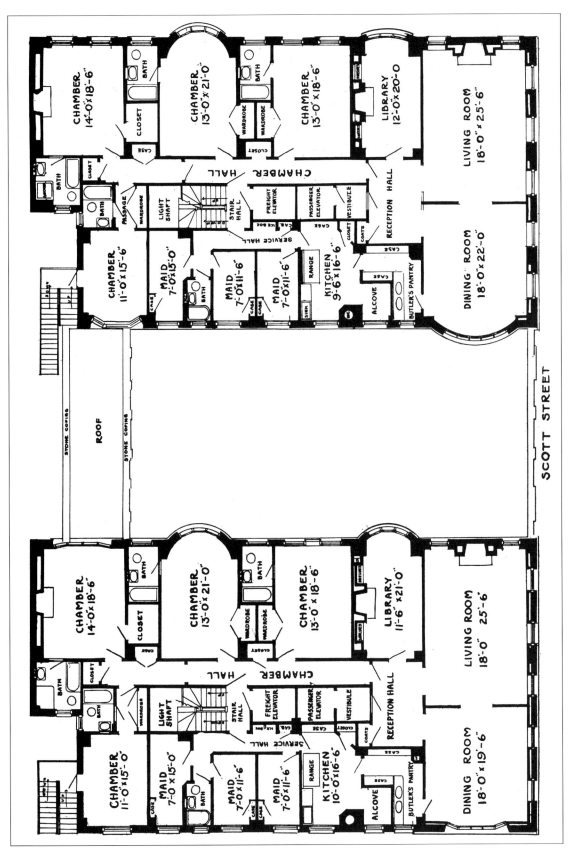

Plan. (Baird and Warner, *Portfolio of Fine Apartment Homes*)

300 North State Street

MARINA CITY

Bertrand Goldberg, Architect | James McHugh Construction Co., Builder | 1959–64

Marina City Towers and the Chicago River, 1960–72. (Hedrich Blessing, courtesy Chicago Historical Society)

These two 60-story reinforced concrete towers mark a key moment in Chicago's rebuilding after World War II. Built at a time of anxiety about the future of American cities, this urban enclave's mingling of offices, apartments, restaurants, shops, recreational spaces, marina, and parking was meant to counter the growing appeal of the suburbs.

The Building Services Employees International Union, led by William McFetridge, purchased the land from the Chicago and North Western Railway and turned to Bertrand Goldberg for a plan. After some initial proposals, Goldberg offered the tallest cylindrical buildings yet constructed, containing almost 900 apartments and space for as many automobiles. Its choice riverfront location and distinctive appearance helped propel the project to success, and gave Chicago another widely recognized architectural icon.

Room sizes were relatively modest, accepting the dominant post-war standards: kitchens were small, there were no formal dining rooms, and heating and cooling elements were visible below the windows. Yet the balconies and superb views helped compensate for the spatial constraints brought on by the unusual design, and the whole made for, in Carl Condit's words, "a staggering exhibition of structural virtuosity" on a site that seemed extraordinarily appropriate for it.

300 North State Street

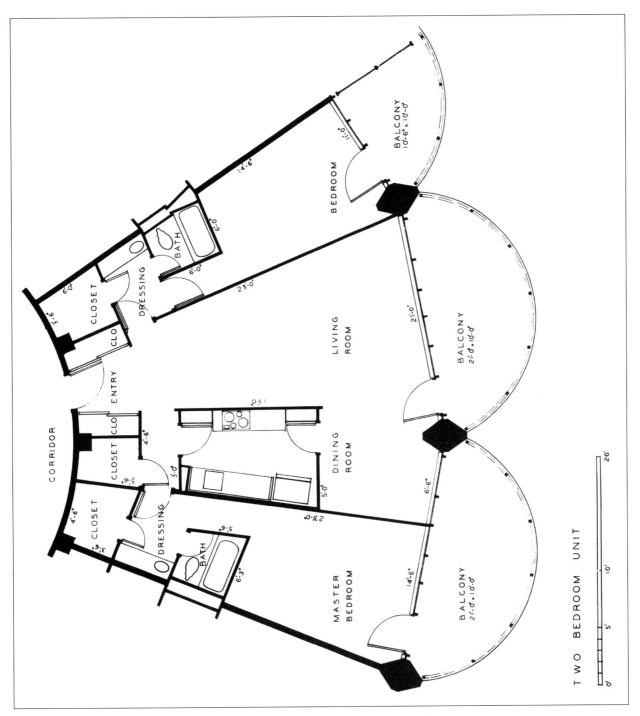

Plan, two bedroom unit, 1960–72. (Hedrich Blessing, courtesy Chicago Historical Society)

300 NORTH STATE STREET

Under construction, looking towards the Wrigley Building, 1960. (Hedrich Blessing, courtesy Chicago Historical Society)

300 NORTH STATE STREET

Balconies, c. 1965. (Hedrich Blessing, courtesy Chicago Historical Society)

300 NORTH STATE STREET

Living Room. Margaret Hutchinson, decorator, for *Family Circle Magazine*, 1964. (Hedrich Blessing, courtesy Chicago Historical Society)

Living room, model residence, c. 1965. (Hedrich Blessing, courtesy Chicago Historical Society)

1320 North State Parkway

Robert S. De Golyer, Architect | Hegemann–Harris Co., Builders | 1925–27

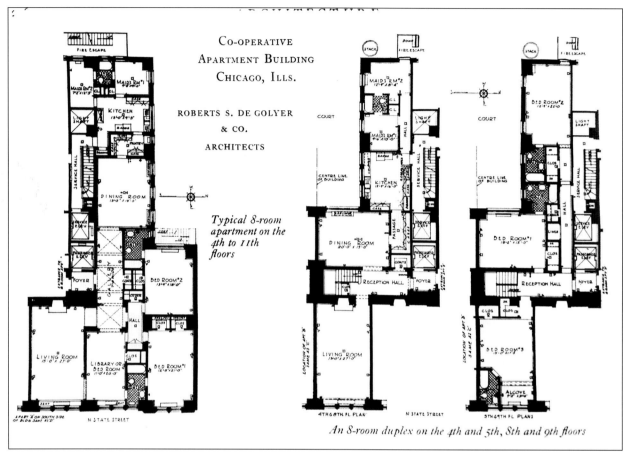

Plans for typical eight room and duplex apartments, 1927. *(Architecture)*

1320 North State was built as cooperative in "Venetian" style, according to its promoters. Purchased from George Porter for $185,000, the site included a house once occupied by Lyman J. Gage, former Secretary of the Treasury. This was another joint project of De Golyer and his engineer office mates H. L. Clute (mechanical) and Smith & Brown (structural).

With model apartments decorated by John A. Colby & Sons, and prices that stretched from $25,000 to $105,000, the building initially was described as containing 40 duplex apartments. In fact, many of the apartments would be simplex, but the largest units with 10 rooms and 7 baths contained as many as 20 closets, the last drawing an expression of wonder from the *Chicago Tribune*. With stone on all sides, its terra-cotta trim and rows of arched windows on upper floors emphasized both its verticality and its Venetian connections.

1320 North State Parkway underwent some corporate changes and was purchased by its tenants in 1949 for $975,000, approximately half of what it cost to build 22 years earlier. It remains a cooperative today.

Exterior, 1927. *(Architecture)*

1530 North State Parkway

Granger & Bollenbacher, Architects | Ralph Sollitt & Sons, Builders | 1929–30

Exterior, 1931. (Hedrich Blessing, courtesy Chicago Historical Society)

The story of this building begins in 1926, when plans were announced by local builder I. J. Mensch for a 15-story gothic apartment building on the site of the Alvin McCord house. Eleven room, five bath apartments were to be standard. Three years later the McCord house was still standing, but a second announcement proved more successful.

This scheme was as lavish as the first, with several duplexes placed atop a string of 11- and 12-room apartments, but the gothic details had turned into French Renaissance. The largest apartment contained 20 rooms and 10 baths, besides some terraces. Brick with a limestone base and trim, 1530 North State Parkway was termed a "Blue Book Co-op" by the *Chicago Tribune*, a reference to the socially prominent purchasers who "flatly decline to let their names be made public." Its slate mansard roof hid water tanks and elevator machinery, a much-appreciated "gesture on behalf of the Chicago Beautiful movement."

Construction began about the time of the 1929 crash, making it one of the last buildings of its type put up in Chicago. Louis Sudler, working with McMenemy & Martin in 1926 when he made the first announcement, had formed his own firm by 1929 and continued to serve as its marketer.

1530 North State Parkway

Plan, 1931.
(Architectural Record)

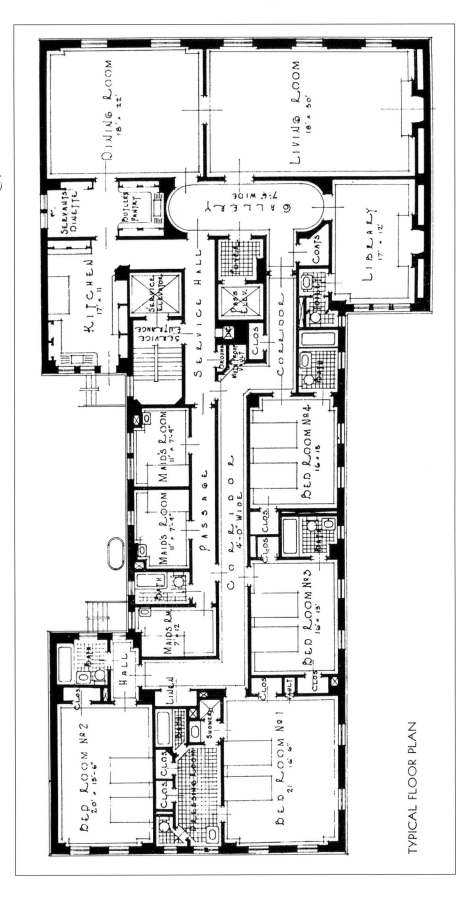

TYPICAL FLOOR PLAN

1530 North State Parkway

View of stair and draped window, King residence, c. 1930s. Walcott and Work, architects.
(Trowbridge, courtesy Chicago Historical Society)

1530 NORTH STATE PARKWAY

Studio, Mrs. James Hopkins residence, 1930s. (Hedrich Blessing, courtesy Chicago Historical Society)

1550 North State Parkway

Marshall & Fox, Architects | 1911–13

Exterior, 1914.
(American Architect)

This was the most extravagantly conceived and executed of Chicago's pre-World War I apartment buildings and remains, even in its divided internal state today, a remarkable structure. Of stone and terra-cotta in an elaborately worked and carefully referenced version of French classicism, its 12 stories face north onto Lincoln Park. Three major public rooms, with orangerie on one side and open bay on the other, stretched more than 100 feet across. The French-labeled floor plans—a device employed shortly thereafter in 1200 Lake Shore Drive—were further evidence of Marshall's sense of grandeur. The dimensions of each of the 10 full-floor apartments exceeded some 8,000 square feet.

In 1920, *The Economist* commented that 1550 North State Parkway "probably has the most distinguished list of tenants of any apartment house in the city." That same year owner Marshall was rumored to want to sell the building to fund expansion of his Edgewater Beach properties. Two tenants, William V. Kelley, president of Miehle Printing Press, and surgeon Arthur Bevan, set in motion what was termed "the most significant joint purchase of real estate ever made in Chicago." Although yearly rentals averaged $9,000 a year, the tenants feared hefty increases with a Marshall sale.

After the building had been sold to Kelley and Bevan the tenants essentially purchased their own apartments with 99 year leases. The new owners and former tenants included Stanley Field, merchant and president of the Field Museum, A. B. Dick, the mimeograph manufacturer, and Dr. Frank Billings, Professor of Medicine at the University of Chicago. After World War II, the huge flats were carved up into four apartments each; some have since been recombined.

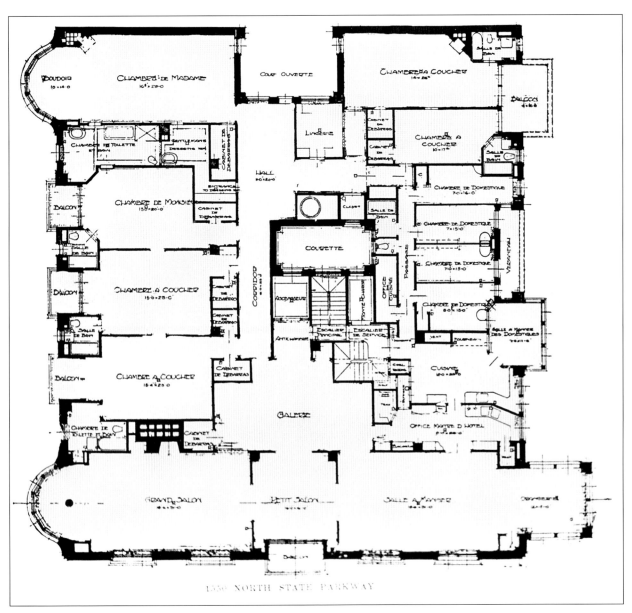

Plan.

1244 North Stone Street

Thielbar & Fugard, Architects | Charles B. Johnson, Builder | 1925

Exterior.
(Baird and Warner,
*Portfolio of Fine
Apartment Homes*)

A nine-story building with eight full-floor apartments and a rooftop penthouse—built originally as an English cottage bungalow for the owner—1244 North Stone Street, as Zurich Esposito suggests, presents what is in some ways a more modest version of Fugard's 20 East Cedar exterior. The brick, limestone, and terra-cotta facade features carved heraldic shields and casement windows whose spandrels have incised Tudor details. On the lower floors, the almost square living rooms enjoy a bay of eight separate windows. In recognition of growing automobile congestion, the residents boasted their own garage. Less conveniently, a long service corridor separated kitchen from butler's pantry and dining room; this cut down cooking smells but must have made meal service a bit laborious.

1244 NORTH STONE STREET

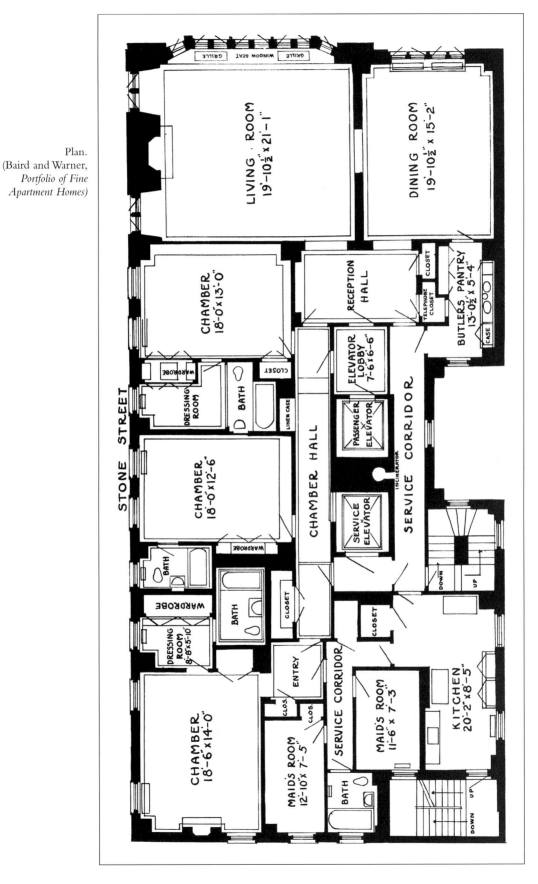

Plan.
(Baird and Warner, *Portfolio of Fine Apartment Homes*)

220 East Walton Place

CASTELLANE APARTMENTS

Fugard & Knapp with Ralph C. Harris, Architects | McLennan Construction Co., Builder | 1919–20

Exterior, 1967.
(Hedrich Blessing, courtesy Chicago Historical Society)

One of a series of Near North buildings originally owned and built by Hugh McLennan, 220 East Walton Place is another example of its architects' interest in Tudor styling, most evident in the two-story limestone entrance with its carved shields and arched windows. A balustrade runs along the top of the 10-story, red brick facade, and is topped by a battlement and carved figures. *The Economist* announced its original cost as $475,000, with apartment rentals of $3,000 a year and up, while the *Chicago Tribune* asserted it would consume $800,000.

Sixteen of the 18 apartments are mirror images of one another, each eight room, four bath flats, with the living rooms and two of the master bedrooms facing south. An eight-room rooftop bungalow, with terrace, pergola, and 30-foot solarium, had been leased in 1919 for $5,000 a year.

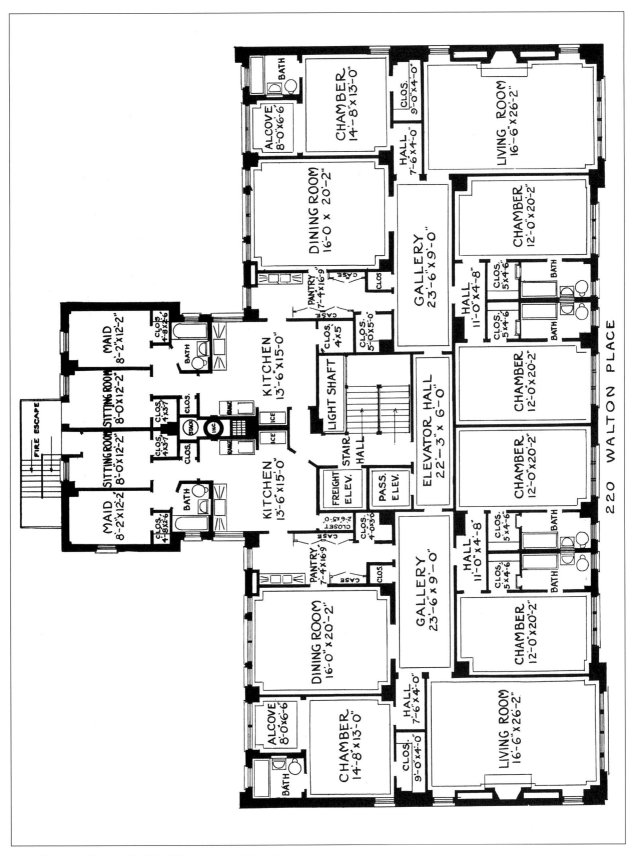

Plan. (Baird and Warner, *Portfolio of Fine Apartment Homes*)

232 East Walton Place

Fugard & Knapp, Architect | McLennan Construction Co., Builder | 1920–21

Exterior, 1939. (Hedrich Blessing, Hogan and Farwell series, courtesy Chicago Historical Society)

Another partnership between developer-builder McLennan and Fugard & Knapp, 232 East Walton Place abandons Tudor Gothic for 18th-century French details, more closely resembling this architectural firm's East Lake Shore Drive buildings one block north. Sober and staid, a limestone base and stone window surrounds contrast with the brick facade; an elaborate cornice tops off the building.

Initially conceived as a rental, plans shifted in response to a growing cooperative mania, and a group of potential tenants was offered shares in the building's equity: two-thirds of the units were to remain rentals, providing dividends to the seven building owners. Slightly larger than their Fugard-designed neighbor just to the west, these apartments maintain the same general orientation to the south.

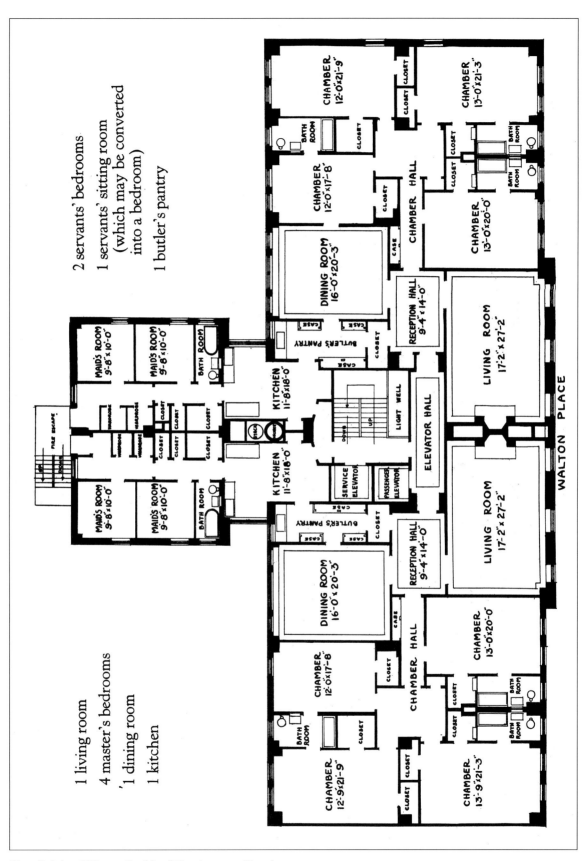

Plan. (Baird and Warner, *Portfolio of Fine Apartment Homes*)

233 East Walton Place

Kenneth Franzheim, Architect, with C. Howard Crane |
McLennan Construction Co., Builder | 1922–23

Exterior, 1933. (Hedrich Blessing, courtesy Chicago Historical Society)

The *Real Estate Indicator* announced that 233 East Walton Place "is one of those few apartment buildings which have not been built on the investment or speculative basis," planned for a group of owners desiring "sane and well-ordered apartment living." Using only a portion of its corner lot to allow for ample light and air, the stone and brick structure sits on a three-story stone base and is topped by a (rebuilt) cornice above its 14th floor. Stone balconettes, panels with classical reliefs, scroll brackets, and flanking urns for the fourth-floor windows soften the austerity of the brick shaft. The full-floor, 11-room apartments each contained a laundry, and the promoters drew attention to "the absence of the typical apartment hall" made possible by the compact plan of the apartments. The chamber corridor, for example, was only 24 feet long.

Another McLennon project, 233 was originally managed by Harold Bradley but was taken over by McMenemy & Martin. The architects Howard Crane and Kenneth Franzheim are better known in Chicago for their elaborately detailed Harris and Selwyn Theaters, built just about this time on North Dearborn Street. In 1938, during the Great Depression, McNally & Quinn proposed a renovation which would have increased rental income by making five apartments out of each full floor unit; the scheme went unrealized.

233 East Walton Place

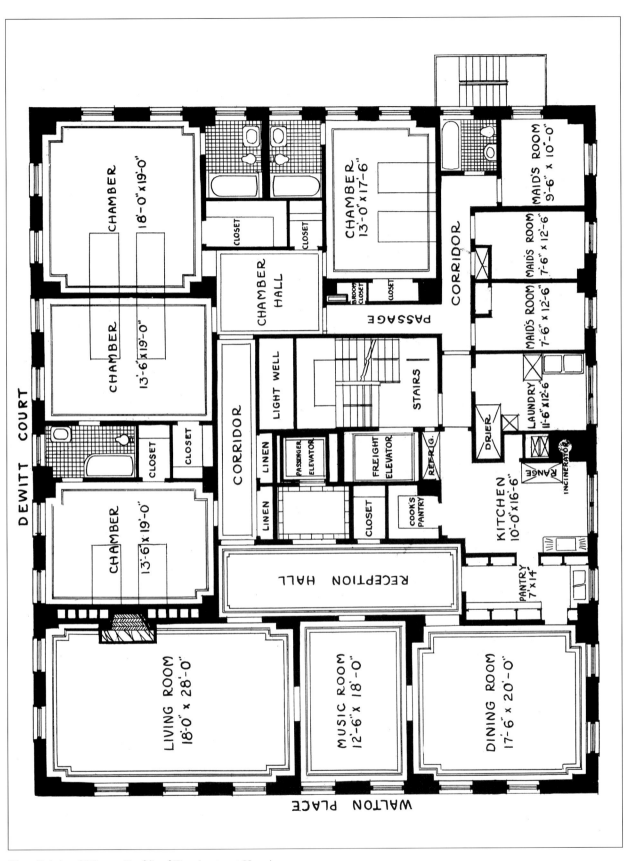

Plan. (Baird and Warner, *Portfolio of Fine Apartment Homes*)

NORTH SIDE

Aerial view of lake front north of Edgewater Beach apartments, looking south, c. 1930s. (Courtesy collection of David R. Phillips)

THIS SECTION IS GEOGRAPHICALLY THE LARGEST of the four divisions and comprises a series of distinct and very different neighborhoods—parts of Lincoln Park, Lakeview, Edgewater, Wrigleyville among them—that lie north of Fullerton Avenue. It extends all the way up to Hollywood, where Lake Shore Drive ends, and some blocks beyond. In 1889, substantial portions of the area voted, as did Hyde Park, to become part of the city of Chicago. The enlargement of Lincoln Park and the lengthening of Lake Shore Drive over some decades stimulated major 1920s high-rise apartment building here. The yacht harbor at Belmont became a favorite vista for some of these buildings, and they form an impressive architectural ridge from about 3000 North, just south of Belmont Avenue, to Irving Park Road.

The Great Depression stopped what would undoubtedly have been more intense development of the lakefront further north. Less exclusive than the Gold Coast, this dense corridor would become still more crowded after World War II, when a series of towering apartment buildings were placed along Sheridan Road and Lake Shore Drive. Many of these were built after passage of the condominium act created a new category of apartment owners, and this is where the most pronounced democratization of the lakefront occurred. The grounds of the Edgewater Beach Hotel, sold off for development, host some particularly tall structures. The older neighborhoods just to the west contain some elegant apartment hotels, some of which have been carefully restored, as well as a wide variety of housing stock, from three- and six-flat buildings to spacious individual homes.

2920 North Commonwealth Avenue

Commonwealth Towers

Maurice L. Bein, Architect | Wahl Construction, Builder | 1929–30

Exterior, 1949. (Hedrich Blessing, courtesy Chicago Historical Society

Russian-born Maurice L. Bein was an inventive and prolific designer of houses, commercial structures, and apartments, who had a particularly inspired feeling for applied decoration. This 14-story building features a lively, multi-colored exterior. Terra-cotta ornamentation, gothic window and entry surrounds, and a central mansard with cornice and two-story windows, give it considerable distinction. A high setback houses terraces and the slight frontal extension of the center bay for the living rooms adds energy to the facade. Within are 24 apartments, most of them three bedroom and three bath, in addition to a couple of larger penthouse units.

2920 North Commonwealth Avenue has been a condominium since the late 1960s. Another vivid example of Bein's decorative talents can be found at Cornell Towers on the South Side at 5346 South Cornell.

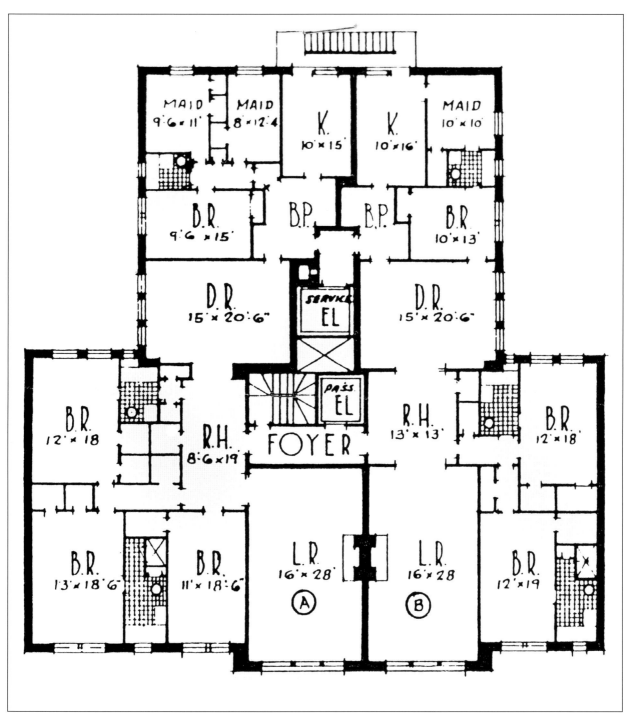

Plan, c. 1980s.

325 West Fullerton Parkway

Andrew Sandegren, Architect | T.B. Swanson, Builder | 1916–17

Exterior.
(Baird and Warner, *Portfolio of Fine Apartment Homes*)

Andrew Sandegren was one of early 20th-century Chicago's more prolific designers of apartment houses. His work can be found all over the city, generally in well-planned, smaller, walk-up buildings. He also created more ambitious and elaborate structures such as this. A series of other spacious apartment buildings erected about the same time are near neighbors: one is by Sandegren himself at 301 West Fulllerton, another by Vitzthum & Teich at 2344 North Lincoln Park West. Some of them bear Prairie School details or Central European influences, and most have sun porches, or breakfast rooms, so popular in this era.

This seven-story, 12-apartment structure, built for Joseph E. Swanson and several others, was described as reflecting the "English Manor house style of the Jacobean period." It originally employed paneling and heavy plaster ceiling beams in its interior. The limestone base and window frames provide a lively counterpoint to the red brick, while the casement windows and living room bays add an elegance to the facade. The land and building represented an investment of more than $300,000, with rents projected at $200 to $350 a month.

325 WEST FULLERTON PARKWAY

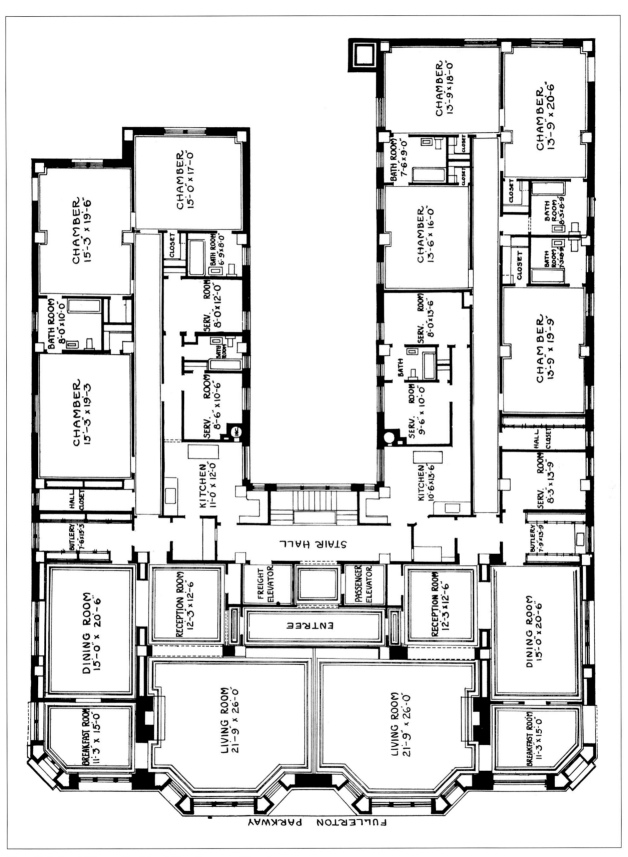

Plan. (Baird and Warner, *Portfolio of Fine Apartment Homes*)

399 West Fullerton Parkway

McNally & Quinn, Architects | 1926–27

Exterior, 1942.
(Hedrich Blessing,
courtesy Chicago
Historical Society)

Seventeen stories tall with 32 apartments and designed as a 100% cooperative, 399 West Fullerton Parkway claimed French Renaissance stylistic antecedents. The reinforced concrete building, faced with cut stone and brick with a couple of mansard roofs along its top, was "open only to families of recognized social and financial standing."

The Kirkham–Hayes Corporation, specializing in cooperatives, promoted the building's location facing Lincoln Park as "so like some ancestral English estate in its pastoral atmosphere that one almost looks for a Baronial Hall, or listens for the baying of the master's hounds." Here was "formality without its chill, and 'hominess' bearing pride of possession." A chauffeurs' room on the first floor and a garage served those not using horses for their excursions. Purchase prices ranged from $13,000 to $24,000 plus a proportionate share of the $950,000 mortgage. Equity, mortgage, and reserve fund added up to $1.6 million. The architects were officers of the 399 Corporation, meant to share in its profits.

The building is one of several high rises standing on the former Loeb estate, which stretched 300 feet along Fullerton Parkway. It was purchased in 1925 by developer Peter F. Reynolds for $380,000. Nellie Loeb was the daughter of Adolphus Busch, the great St. Louis brewer.

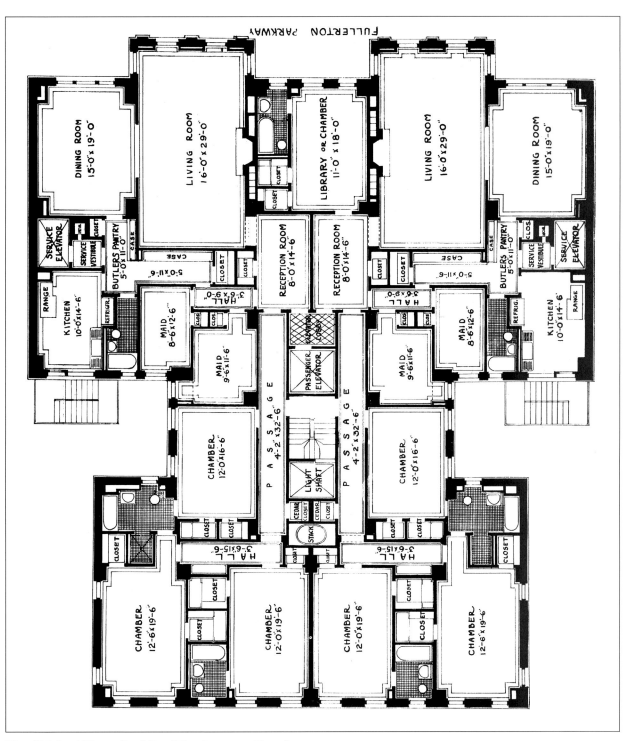

Plan. (Baird and Warner, Portfolio of Fine Apartment Homes)

660–700 West Irving Park Road

THE PATTINGTON

David E. Postle, Architect | Telford & McWade, Builder | 1902–03

Exterior. (Baird and Warner, *Portfolio of Fine Apartment Homes*)

While the rooms are smaller than in some grander buildings, the Pattington remains Chicago's most impressive open-court apartment complex of its day. Built for James E. Patton of Milwaukee, its two connected courtyards reflect a physical layout that would become extremely popular among local flat builders, although rarely of this size or elegance. Ten entrances enable residents of the more than 70 apartments to retain some level of privacy while reducing traffic on individual stairwells and landings. In this walk-up, freight elevators were intended to ease the task of moving heavy furniture and appliances. The gold brick and stone building, running 422 feet along Irving Park, has some refined neoclassical ornamentation, including column-flanked portals and a balustraded walkway.

Built for rental purposes, the Pattington incorporated concrete as part of its fireproofing method, used previously, promoters declared, only for industrial or commercial purposes. When it was sold in 1923 to J. B. Waller, *The Economist* estimated the annual rental for the apartments was some $150,000, while the garages (built in 1910 or later) brought in another $40,000. The Pattington has been a condominium since 1977.

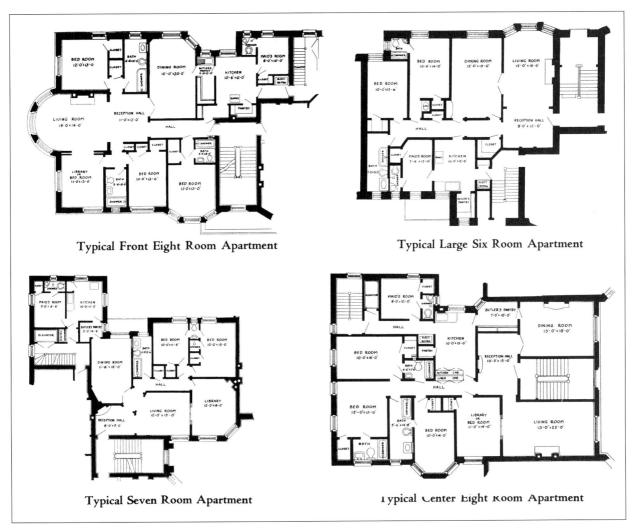

Plan. (Baird and Warner, *Portfolio of Fine Apartment Homes*)

3240 North Lake Shore Drive

SHERIDAN–MELROSE APARTMENTS

McNally & Quinn, Architects | A. Lindstrom, Builder | 1927–29

Exterior. (Baird and Warner, *Portfolio of Fine Apartment Homes*)

Perched on the northwest corner of what was then Sheridan Road and Melrose Street, 3240 North Lake Shore Drive is at the intersection of the Outer Drive and Sheridan Road. Backers boasted that its location permitted spectacular views north, south, and east, and especially of the nearby yacht harbor and recently extended Lincoln Park. There were 67 apartments in all.

The experienced architectural team of Frank McNally & J. Edwin Quinn here produced a "modern version of French Renaissance," a 20-story brick and stone-trimmed structure with apartments ranging up to nine rooms. Above the 16th floor cornice is a large four-story section that does not run parallel to the Sheridan Road side, creating a curious visual effect. It contained some duplex apartments, two with generous terraces. An 80-car garage, cedar closets, paneled libraries, wood-burning fireplaces, and landscaped gardens were expected to increase the appeal of this 100% cooperative.

The developers issued a booklet "Selection and its Reward," containing endorsements from 13 happy tenant-owners, each of whom wrote his praise on his own business letterhead, a win-win advertising occasion. A rental building today, 3240 is one of the few grand buildings of the 1920s that is neither cooperative nor condominium.

3240 North Lake Shore Drive

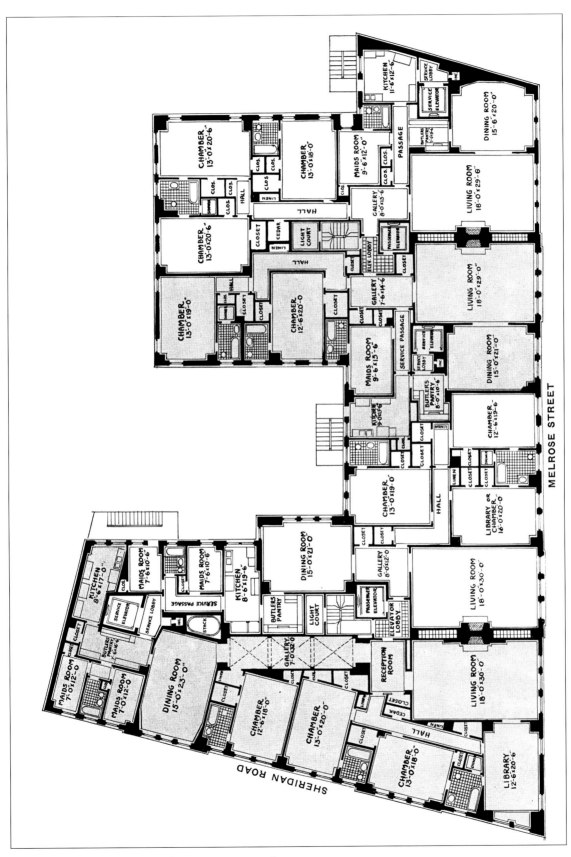

Plan. (Baird and Warner, *Portfolio of Fine Apartment Homes*)

3300 North Lake Shore Drive

SHERIDAN—ALDINE APARTMENTS

Rissman & Hirschfeld, Architects; Edwin D. Krenn, Associate Architect | McLennan Construction, Builder | 1926–27

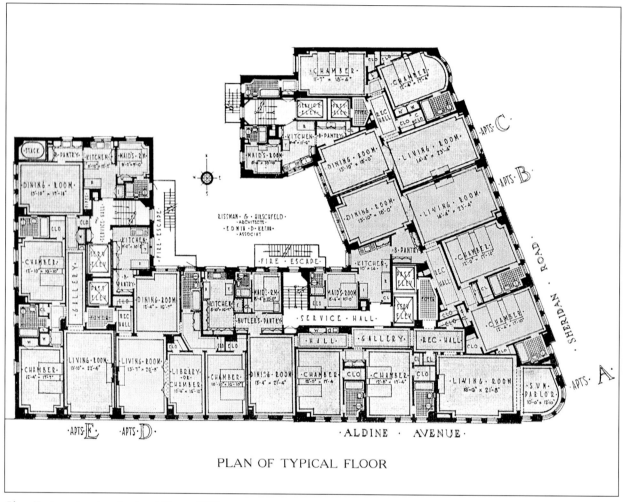

Plan. (Sexton, *American Apartment Houses*, 1929)

This 17-story, Italian Renaissance-inspired structure was part of the real estate empire of the Edith Rockefeller McCormick Trust, which purchased the land in 1925. Mrs. McCormick, daughter of John D. Rockefeller, lived for a time in the building. Edwin Krenn headed the trust's property development section, and also performed occasional design work. Krenn & Dato, another arm of the trust, provided the $1.2 million mortgage and handled rentals and sales. Like many other development operations, this all collapsed in the 1930s.

The principal architects, Maurice B. Rissman and Leo S. Hirschfeld, devised a series of significant Chicago apartment buildings, several of them quite large by contemporary standards. 3300, according to one early announcement, intended to sell some 27 apartments, with the remainder of the 80 or so units to have been rented. Two massive entrances, one off Aldine with immense hanging lanterns, the other on Lake Shore Drive, pierce the rusticated stone base, and stone urns cap the balustrade topping the building. The corner bays enclosing the large sun porches echo motifs of neighboring buildings. Today 3300 is a condominium.

Exterior, 1948. (Hedrich Blessing, courtesy Chicago Historical Society)

3314 North Lake Shore Drive

LE GRIFFON

L. G. Hallberg & Co., Architect | Jens Jensen and Son, Builder | 1916–17

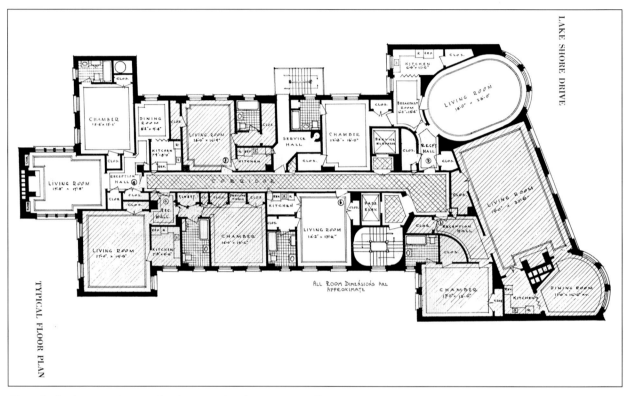

Plan of redevelopment. (*3314 Lake Shore Drive*, brochure, private collection)

Swedish-born L. G. Hallberg designed one of Chicago's first "high class" apartment buildings, the Mentone Flats, in 1882. Indeed, historian Carroll William Westfall argues it might literally have been the first. The gothicism favored by Hallberg for the Mentone was transformed by his firm into elaborate neoclassicism some 35 years later.

3314 North Lake Shore Drive—originally 3310 Sheridan—despite its relatively small footprint and modest height, is one of the most monumental apartment structures on North Lake Shore Drive. The brackets, balustrades, cartouches, crests, lanterns, festoons, scrolls, and carvings constitute a virtuoso performance of neoclassical themes as brick, glazed terra-cotta, and gray limestone play off one another in their own distinctive accents. Built for Charles B. Smith, of the Stewart-Warner Speedometer Company, this was, in fact, the first shoreline apartment "high rise" constructed north of North Avenue.

When it opened, each story contained a single 18-room, 5-bath apartment, typically at a mid-1920s rental of $10,000 a year. Residents included members of major Chicago merchant families, including Spiegel, Ward, Peacock, and Goldblatt. At some later point, floors were reorganized into smaller units, with the large formal rooms oddly out of place in such reduced circumstances. In 1951, when the building was sold to William H. Seide for under $400,000, it contained some 49 units. In the early 1980s there was further internal remodeling and several attempts at condominium conversion, one of them ultimately successful in 1983. There are currently more than 30 apartments in the building.

Exterior. (*3314 Lake Shore Drive*, brochure, private collection)

3400 North Lake Shore Drive

HARBOR APARTMENTS

Peter J. Weber, Architect | Mueller Construction, Builder | 1919–21

Exterior rendering by Peter J. Weber, c. 1915/17, pencil and gouache on illustration board. (The Art Institute of Chicago, Gift of Bertram A. Weber)

In its original presentation, one of the first major projects to be erected after World War I, this extravagant building was designed to appeal to very wealthy Chicago families. Built for Hugo J. Goetz, president of the Para Auto Tire Company, who moved into the rooftop bungalow or "aerovilla," the nine-story brick and limestone structure below it was planned for one 16-room and two 12-room apartments on each floor. These last two faced Roscoe Street to the building's south, while the larger apartments overlooked the lake. After entering one of the two entrances, residents were escorted up by "Elevator pilots" to their palatial establishments. A "servant service bureau" supplied emergency help to those temporarily without butlers and maids.

Early tenants—who paid advances on their five- and ten-year leases before the building was built—included Frederick Bartlett the realtor, John F. Jelke, George Rasmussen of the National Tea Company, and, somewhat later, J. Ogden Armour. Col. Robert H. Morse, of Fairbanks, Morse, planned to put together two units and create the largest apartment in Chicago: 21 rooms with 9 baths. Some residents, Morse among them, spent many tens of thousands decorating the interiors.

While lobby details recall this splendor, along with some apartment paneling here and there, the building now contains something close to twice the original number of 25 units, typically five to a floor. The facade continues to express the beaux-arts classicism of Peter J. Weber, celebrated for his far more exuberant Chocolat Menier Pavilion at the 1893 Columbian Exposition.

3400 NORTH LAKE SHORE DRIVE

Plan.

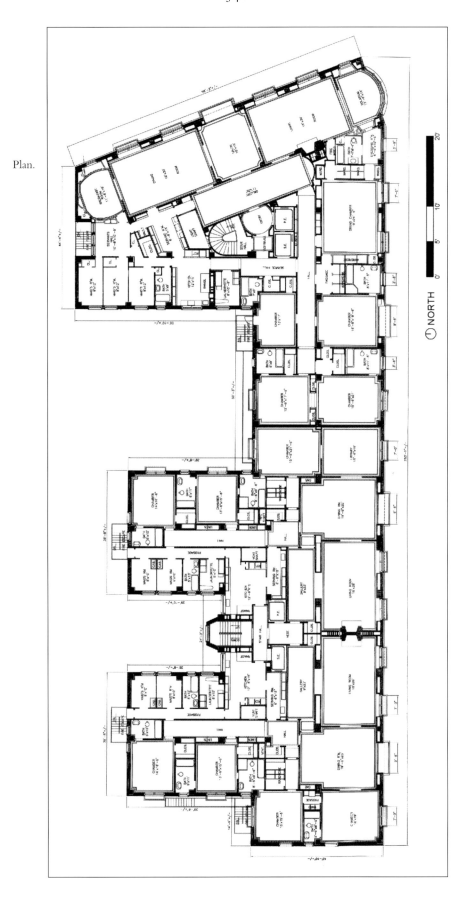

3500 North Lake Shore Drive

CORNELIA APARTMENTS

Robert S. De Golyer, Architect | Avery Brundage, Builder | 1926

Exterior.
(Sexton, *American Apartment Houses*, 1929)

With one of the more extraordinary rooflines among Chicago apartment buildings, the Cornelia moves upward from its two-story rusticated limestone base, through stone and terra-cotta-trimmed brick floors—whose window treatments vary in a succession of bands—to the 15th floor, after which an impressive two-story mansard-roofed pavilion completes the whole 17-story structure. "If the Little Corporal were to take a jaunt down Sheridan Road in about a year," observed the *Chicago Tribune,* which confused its Napoleons a little, "he might see something familiar." In fact, the Cornelia had Second Empire referencing and would have caught the eye of Napoleon III rather than that of Napoleon Bonaparte.

The two- and three-bedroom apartments are serviced by two separate elevator foyers, and each unit enjoys a large gallery and at least one maid's room. The efficient planning and comfortable dimensions of the more than 60 units mark this as a De Golyer building.

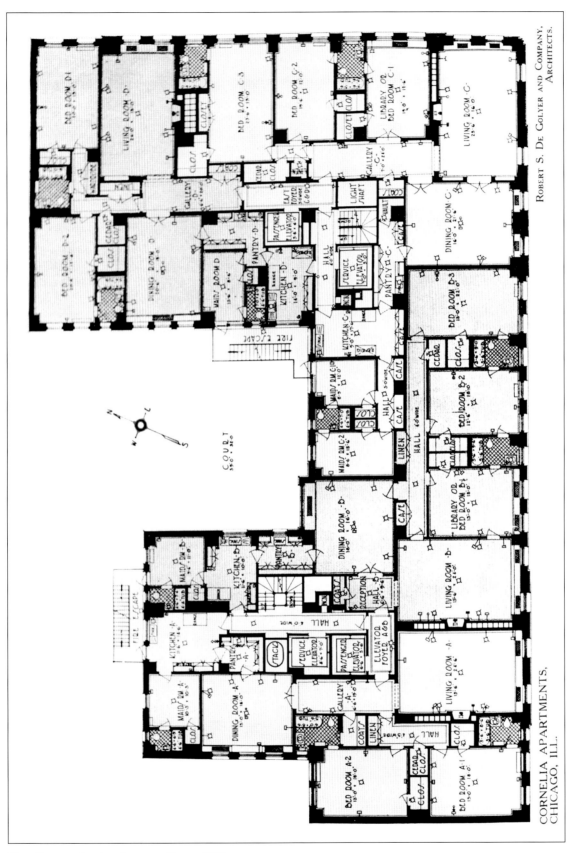

Plan. (Sexton, *American Apartment Houses*, 1929)

3750 North Lake Shore Drive

Robert S. De Golyer, Architect | John A. Lundstrom & Co., Builder | 1926–27

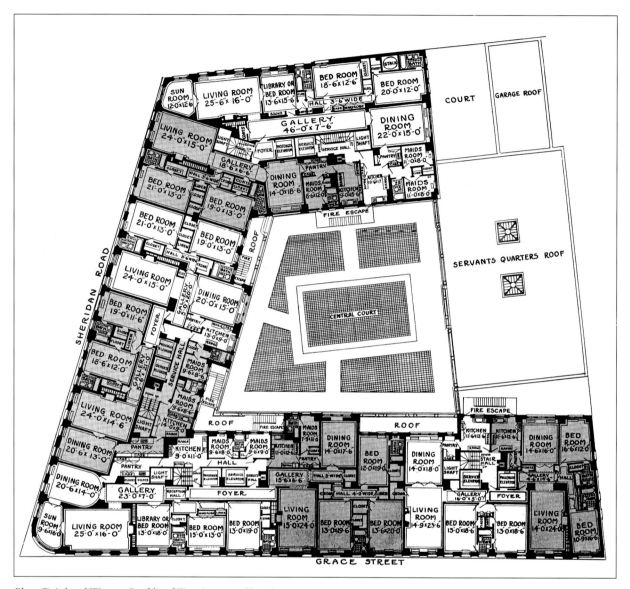

Plan. (Baird and Warner, *Portfolio of Fine Apartment Homes*)

The rounded northeast corners of this 17-story building, its massive size, and the contrast between its red brick and the long, white vertical quoins give it a prominent place on Lake Shore Drive. Emil W. Carlson owned the southwest corner of Sheridan Road and Grace Street, and a few years earlier Walter Ahlschlager was supposedly designing the apartment house. But De Golyer received the commission and divided the 120 apartments among four separate elevator entries; they included 30 nine-room units.

Built as an unequal U or a slightly indented V, 3750 North Lake Shore Drive, like another De Golyer design on the south side, the Powhatan, features an enclosed swimming pool, in this case located in a central, glass-enclosed court off the lobby. Shower rooms for hardier Lake Michigan bathers were also provided. Described, in 1926, as Chicago's "largest and finest" apartment building, 3750 was built as a cooperative and is one today.

Exterior, 1991. (Courtesy Commission on Chicago Landmarks)

3800 NORTH LAKE SHORE DRIVE

SHERIDAN–GRACE APARTMENTS

B. Leo Steif, Architect | Avery Brundage, Builder | 1926–27

Exterior.
(Baird and Warner, *Portfolio of Fine Apartment Homes*)

Planned and completed at just about the same time as 3750, its immediate neighbor across Grace Street to the south, and, like it, 17 stories high, 3800 North Lake Shore Drive is quite different in external appearance. The irregularly shaped site supports a semi-circular Tudor Gothic structure, which is basically only two rooms deep. A two story, limestone base contrasts with the rough red brick that dominates the facade; stone and terra-cotta, particularly on some of the upper floors, provide further accents.

The building and land were valued at more than $3 million, and builder Avery Brundage headed the corporation liable for the more than $2 million in bonds. The 86 apartments included two 10-room duplexes that occupied the 16th and 17th floors. A 100-car garage and wood-burning fireplaces added further appeal. But it was the building's outline and gothic details that captivated the press. "A giant old English castle silhouetted against a purpling sunset" is what romantic Chicagoans will see from the new Lincoln Park extension, wrote Philip Hampson in the *Chicago Tribune*. A "fairy whispered into Mr. Steif's ear and induced him to take water tanks, pent houses, square corners, and other unsightly components of the ordinary tall apartment building, shake them up in a magic bottle...and turn them into objects" that would simulate a castle. Oriels, gables, chimneys, stone window surrounds, added to the larger effect.

Steif, who had worked earlier in Walter Ahlschlager's office, designed several hotels and large apartment houses in Chicago, including the Barclay at 4940 East End in the Chicago Beach area, and the startlingly colored and emphatically moderne 10 West Elm. Building contractor and Olympics leader Avery Brundage lived for a time in 3800.

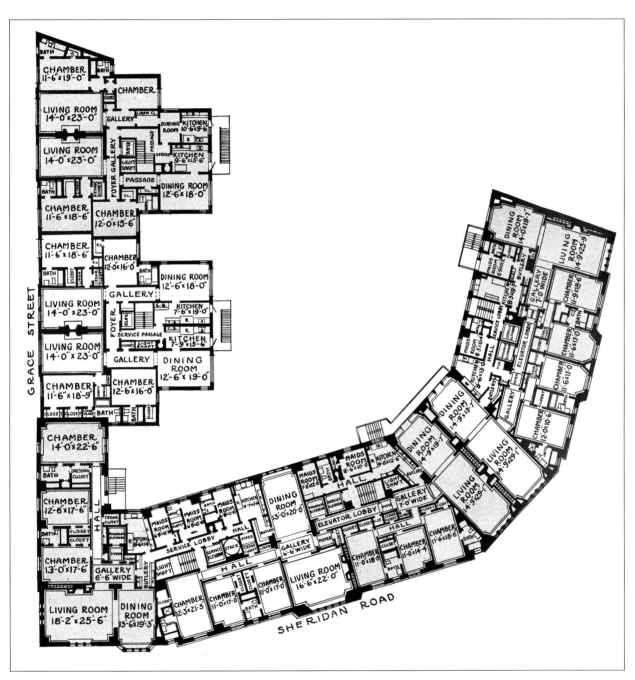

Plan. (Baird and Warner, *Portfolio of Fine Apartment Homes*)

3920 North Lake Shore Drive

Lake shore towers

Roy F. France, Architect | C. Erickson & Co., Builder | 1926–27

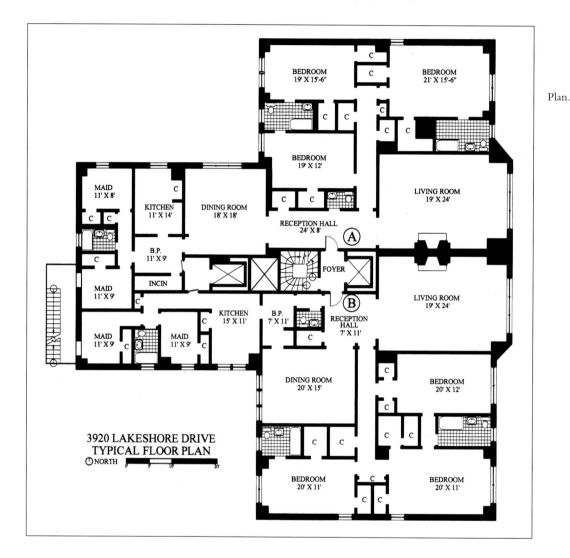

Plan.

The builder of Lake Shore Towers, Dr. Max Thorek, was an energetic, multi-sided talent, genuinely gifted but with a flair for self-promotion. Hungarian-born and Chief of Surgery at the American Hospital, which he helped to found and administer, he was a well exhibited amateur photographer, and first violinist in the Chicago Business Men's Orchestra, and was a widely published and a successful teacher. Thorek owned Lake Shore property which suddenly became more valuable with the extension of Lincoln Park and Lake Shore Drive.

Roy France, the architect, actually purchased the plot from Thorek and headed the building corporation, but Thorek held the mortgage and moved into the duplexed, terraced penthouse. Originally announced as a 12-story Italian Renaissance structure with three apartments to a floor, the building was completed as an 16-story "French Gothic" exercise, with two apartments to a floor, all in all some 30 eight-room apartments, plus the 11-room bungalow at its top. Planned to be 100% cooperative, the building went bankrupt in the 1930s, and was sold in 1947 for $750,000, little more than half of its 1927 value. In 1951 the tenants bought it and converted it to cooperative status. It remains one today.

Architect Roy France put up many other apartment houses and hotels in Chicago, including the Chatelaine Tower on Chestnut Street and the Patrician on West Fullerton, but is even better known for his art deco hotels in Miami Beach.

3920 NORTH LAKE SHORE DRIVE

Exterior.

2430 North Lakeview Avenue

Rebori, Wentworth, Dewey & McCormick, Architects |
Dahl, Stedman Company, Builder | 1926–27

Chamber and lake window, Charles Goodspeed residence. David Adler, architect, 1927.
(Trowbridge, courtesy Chicago Historical Society)

This restrained exercise in Georgian revival presents a facade of Indiana limestone with some contrasting brick. Eighteen stories high, it stands on the site of the Henry Chapin home and is the southernmost of three contiguous cooperatives built on Lakeview at about the same time. All of the apartments, except for one full-floor simplex—designed for the Chapins, who were part of the building syndicate—are duplexes, 17 in all.

2430 North Lakeview Avenue was planned to provide as much privacy and luxury as an apartment house could afford, "interiors familiar to most of us only through the kindness of the movies," wrote Philip Hampson in the *Chicago Tribune*. The scale of the 14-room apartments, their curved staircases, large libraries, sewing rooms and numerous closets, echoed the neoclassical elegance of the exterior. Particular care was taken with sound deadening between apartments, emphasized the promoters, and an elaborate iron and glass entry canopy acknowledged arrivals on foot or by automobile. Today's ample parking area behind the building was planned as a garden with trellises, fountain, and teahouse.

Built as a cooperative for socially prominent Chicagoans who included architect A. N. Rebori, Leander McCormick, and Robert J. Thorne, the building survived the Depression intact and remains a cooperative today.

Exterior, 1991. (Courtesy Commission on Chicago Landmarks)

2430 North Lakeview Avenue

Entrance hall and stairs,
Charles Goodspeed residence.
David Adler, architect;
Jan Juta, decorator, 1927.
(Trowbridge, courtesy
Chicago Historical Society)

Dining room and fireplace, Charles Goodspeed residence. David Adler, architect, 1927.
(Trowbridge, courtesy Chicago Historical Society)

Corner of room, Charles Goodspeed residence. David Adler, architect, 1927. (Trowbridge, courtesy Chicago Historical Society)

2430 NORTH LAKEVIEW AVENUE

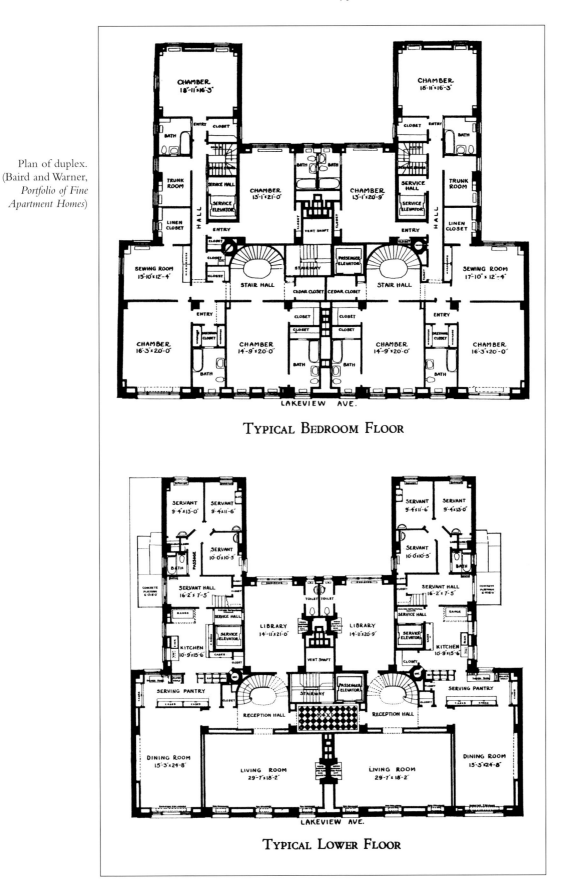

Plan of duplex. (Baird and Warner, *Portfolio of Fine Apartment Homes*)

2440 North Lakeview Avenue

Rissman & Hirschfeld, Architects | Avery Brundage, Builder | 1926–27

Exterior, 1966. (Robert Harr/Hedrich Blessing, courtesy Chicago Historical Society)

As an indication of changing standards, it may be noted that when 2440 North Lakeview Avenue was announced in 1926, its 107 apartments made it "the largest of its kind in the middle west," its kind, presumably, being a semi-cooperative. With the land, the cost of the project came to some $4 million.

The larger apartments, a couple of them duplexes with two-story living rooms, were intended to be sold, while the smaller units were to be rented. Separate entrances and lobbies were planned for owners and their tenants. The popular "Tudor Gothic" style was invoked in the brick, limestone, and terra-cotta structure. *Chicago Tribune* critic Al Chase declared its styling made the newest Chicago buildings "look as old fashioned as a last year's straw hat" with its "modern set-back style of architecture, now almost universally used in Manhattan and popular throughout most of the other big cities outside Chicago." The setbacks permitted rooftop paraphernalia to be hidden. The usual 1920s luxury items—colored tile baths, separate shower stalls, wood-burning fireplaces, vaulted galleries—were supplemented by an elaborate sunken English garden.

The promotional brochure pointed to the exclusive neighborhood, listing the names of prominent Chicagoans already living in apartments on either side of 2440. Aside from the two 11-room duplexes, 2440 originally included some 30 eight-room apartments, and 33 of six rooms. Reorganized in 1950, many tenants bought their apartments—one 11-room unit sold for $46,000 that year—and 2440 remains a cooperative today.

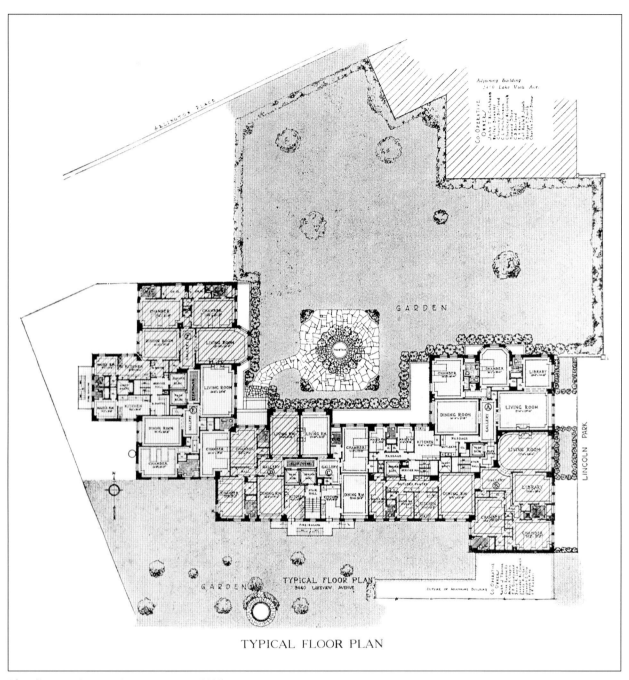

Plan. (Sexton, *American Apartment Houses*, 1929)

2450 North Lakeview Avenue

Howard Van Doren Shaw, Architect | 1922–24

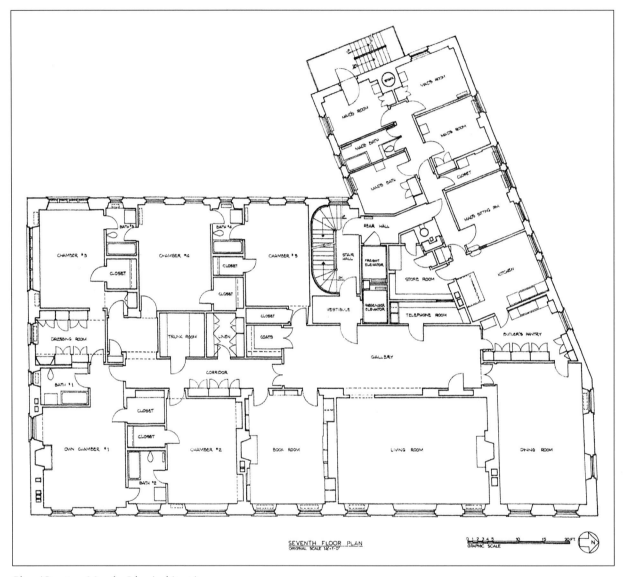

Plan. (Courtesy Murphy Jahn Architects)

This 13-story neoclassical brick building, with a rusticated limestone base and a trio of carved keystones, was Shaw's final Chicago apartment house, and it is quite different in spirit from the Tudor–Gothic 1130 Lake Shore Drive completed more than a decade earlier. The large, 8,000 square foot, five-bedroom apartments, one to a floor, had separate service wings and impressive galleries. Built as a cooperative, with apartments arranged to meet owners' wishes, the building immediately became one of the city's most prestigious addresses. *The Economist* listed the subscribers before the building was up and described them as millionaires. Two of its more modestly endowed tenant–owners were architect Shaw and *Chicago Tribune* cartoonist John T. McCutcheon. Others included Art Institute benefactor Kate Buckingham, who installed in her apartment portions of her family's Prairie Avenue home, and two Art Institute presidents, Charles Hutchinson and Chauncey McCormick, besides prominent bankers and attorneys. Occupying a large plot of land, the building had room left for landscaping and, some decades later, construction of a string of handsomely designed garages.

Exterior. (Courtesy Ryerson and Burnham Libraries, The Art Institute of Chicago, Howard van Doren Shaw Collection. All rights reserved.)

Dining room, Howard Van Doren Shaw residence, c. 1925. (Courtesy Ryerson and Burnham Libraries, The Art Institute of Chicago, Howard Van Doren Shaw Collection. All rights reserved.)

2450 NORTH LAKEVIEW AVENUE

McCutcheon residence, 1939. (Hedrich Blessing, Courtesy Chicago Historical Society)

2600 North Lakeview Avenue

MARLBOROUGH APARTMENTS

Robert S. De Golyer, Architect | Paschen Brothers, Builder | 1922–24

Exterior. (Trowbridge, courtesy Chicago Historical Society)

The Marlborough was planned as a semi-cooperative, containing slightly more than 100 apartments but with only eight owners—they were to get the "super de luxe suites, containing the last word in luxury." The remaining 97 units, however, would not be rented to just anyone. Harold Bradley, the renting agent, "who probably knows as much about social register families and their standing as tenants as anyone else along the Gold Coast," was to pass on their claims "with a thoroughness which should set a high standard of exclusiveness...." In view of Bradley's coming economic problems (see 20 East Cedar), this was certainly an ironic arrangement.

The brick building on the northwest corner of Lake View and Deming originally had two parts. 400 Deming Place faced south, with "servantless" units. "There is a very real demand in Chicago from...tenants who have means and live well, but require only small living quarters," declared the promoters. The Lakeview section, with larger apartments, was designed with setbacks overlooking Lincoln Park, enhancing the views of most residents. A series of separate entries reduced the impact of so many apartments, and while every apartment was unfurnished and had a full, if often small, kitchen, the Marlborough originally included a full dining room and room service.

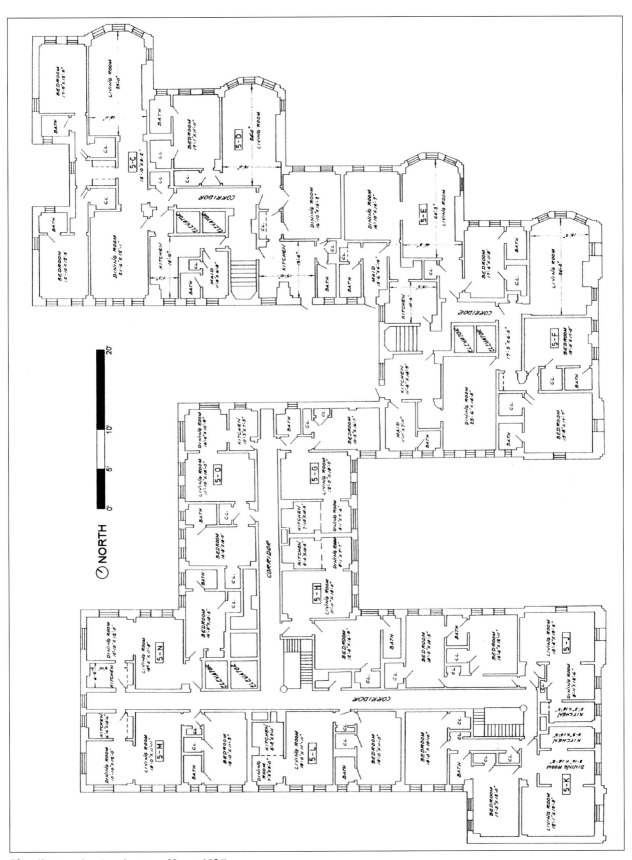

Plan. (Sexton, *American Apartment Houses*, 1926)

5000 North Marine Drive

THE AQUITANIA

Harris & Jillson, Architects | Paschen Brothers, Builder | 1922–23

Exterior.
(Baird and Warner, *Portfolio of Fine Apartment Homes*)

The Aquitania was presented as the first of five similar apartment buildings, all 15 stories high, to adjoin one another along Edgewater's lakeshore. Visions of a Streeterville North—the counterpart to Hyde Park's Streeterville of the South—stimulated the appetite of the Aquitania's owner, George K. Spoor, president of Chicago's greatest movie studio, Essanay Film Manufacturing, and briefly the employer of Charlie Chaplin. Spoor had title to an extended strip of lakefront from Argyle Street to Ainslee and lived nearby.

The Aquitania, named for the ocean liner, was the only one of the five to go up, a red brick building with its first three floors and top three floors respectively clad in limestone or trimmed extensively in stone and terra-cotta. Urns once surmounted a balustrade at the building top to emphasize the classicism of the exterior. Dion O'Banion, notorious as the city's leading gangster florist, was an Aquitania resident.

The 82 apartments are reached by two elevator corridors, and as befit a corner building, two entrances were provided. An interior remodeling of the first floor created one of Chicago's most arresting art moderne lobbies, featuring murals by Louis Weinzelbaum. Although some early descriptions labeled the Aquitania a hotel, advertisements included the phrase "Not a Hotel" because the rented apartments were unfurnished. "No other building in Chicago could compare with it," boasted the promoters, "and only a few along Park Avenue."

5000 North Marine Drive

Plan. (Baird and Warner, *Portfolio of Fine Apartment Homes*)

421 West Melrose Street

THE EDDYSTONE

Holabird & Root, Architects | Lind Construction Co., Builder | 1928–29

Rendering, exterior, c. 1927. (Brochure, courtesy Ryerson and Burnham Libraries, McNally and Quinn Collection, The Art Institute of Chicago. All rights reserved.)

This was to have been the first unit of an immense cooperative apartment project, planned to house more than 2,000 people. Built on the site of the Chase homestead for Albert W. Swayne, one of the major promoters of cooperative buildings in Chicago, its central tower would have risen 420 feet high, and projected amenities were to include playrooms, a restaurant, private dining rooms, a handball court, a swimming pool, gymnasium, and a two-level, 250-car garage. Serving the complex were to have been 19 freight and 19 passenger elevators.

The total investment required was huge, estimated to be $12 million. Instead, the Depression intervened, and the Eddystone, with its 85 apartments, remained the only realized portion of the project. Although a number of its apartments sold, the building itself failed during the 1930s; it became a rental and then was converted to a condominium.

421 WEST MELROSE STREET

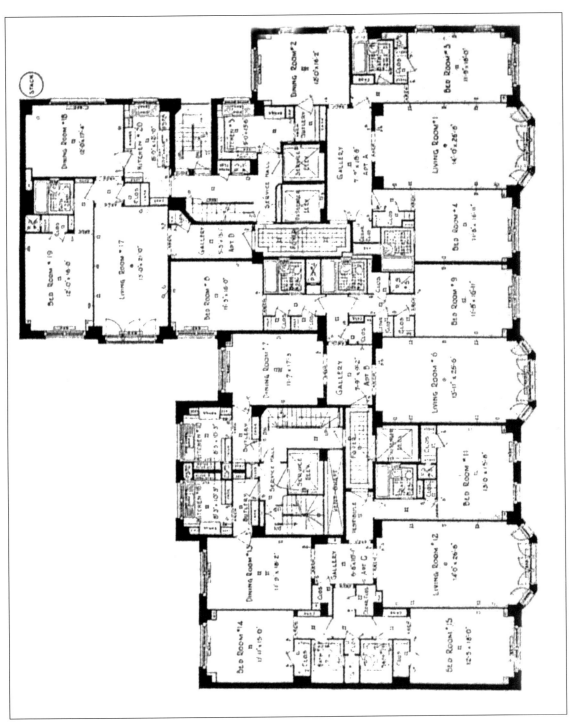

Plan.

327

421 WEST MELROSE STREET

Projected exterior, rendering, c. 1927. (Brochure, courtesy Ryerson and Burnham Libraries, McNally and Quinn Collection, The Art Institute of Chicago. All rights reserved.)

2800 NORTH PINE GROVE AVENUE

THE BREWSTER

Enoch Hill Turnock, Architect | 1893

Exterior, 1982.
(Bob Thall, courtesy
Commission on
Chicago Landmarks)

The Brewster is a rare survivor from a lively era of hotel and apartment construction in the 1890s, and was originally called the Lincoln Park Palace. A palace it remains. While its architect had worked for William Le Baron Jenney, pioneer of skeleton frame building construction, and had applied these methods to the eight-story rectangular building, its massively thick, cyclopean stone front suggests older construction methods. Rich decorative carvings and projecting window bays, along with the arresting pink color, give the Brewster a strong presence on Diversey Parkway and a monumental quality on Pine Grove.

The interior, however, is a daring ballet of metal and glass: a naturally lit atrium with open elevator, staircase, and bridges offers access to the apartments. The walkways consist of glass prisms which intensify the impression of light. It is one of the most exciting of such interiors in the city, and as such has been used in several motion pictures. The apartments themselves, while elegantly appointed, were and are relatively small in size and in number of rooms.

Legend has Charlie Chaplin living in the Brewster during his brief Chicago sojourn for Essanay Films. Remodelled twice, the Brewster is today a condominium. English-born Turnock spent his last years in Elkhart, Indiana, where he built one of the area's great mansions, Ruthmere, for a local notable.

Interior, 1982. (Bob Thall, courtesy Commission on Chicago Landmarks)

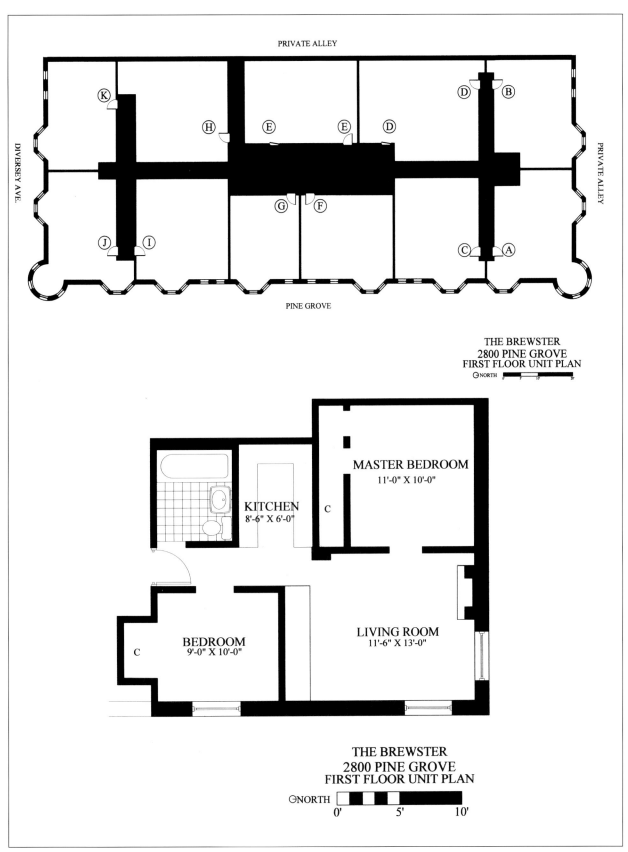

Plans.

3000 North Sheridan Road

Robert S. De Golyer, Architect | H. Janisch, Builder | 1927

LEFT: Exterior. (Brochure, courtesy Ryerson and Burnham Libraries, McNally and Quinn Collection, The Art Institute of Chicago. All rights reserved.).

ABOVE: Advertisement, Janisch, 1929. *(Illinois Society of Architects Handbook).*

This was another of the many apartment projects jointly undertaken by developer W. C. Bannerman and architect Robert De Golyer. Placed on the corner of Sheridan Road and Wellington Avenue, and designed in the "early English Renaissance style," another term for Tudor, the 18-story brick building with limestone trim was planned as a 100% cooperative with 94 apartments. A rooftop bungalow and a 44-foot long gymnasium for the tenant-owners were among its features. Each floor from the second to the 13th housed six apartment units; the upper four floors had different arrangements. Two picturesque corner towers on the Sheridan Road side give the building a distinctive profile, pleasing Al Chase of the *Chicago Tribune,* both because they differentiated it from the usual "box type" apartment house and because they concealed the unsightly rooftop tanks.

The L-shaped building, with its long side running along Sheridan, has three sets of elevators, offering even the small apartment owners a good deal of privacy. Developers emphasized its domesticity: the building office, switchboard, and mail rack were secluded "so that the entrance lobbies are not given the atmosphere of a hotel," while the plaster walls in the elevator foyers were marked off in a masonry pattern "to give the impression of an outer vestibule in a private residence."

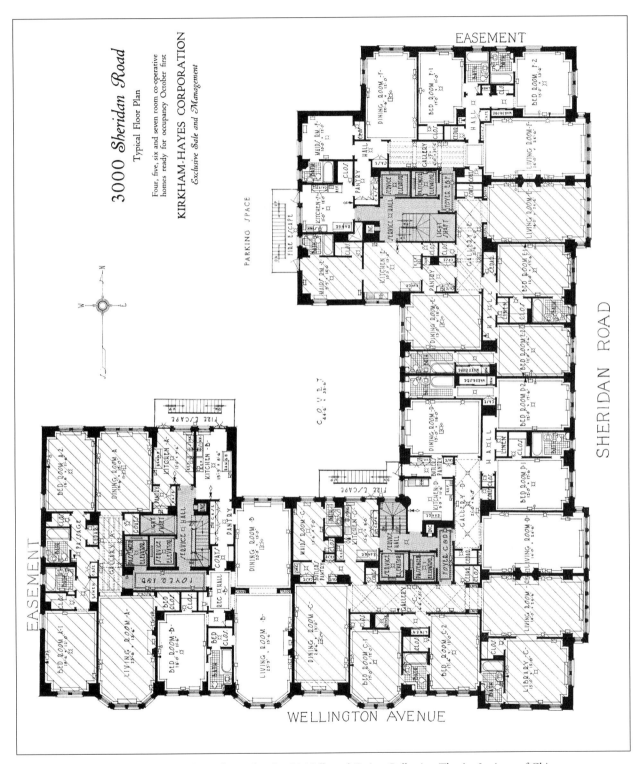

Plan. (Brochure, courtesy Ryerson and Burnham Libraries, McNally and Quinn Collection, The Art Institute of Chicago. All rights reserved.)

3100 North Sheridan Road

BARRY APARTMENTS

Robert S. De Golyer, Architect | Paschen Brothers, Builder | 1924–25

Exterior. (Trowbridge, courtesy Chicago Historical Society)

The Barry was planned as still another semi-cooperative, according to the *Chicago Tribune,* with 25—*The Economist* announced only 14—of its 67 apartments to be sold, and the remainder rented. Whether or not these sales took place is unclear; just months after its completion, owner Thomas Collins claimed that the Barry was fully leased and ads for "The Most Luxurious Apartment Building on the North Shore" were promoting rentals of nine-room units.

The restrained classicism of De Golyer's building, in brick with a stone base, pedimented windows on the 2nd floor, and a two-story "New York setback" above the 12th, gives it a more severe appearance than most of his other apartment houses. Yet it took six months for real estate buffs and newspaper readers to find out what the building would look like. The *Tribune* claimed to have spent a fortune on telephone calls to get a rendering from developer Collins, who apparently had ignored local talent for the art work and had gone to Boston—"not the fastest city in the world"—for his artist, Richard M. Powers.

With apartments ranging from four to nine rooms, including six penthouses with terraces, and with full kitchens and wood-burning fireplaces, the Barry certainly was distinguished from other rentals in the area by reason of its roominess. Several of the larger flats were duplexes, and the nine-room apartments were promised with two-story living rooms. William Hale Thompson, Chicago's notorious mayor, lived here for a time. Auctioned off in late 1950, with a $900,000 minimum bid, the Barry today is a condominium.

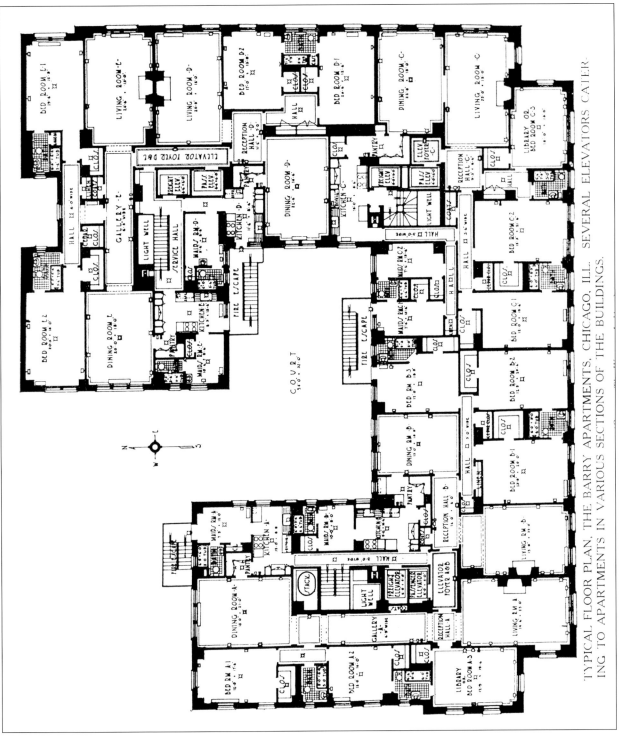

Plan. (Sexton, *American Apartment Houses*, 1929)

5510 North Sheridan Road

THE RENAISSANCE

Quinn & Christiansen, Architects | H. Janisch, Builder | 1926–27

Exterior.
(Baird and Warner, *Portfolio of Fine Apartment Homes*)

A 17-story T-shaped structure of red brick with stone trim, the Renaissance is topped by a striking gabled mansard roof, whose chimneys and towers contain the French Renaissance details the architects claimed they were referencing. Along with extensive carved floral decorations at ground level, two automobile portals leading to and from the three-story garage flank the main entrance. Originally, the building contained 32 similarly laid-out apartments, two to a floor; set back from the lower part of the tower on the top four floors are eight of these apartments, and they are slightly smaller.

Everett Quinn and R. C. Christiansen designed several other luxury apartment houses, 6700 South Crandon and 431 West Oakdale among them, but they also designed hotels, warehouses, and factories for clients that included the Sheraton Chicago Hotel and the National Biscuit Company. The contractor, Janisch, who often worked with them, was president of the 5510 corporation. Built as a cooperative, 5510 North Sheridan Road is today a condominium.

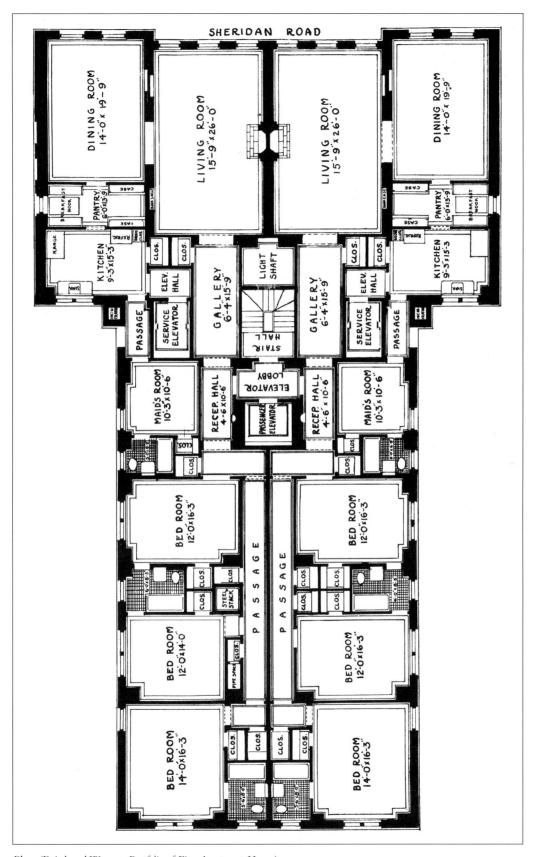

Plan. (Baird and Warner, *Portfolio of Fine Apartment Homes*)

5555 North Sheridan Road

EDGEWATER BEACH APARTMENTS
Benjamin H. Marshall, Architect | W.B. Ewers, Builder | 1927–28

Exterior, 1960. (Hedrich Blessing, courtesy Chicago Historical Society)

These apartments, at first called the Bryn Mawr Beach Apartments, were part of a larger complex that included the Edgewater Beach Hotel. The hotel's two buildings, so long a center of conventions and local entertainment, no longer stand. Ingeniously designed to maximize the light and views of the 16 apartments on each floor and to prevent long corridors, the reinforced concrete, steel-framed structure is faced with granite, limestone, stucco, and terra-cotta. The stucco is painted pink, and the general stylistic details reflect a blend of neoclassical references. Changes have affected the original entrance marquee; its giant urn-garnished colonnade, now gone, suggested the formal Edwardian elegance of some London hotels, while the building itself evoked, and still evokes, a Mediterranean flavor.

One of Benjamin Marshall's most elaborate designs, 20 stories high, with more than 300 unfurnished apartments, ranging from four to seven rooms, the Edgewater Beach came complete with garage, restaurant, swimming pool, gardens, tennis courts, exercise rooms, retail stores, beachfront, and a suitably ornate lobby. There were so many extravagances that the *Chicago Tribune* opined that it sounded like "a cinema ideal of a prewar Russian duke's palace...." The beachfront and the tennis courts are gone, but the other features remain. Residents included judges, politicians like Mayor Martin Kennelly, and "Papa Bear" George Halas.

In 1949, the Edgewater Beach was auctioned off to a group of investors for the record price of $4.6 million. Not long thereafter it became a cooperative and remains one today.

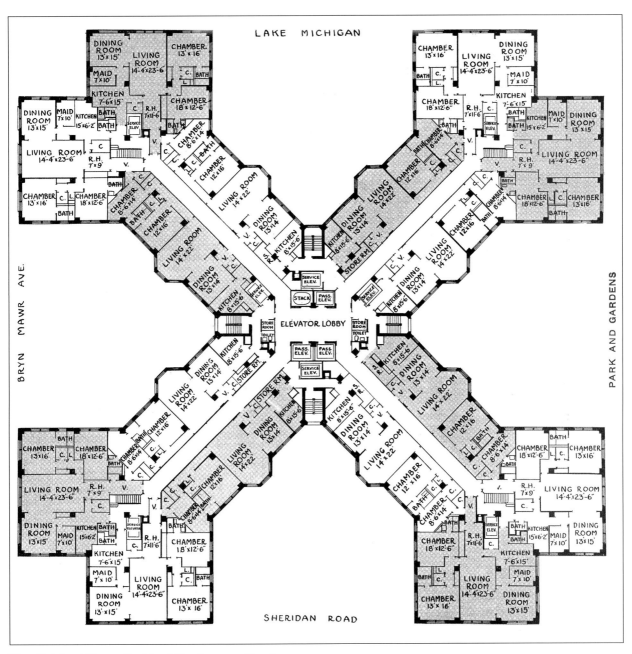

Plan. (Baird and Warner, *Portfolio of Fine Apartment Homes*)

Living room. Carson, Pirie, Scott, decorators. (Trowbridge, courtesy Chicago Historical Society)

Exterior rendering. (Sexton, *American Apartment Houses*, 1929)

442 West Wellington Avenue

R.A. Northquist, Architect | J.H. Boutet, Builder | 1926–27

Exterior.

This 13-story brick building, with a limestone accented entrance and base, does not command a direct view of the lake, unlike so many other entries in this book. Rather, it is a somewhat more luxurious version of high-rise apartment buildings that can be found on any number of east-west streets in Chicago, among them nearby Surf Street, Oakdale Avenue, Briar Place, Stratford Place, and Aldine Avenue. It is built around family needs, as its large yard and playground make clear.

R. A. Northquist designed a number of apartment complexes in the Lincoln Park area, on Bissell and Dayton Streets, and served as the engineer for other projects. The spacious 8-room, 3–bath apartments with their long corridors leading to the three master bedrooms, are a larger, more lavish adaptation of the conventional six flat design. When the building was first renting, in 1927, apartments of up to 15 rooms with eight baths were available. 442 West Wellington has been a cooperative since 1948.

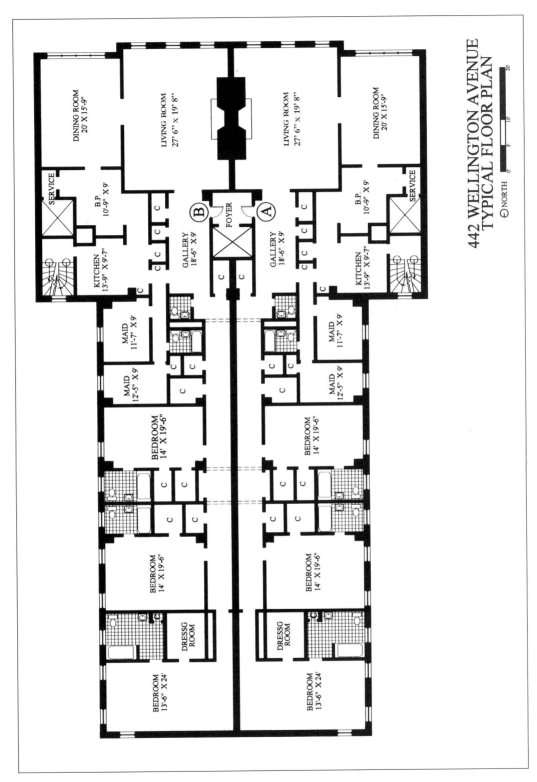

Plan.

Selected Bibliography and Building References

The primary sources for this text, along with the pictorial archives of the Chicago Historical Society and The Art Institute of Chicago, have been hundreds of issues of *The Economist* and its successor *Realty and Building*, the *Chicago Tribune*, *American Contractor*, *Chicago Realtor*, the *Chicagoan*, *Architectural Record*, *Architectural Forum*, *Western Architect*, and other journals. These were supplemented by monographs, yearbooks, interviews, summaries submitted to the Commission on Chicago Historical and Architectural Landmarks as well as their publication series, applications for national landmark status, and the oral history program of The Art Institute of Chicago's Department of Architecture. I am indebted to all of these, as well as to some particularly useful sources, most of them secondary, for the study of Chicago apartment houses, that are listed below.

Berger, Miles. *They Built Chicago*. Chicago: Bonus Books, Inc., 1992.
Blaser, Werner. *Mies van der Rohe. Lake Shore Drive Apartments*. Basel: Birkhauser. 1999.
Bluestone, Daniel. "Chicago's Mecca Flat Blues." *Journal of the Society of Architectural Historians*, 57 (Dec., 1998), 382-401.
Bruegmann, Robert. *The Architects and the City*. Chicago. University of Chicago Press, 1997
_____. *Holabird & Roche/Holabird & Root: An Illustrated Catalog of Works, 1880-1940*.
    New York: Garland, 1991.
Building for the Future. Chicago: W. L. Van Dame Co., 1918
Condit, Carl W. *Chicago 1910–1929*. Chicago: University of Chicago Press, 1973.
_____. *Chicago 1930-1970*. Chicago: University of Chicago Press, 1974.
Conway, Paul Raymond. *The Apartment House Dweller: A Study of Social Change in Hyde Park*.
    Master's Esaay, University of Chicago, 1926.
Craib-Cox, John. "Houses in the Sky." *Architectural Review*, 162 (1977), 228–231.
Hilliard, Celia. " 'Rent Reasonable to Right Parties': Gold Coast Apartment Buildings 1906–1929."
    Chicago History 8 (Summer, 1979), 66–77.
Directory to Apartments of the Better Class along the North Side of Chicago. Chicago: A. J. and H. Bradley. 1917.
Esposito, Zurich. *The Development of Apartment House Design and the Luxury Apartment House Designs of
    John Reed Fugard*. Master of Science Thesis, School of The Art Institute of Chicago, 1995.
Greene, Virginia A. *The Architecture of Howard Van Doren Shaw*. Chicago: Chicago Review Press, 1995.
Hoyt, Homer. *One Hundred Years of Land Values In Chicago*. Chicago: University of Chicago Press, 1933.
Kunz, Olive Anna France. *Co-Operative Apartments*. Master's Essay, University of Chicago, 1931.
Mayer, Harold M. and Richard C. Wade. *Chicago: Growth of a Metropolis*. Chicago: University of Chicago Press, 1969.
Moulton, Robert H. "A $40,000 Bungalow on the Roof of a Chicago Apartment House,"
    Architectural Record 42 (Aug., 1917), 149-152.
A Portfolio of Fine Apartment Homes. Chicago: Baird & Warner, Inc. 1928.
Randall, Frank R. *History of the Development of Building Construction in Chicago*. Urbana:
    University of Illinois Press, 1949.
Schulze, Franz, ed. *An Illustrated Catalogue of the Mies van der Rohe Drawings in the Museum of Modern Art*.
    New York: Garland, 1992. Vols. 13-14.
Sexton, R. W. *American Apartment Houses of Today*. New York: Architectural Book Publishing Co., 1926.
_____. *American Apartment Houses, Hotels and Apartment Hotels of Today*. New York:
    Architectural Book Publishing Co., 1929.
Sinkevitch, Alice, ed., *A.I.A. Guide To Chicago*. San Diego: Harcourt Brace, 1993.
Spray, John C. *Chicago's Great South Shore*. Chicago: South Shore Publishing Co., 1930.

Stamper, John W. *Chicago's North Michigan Avenue*. Chicago: University of Chicago Press, 1991.
Stoller, Ezra. *The John Hancock Center*. New York: Princeton Architectural Press, 2000.
Stratton, Michael. *The Terracotta Revival*. London: Gollancz. 1993.
Westfall, Carroll William. "Chicago's Better Tall Apartment Buildings, 1871-1923," *architectura*, 21 (Jan., 1992), 177-208.
_____. "From Homes to Towers: A Century of Chicago's Best Hotels and Tall Apartment Buildings" in *Chicago Architecture, 1872-1922*. Munich: Prestel, 1987, 266-289.
_____. "The Golden Age of Chicago Apartments," *Inland Architect*, (Nov., 1980),
_____. "Home at the Top: Domesticating Chicago's Tall Apartment Buildings," *Chicago History*, 14 (Spring, 1985), 20-39.
de Wit, Wim. "Apartment Houses and Bungalows: Building the Flat City." *Chicago History* 12 (Winter, 1983-84), 18-29.
Wrobleski, Donald von Fennig. *The Architectural History of 1260 North Astor Street*. Chicago: Privately printed, 1994.

PRIMARY REFERENCES

6700 S. Crandon—*Chicago Tribune*: 05-05-28, pt 3, p.1
6901 S. Oglesby—*The Economist*: v. 79, 04-14-28, p. 928
2666 E. 73rd—*Chicago Tribune*: 09-09-28, pt 3, p.1
2231 E. 67th—*Chicago Tribune*: 08-29-26, pt 3, p.1; 07-24-27, pt. 3, p.3; *The Economist*: v. 76 07-10-25, p.108
7000 South Shore Drive—*Chicago Tribune*: 08-08-26, pt 3, p.1;
    The Economist: v. 76, 09-25-26, p.85; v. 77, 02-12-17, p. 440
7321 South Shore Drive—*Chicago Tribune*: 03-16-28, pt 1, p.14; 08-14-27, pt. 3, p.1;
    The Economist: v. 74, 07-11-25, p. 112; v. 77, 05-28-27, p.1455
5000 S. Cornell—*Chicago Tribune*: 04-21-20, pt 3, p.1
5421 S. Cornell—*Chicago Tribune*: 08-28-27, pt 3, p.1; 08-05-28, pt. 3, p.1; *The Economist*: v. 78, 09-10-27, p.592
5801 S. Dorchester—*Chicago Tribune*: 01-29-28, pt 3, p.1; *The Economist*: v. 78, 08-20-27, p. 466
5000 S. East End—*Chicago Tribune*: 08-05-28, pt 3, p. 1; 08-28-27, pt. 3, p. 1; *The Economist*: v. 78, 09-03-27, p.593
5555 S. Everett—*Chicago Tribune*: 06-25-24, pt 2, p.13;
    The Economist: v. 71, 01-25-24, p.44; 06-21-24, p.1528; v.78, 09-03-27, p.593
1640 E. 50th—*Chicago Tribune*: 09-23-28, pt 3, p.1; 08-28-29, pt 3, p.1
1648 E. 50th—*Chicago Tribune*: 09-25-27, pt 3, p.1; 04-15-28, pt 3, p.4; *The Economist*: v. 78, 10-01-27, p 827
1321 E. 56th—*Chicago Tribune*: 02-17-29, pt 3, p.1
5454 South Shore Drive—*Chicago Tribune*: 04-05-25, pt 14, p.2; 06-07-25, pt 10, p.24
    The Economist: v.73, 03-14-25, p. 683
5490 South Shore Drive—*Chicago Tribune*: 09-22-26, pt. 2, p. 6; 10-08-16, pt 2, p.8;
    The Economist: v. 73, 03-14-25, p. 683
5830-44 S. Stony Island—*Chicago Tribune*: 02-02-27, pt. 3, p.2; *The Economist*: v. 67, 06-03-22, p. 1278
1200 N. Astor—*The Economist*: v. 69, 05-119-23, p. 1177
1209 N. Astor—*Chicago Tribune*: 07-22-23, pt. 2, p.14; 07-20-24, pt. 2, p.9; 07-20-24, pt. 2, p. 9;
    The Economist: v. 75 05-08-26, p. 1358
1260 N. Astor—*Chicago Tribune*: 05-04-30, pt. 2, p.15
1301 N. Astor—*Chicago Tribune*: 09-11-27, pt 3, p.1; *The Economist*: v. 78, 09-10-27m p. 653
1325 N. Astor—*Chicago Tribune*: 03-11-28, pt 3, p.1
20 E. Cedar—*Chicago Tribune*: 04-25-20, pt.2, p.6; American Contractor: 06-17-22, p. 42
70 E. Cedar—*Chicago Tribune*: 06-06-26, pt. 3, p.1
161 E. Chicago—*Chicago Tribune*: 12-23-84, sec. 13, pp. 1, 12-14; Sun-Times: 01-11-85, pp. 2-3
1366 N. Dearborn—*Chicago Tribune*: 11-28-26, pt 3, p.2
175 E. Delaware—*Realty & Building*: v. 156, 09-03-66, p.1
257 E. Delaware—*Chicago Tribune*: 01-25-17, pt 2, p.8; 03-11-17, pt 9, p.24
179 E. Lake Shore Drive—*Chicago Tribune*: 02-05-28, pt 3, p.1; 09-02-28, pt 2, p.7
219 E. Lake Shore Drive—*Chicago Tribune*: 12-04-21, pt 10, p.20
505 N. Lake Shore Drive—*Realty & Building*: v. 157, 02-11-67, p.2
680 N. Lake Shore Drive—*Chicago Tribune*: 02-08-25, pt 2, p.11
936 N. Lake Shore Drive—*Realty & Building*: v. 157, 04-08-67, p.1
999 N. Lake Shore Drive—*Chicago Tribune*: 04-03-29, pt 3, p.1;
    The Economist: v. 46, 09-30-11, p.583; v. 63, 02-21-20, p.421

SELECTED BIBLIOGRAPHY AND BUILDING REFERENCES

1040 N. Lake Shore Drive—*Realty & Building*: v. 152, 8-22-64, p.1
1120 N. Lake Shore Drive—*Chicago Tribune*: 09-21-24, pt. 2, p.12;
    The Economist: v. 71, 04-12-24, p.907; v. 72, 09-20-24, pp. 706, 734
1130 N. Lake Shore Drive—*Chicago Tribune*: 10-03-20, pt. 2, p.12
1242 N. Lake Shore Drive—*Chicago Tribune*: 04-28-29, pt. 3, p.1
1420 N. Lake Shore Drive—*Chicago Tribune*: 06-24-28, pt. 3, p.1
1430 N. Lake Shore Drive—*Chicago Tribune*: 08-28-27, pt. 3, p. 1
1448 N. Lake Shore Drive—*Chicago Tribune*: 08-15-26, pt 3, p.3; 03-13-27, pt. 3, p.3; 04-17-27, pt 3, p.1
1500 N. Lake Shore Drive—*Chicago Tribune*: 12-11-27, pt 3, p.1; 07-15-28, pt 3, p.1
1540 N. Lake Shore Drive—*Chicago Tribune*: 08-13,25, pt. 2, p.21; 08-30-25, pt 2, p. 12
    The Economist: v. 73, 03-14-25, p.681
2130 N. Lincoln Park West—*Chicago Tribune*: 03-21-26, pt 3, p.1; *The Economist*: v. 78, 08-27-27, p.528
2300 N. Lincoln Park West—*Chicago Tribune*: 03-19-22, pt 10, p.30
900 N. Michigan—*Chicago Tribune*: 08-09-25, pt 2, p.13; *The Economist*: v. 73, 02-07-25, p.355
940-80 N. Michigan—*Chicago Tribune*: 04-14-85, pt 16, p.2
60-70 E. Scott Chicago—*Chicago Tribune*: 10-03-20, pt. 2, p. 12
1320 N. State—*Chicago Tribune*: 08-09-25, pt 2, p.14; 10-31-26, pt 3, p.1
    The Economist: v. 73, 02-21-25, p.485; v. 74, 11-07-25, p. 1265
1530 N. State—*Chicago Tribune*: 05-12-29, pt 3, p.1
1550 N. State—*Chicago Tribune*: 05-16-20, pt 10, p.28;
    The Economist: v. 62, 05-15-20, p.1089; v. 64, 07-31-20, p. 225
1244 N. Stone—*Chicago Tribune*: 06-16-25, pt 2, p.14
220 E. Walton—*Chicago Tribune*: 10-03-20, pt. 2, p.12
2920 N. Commonwealth—*Chicago Tribune*: 03-24-20, pt 3, p.1
325 W. Fullerton—*Chicago Tribune*: 01-14-17, pt 2, p.5; *The Economist*: v. 55, 04-15-16, pp. 760, 762
399 W. Fullerton—*Chicago Tribune*: 08-01-26, pt 3, p.1; 07-22-28, pt 3, p.1
660-700 W. Irving Park—*The Economist*: v. 29, 08-09-02, p.186; v. 70, 09-01-23, p. 472
3300 N. Lake Shore Drive—*Chicago Tribune*: 12-22-25, pt 2, p. 30; 12-17-25, pt 3, p.1
3400 N. Lake Shore Drive—*Chicago Tribune*: 08-24-19, pt 2, p. 8
    The Economist: v. 62, 07-26-19, p. 213; 8-23-19, p. 289; v. 65, 01-22-21, p. 203; v. 67, 05-15-22, p. 860
3500 N. Lake Shore Drive—*Chicago Tribune*: 02-07-26, pt 3, p.1;
    The Economist: v. 74, 10-31-25, p. 1164; 11-21-25, p. 1362
3750 N. Lake Shore Drive—*Chicago Tribune*: 05-23-26, pt 3, p.1
3800 N. Lake Shore Drive—*Chicago Tribune*: 08-22-26, pt 3, p.1; 12-19-26, pt. 3, p1
3920 N. Lake Shore Drive—*Chicago Tribune*: 06-26-27, pt 3, p1; 06-06-26, pt 3, pp. 1-2
2430 N. Lakeview—*Chicago Tribune*: 12-05-26, pt 3, p.1
2440 N. Lakeview—*Chicago Tribune*: 08-15-26, pt. 3, p.1; *The Economist*: v. 75, 04-24-26, p.1204
2450 N. Lakeview—*The Economist*: v. 68, 080-26-22, p.479
2600 N. Lakeview—*Chicago Tribune*: 06-19-22, pt 2, p.16
421 W. Melrose—*The Economist*: v. 79, 01-28-28, p. 343; 03-03-28, p. 546
5000 N. Marine—*Chicago Tribune*: 04-05-24, pt 1, p.11; 06-25-22, pt 9, p.24
3000 N. Sheridan—*Chicago Tribune*: 02-06-27, pt 3, p.1
3100 N. Sheridan—*Chicago Tribune*: 09-28-24, pt 10, p.28; *The Economist*: v. 75, 04-03-26, p. 943
3240 N. Sheridan—*Chicago Tribune*: 09-18-27, pt 3, p.1
5510 N. Sheridan—*Chicago Tribune*: 11-27-27, pt 3, p.1
5555 N. Sheridan—*Chicago Tribune*: 09-04-27, pt 3, p.1

Index

Adams, Cyrus, 34
Adler, David, 30, 105, 108-109, 310, 312-314
Ahlschlager, Walter, 20, 21, 27, 60, 304, 306
Allerton, Robert M., 105
Alschuler, Alfred S., 96
American Furniture Mart, 23, 168-169
American Hospital, 308
Anderson, A. & E., Co., 40
Aquitania, The, 34, 324-325
Architectural Forum, 105
Architectural Record, 178
Armour, A. Watson, 27
Armour, J. Ogden, 300
Arpen Group, 23
Arquette, Geo. L., 54
Art Institute of Chicago, The, 190, 318
Arts Club, 64
1200 N. Astor St., 94-95
1209 N. Astor St., 96-97
1260 N. Astor St., 98-103
1301 N. Astor St., 98, 105-111
1325 N. Astor St., 112-117
1335 N. Astor St., 22, 23
1350 N. Astor St., 22
Baird & Warner, 18, 25, 27, 188, 208
Bannerman, William C., 27, 48, 206, 332
Baptist Theological Union, 56
Barclay, The, 306
Barry Apartments, 334-335
Bartlett, Frederic Clay, 105
Bartlett, Frederick H., 300
Bedgbo, Nelson, 254
Bein, Maurice L., 18, 286
Belden-Stratford Hotel, 230
Beman, Solon S., 15
Berger, Miles, 27, 206
Bergman, Ruth, 18, 210
Bevan, Dr. Arthur, 274
Billings, Dr. Frank, 274
Blair, Chauncey, 210
Blois, Chateau at, 208
Booth Hansen, 31, 114, 155, 157, 242
Boutet, J. H., 342
Bradley Apartments, 118-121
Bradley, Harold, 17, 18, 118, 260, 282, 322
Brand Brewery, 118
Breakers, The, 152-155
Brewster The, 329-331
Brown, Charles A., 118

Brundage, Avery, 27, 58, 60, 90, 208, 220, 302, 306, 316
Bryn Mawr Beach Apartments, 338
Bryson Flats, 15, 16
Buck, John, 27
Buckingham, Kate, 318
building brochures, 28-29
Building Services Employees International Union, 262
Burnham, Daniel, 14, 202
Busch, Adolphus, 290
Calkins, Earnest Elmo, 25
Candela, Rosario, 196, 210
Campbell Apartments, 254-255
Campbell, George, 254
Carlson, Emil, 304
Carlyle, The, 23, 26, 184-185
Carson Pirie Scott & Co., 29, 340
Carter, Edward G., 82
Castellane Apartments, 278-279
20 E. Cedar St., 118-121, 276, 322
70 E. Cedar St., 122-123
Celotex Co., 242
Chapin, Henry, 310
Chaplin, Charlie, 324, 329
Chase, Al, 20, 27, 52, 112, 210, 316, 332
Chatelaine Tower, 308
Chicago and North Western Railway, 262
40-50 E. Chicago Ave., 124-125
161 E. Chicago Ave., 126-129
4950 S. Chicago Beach Dr., 66-71
Chicago Beach Hotel, 58, 66
Chicago Beach tract, 58, 306
Chicago Business Men's Orchestra, 308
Chicago Club, 56
Chicago Face Brick Association, 33
Chicago Real Estate Board, 25
Chicago Tribune, 19, 20, 27, 42, 46, 52, 54, 60, 66, 72, 112, 118, 130, 190, 202, 206, 208, 210, 238, 260, 268, 270, 278, 302, 306, 310, 316, 332, 334, 338
Chicagoan, 18, 32, 210
Childs & Smith, 208
Childs, Frank A., 208
Christiansen, R. C., 38, 336
Claar, Elmer A., 25
Clute, H. L., 58, 268
Cloisters, The, 56-57
Coastland, The, 42-43

Index

Cobb, Henry Ives, 196
Colby, John A. & Sons, 29, 268
Colgate-Palmolive Co., 242
Collins, Thomas, 27, 334
Comiskey, Charles, 60
Commonwealth Hotel, 33
Commonwealth Towers, 286-287
2920 N. Commonwealth Ave., 286-287
Condit, Carl, 35, 156, 242, 262
condominium legislation, 26, 34, 37, 184
Conger, Cornelia, 115
Conley & Carlson, 52
Container Corporation of America, 182
Co-operative Association of Chicago, 25
cooperatives, 24-26, 34
Consumer Price Index, 32
Cornelia Apartments, 302-303
Cornell Towers, 18, 286
5000 S. Cornell Ave., 52-53
5346 S. Cornell Ave., 286
5421 S. Cornell Ave., 54-55
Corrigan, E. W., 146
Costello, Harold, 27, 40
Craib-Cox, John, 18, 33
6700 S. Crandon Ave., 29, 38-39, 44, 336
Crane Construction Co., 164, 256
Crane, C. Howard, 282
Crane, R. T., 220
Crane Tower, 60
Dahl-Stedman, Co., 112, 310
Dahlberg, Bror C., 242, 242-245
Danforth, S. Chester, 28
1366 N. Dearborn Pkwy., 130-131
Dearborn Park, 27
Dearborn Schiller, The, 29, 130-131
Deering, James, 206
Decker, H. H., 25
De Golyer, Robert S., 19, 21, 27, 30, 48, 58, 66, 182, 196, 206, 254, 268, 302, 304, 322, 332, 334
Del Prado Hotel, 60
132 E. Delaware Pl., 132-135, 238
175 E. Delaware Pl., 137-141
227 E. Delaware Pl., 29
230 E. Delaware Pl., 17
257 E. Delaware Pl., 142-143
Dick, A. B., 274
Doerr, William P., 18
5801-11 S. Dorchester Ave., 56-57
Dovenmuehle, 184
Drake Brothers, 27, 248
Drake Hotel, 148
Drake Tower, 18, 33, 34, 148-151
Drama League of Chicago, 226
Draper & Kramer, 27
Dunning, N. Max, 168
4940 S. East End Ave., 306
5000 S. East End Ave., 58-59

East Point, 23
Eberson, John, 86
Economist, The, 17, 94, 226, 238, 274, 278, 292, 318, 334
Eddystone, The, 326-328
Edgewater Beach Apartments, 34, 164, 274, 338-341
Edgewater Beach Hotel, 338
Edlund, E., 38, 42
Egan, James J., 124
Elite Dictionary and Club List of Chicago, 15
Elkins, Frances, 108-109
Elliman & Co., Douglas, 210
10 West Elm St., 18, 306
Elm Tower, 23
Ely residence, 108-109
Eppenstein and Schwab, 88
Eppenstein, James, 185
Epstein & Sons International, A., 23-24
Erickson, C. & Co., 308
55 E. Erie St., 144-145
Esposito, Zurich, 260, 276
Essanay Film Manufacturing Co., 324, 329
Esser, Curt A., 64
5555 S. Everett Ave., 60-63
Ewers, W. B., 338
Fairbanks, Morse & Co., 300
Faulkner, Charles Draper, 42
Federal Housing Authority, 14, 26
Ferriss, Hugh, 105
Field, Stanley, 274
1640 E. 50th St., 64-65
1648 E. 50th St., 66-71
1321 E. 56th St., 72-73
1644 E. 56th St., 74-77
Fitzgerald Construction, 130
Flamingo Hotel, 54
"Flaxinuum," 226
Fordham Co., 146
Fox, Charles E., 38
France, Roy, 30, 118, 308
Franzheim, Kenneth, 282
Freer, Archibald, 202
French, J. B., 238
Fridstein, Meyer, 78, 230
Fridstein, Meyer & Co., 78, 230
Fugard & Knapp, 118, 160, 162, 260, 278, 280
Fugard, John Reed, 30, 118, 162, 260, 276
Fujikawa Johnson & Associates, 144
301 W. Fullerton Pkwy., 288
325 W. Fullerton Pkwy., 288-289
399 W. Fullerton Pkwy., 29, 290-291
Gables Apartments, 16
Gage, Lyman J., 268
Garden, Hugh M. G., 232
Garard Trust, 25
General Electric Refrigerators, 29

Glass Houses, 22, 170-177, 254
65 E. Goethe St., 146-147
Goetz, Hugo J., 300
Goldberg, Bertrand, 262
Goode, James, 30
Gotham, The, 54
Gottschalk, G. H., 27, 78, 82, 230
Graham, Bruce, 137, 248
Granger & Bollenbacher, 270
Granville Tower, 23
Greenebaum Sons Investment Co., 25
Greengard, B. C., 27
Greenwald, Herbert, 27, 86, 170
Gregori, Raymond, 15, 18
Halas, George, 338
Hallbauer–La Bahn, 96
Hallberg, L. G. & Co., 298
Hallberg, Lawrence G., 15, 16, 298
Hamlin, Peter, Construction, 66
Hampson, Philip, 19, 28, 46, 202, 306, 310
Harbor Apartments, 300-301
Harris & Jillson, 324
Harris, Ethel and Mortimer, 224-225
Harris, Ralph C., 278
Harris Theater, 282
Hasbrouck, Hunderman, 23
Hausner & Macsai, 23
Hedrich Blessing, 31
Hegemann-Harris Co., 242, 268
Heinrich, John, 164
Henry, Charles F., 27, 118
High, George, 196
Hirschfeld, Leo S., 22, 23, 223, 296
Hirschfeld, Pawlan & Reinheimer, 30, 184, 256
Hoguelet brothers, 27
Holabird & Roche, 21, 94, 232
Holabird & Root, 14, 242, 326
Holabird, John, 188
Holabird, William, 94, 188
Holsman, Henry K., 34, 44, 72
Holsman & Holsman & Klekamp, 86, 170
Hotel St. Benedict Flats, 15, 124-125
Hood, Raymond, 118
Hooper & Janusch, 202
Hooper, William T., 202
Hopkins, Mrs. James, 273
House Beautiful, 190
Houston, Texas, 23
Hunt, Jarvis, 202, 238
Hunt, Richard Morris, 238
Hutchinson, Charles, 318
Huszagh & Hill, 220
Huszagh, Ralph, 21, 220
Hutchinson, Margaret, 266
Ida B. Wells Homes, 22
Indiana Limestone Co., 226
Ingram, Horace Colby, 160

Inland Architect, 200
Inland-Robbins Co., 250
Insull, Samuel, 186, 196
Intercontinental Hotel, 60
660-700 W. Irving Park Rd., 292-293
Jackson Shore Apartments, 82-85
Jackson Towers, 20, 60-63
Jane Addams Houses, 21
Janisch, H., 46, 122, 332, 336
Janusch, Fred, 202
Jacques Restaurant, 238
Jelke, John H., 300
Jenney, William Le Baron, 14, 23, 329
Jensen, Jens & Son, 298
John Hancock Center, 137-141
Johnson, Axel H., 142
Johnson, Charles B., 274
Johnson, Charles B. & Son, 64, 66
Julia Lathrop Homes, 21
Juta, Jan, 312
Keep, Chauncey, 220
Kelley, William V., 274
Kelly Steel Erectors, 132
Kennelly, Martin, 338
Khan, Fazlur, 137
King residence, 272
Kirkham-Hayes Corporation, 25, 37, 290
Klafter, David Saul, 202
Klutznick, Philip, 27
Knapp, George, 118
Kohn Pedersen Fox, 132
Krenn & Dato, 296
Krenn, Edwin D., 296
Kroc, Ray, 196
Krueck & Sexton Architects, 31, 129, 176-177
Lagrange, Lucien, 23, 146, 236
Lake Point Tower, 164-167
Lake Shore Apartments, 182-183
Lake Shore Athletic Club, 238
179 E. Lake Shore Dr., 33, 34, 148-151
199 E. Lake Shore Dr., 17, 152-155
209 E. Lake Shore Dr., 156-159, 178
219 E. Lake Shore Dr., 160-161, 162
229 E. Lake Shore Dr., 162-163
505 N. Lake Shore Dr., 164-167
680 N. Lake Shore Dr., 168-169
860-880 N. Lake Shore Dr., 170-177
900 N. Lake Shore Dr., 21
936 N. Lake Shore Dr., 17, 31, 178-181
942 N. Lake Shore Dr., 31, 178
999 N. Lake Shore Dr., 152, 182-183, 242
1040 N. Lake Shore Dr., 184-185
1100 N. Lake Shore Dr., 17, 186-187
1120 N. Lake Shore Dr., 19, 25, 188-189
1130 N. Lake Shore Dr., 190-193, 318
1200 N. Lake Shore Dr., 194-195, 274
1242 N. Lake Shore Dr., 196-199

Index

1418 N. Lake Shore Dr., 200-201
1420 N. Lake Shore Dr., 202-205
1430 N. Lake Shore Dr., 29, 34, 206-207
1448 N. Lake Shore Dr., 21, 208-209
1500 N. Lake Shore Dr., 21, 196, 210-219
1540 N. Lake Shore Dr., 34, 220-225
3240 N. Lake Shore Dr., 294-295
3300 N. Lake Shore Dr., 296-297
3314 N. Lake Shore Dr., 298-299
3400 N. Lake Shore Dr., 300-301
3500 N. Lake Shore Drive, 302-303
3750 N. Lake Shore Dr., 21, 304-305, 306
3800 N. Lake Shore Dr., 21, 306-307
3920 N. Lake Shore Dr., 308-309
1000 Lake Shore Plaza, 22
Lake Shore Towers, 308-309
Lake Shore Trust & Savings Bank, 118
2430 N. Lakeview Ave., 310-315
2440 N. Lakeview Ave., 316-317
2450 N. Lakeview Ave., 318-321
2600 N. Lakeview Ave., 322-323
Lanquist & Co., 190
La Tour Restaurant, 256
Lawson, Victor, 210, 220
Le Griffon, 298-299
Lehmann estate, 27, 60
Leichenko & Esser, 64
Leichenko, Peter M., 64
Lilienthal, 226
Lincoln Park Palace, 329
2130 N. Lincoln Park West, 226-229
2300 N. Lincoln Park West, 230-231
2344 N. Lincoln Park West, 288
Lind Construction Co., 48, 326
Lindbergh Beacon, 242
Lindstrom, A., 294
Loeb, Nellie, 290
Loebl, Schlossman & Bennett, 232
Loebl, Schlossman, Dart & Hackl, 250
Loewenberg & Loewenberg, 23
Lohan Associates, 168
Lott Hotel Co., 230
Lundstrom, John A. & Co., 304
McClurg, Mrs. Ogden, 156
McClurg, Ogden, 182
McConnell Apartments, 94-95
McConnell, John, 94
McCord, Alvin, 270
McCormick, Chauncey, 318
McCormick, Cyrus, Jr., 238, 241
McCormick, Edith Rockefeller, 296
McCormick, Edith Rockefeller Trust, 27, 296
McCormick, Leander, 310
McCormick, Robert Hall, 98, 101-102
McCutcheon, John T., 318
McFetridge, William, 262
McHugh, James Construction Co., 236, 262

Mack, John, 27
McLennan Construction Co., 27, 118, 160, 178, 260, 278, 280, 282
McLennan, Hugh, 27, 160, 278
McMenemy & Martin, 270, 282
McNally & Quinn, 27, 46, 122, 130, 210, 213-217, 282, 290, 294
McNally, Frank, 46, 294
McNulty Construction Co., 72
McNulty, William G., 52
McQuay Radiators, 29
Maher, Philip B., 18, 20, 27, 98, 105, 110
Malibu East, 23
Mandel, Mrs. Frederick, 120
Mandel, Leon, estate, 27
Manhattan Building, 23
Mann, William D., 118
Manor House, 16, 17
Maple Tower, 23
Marina City, 22, 262-267
5000 N. Marine Dr., 34, 324-325
Marlborough Apartments, 322-323
Marshall Apartments, 186-187
Marshall, Benjamin H., 16, 27, 30, 48, 148, 156, 164, 186, 194, 200, 274, 338
Marshall & Fox, 17, 118, 152, 182, 186, 194, 230, 274
Marx, Samuel A., 31, 116-117, 224-225
Mayfair Construction Co., 200
Mecca Flats, 15
Medinah Club, 60
Meeker, Arthur, 186
Melemore Construction Co., 162, 178
421 W. Melrose St., 326-28
Mensch, I. J., 270
Mentone Flats, 15, 298
6 N. Michigan Ave., 232-235
800 N. Michigan Ave., 236-237
900 N. Michigan Ave. (demolished), 132, 238-241
900 N. Michigan Ave., 31, 132-35, 238
919 N. Michigan Ave., 242-247
940-940 N. Michigan Ave., 248-249
Midway Gardens, 66
Miehle Printing Press Co., 274
Mies van der Rohe, Ludwig, 22, 64, 86, 164, 170, 254
Montgomery Ward Tower Building, 23, 232-235
Moore, W. J., 62
Morgan, Charles L., 18, 27, 64, 66
Morse residence, 196
Morse, Col. Robert H., 300
Morton, Sterling, 196
Mueller Construction Co., 300
Mumford, Lewis, 14
Museum of Science and Industry, 60, 74
Narragansett, The, 30, 34, 64
National Biscuit Company, 336

INDEX

National Tea Co., 300
Nelson Construction Co., 202
Netherlands Hotel, Cincinnati, 60
Newburg, Gustav K. Construction, 126
Newton, Perry I., 115
Nimmons, George C., 168
Norcross, Frederic, 105
Northquist, R. A., 342-3
Northwestern Terra Cotta, 18
Northwestern University, 208
Noyes, La Verne, 190
Nyden, John A., 16, 19, 27, 31, 34, 137
431 W. Oakdale Ave., 336
O'Banion, Dion, 324
6901 S. Oglesby Ave., 40-41
Olsen, Paul Frederick, 18, 27, 30, 40, 90
Olympia Centre, 126-129
Oman & Lilienthal, 34, 226
One Magnificent Mile, 248
Ontario Flats, 15
Ouilmette Construction Co., 98
Outer Drive East, 22, 34, 256-259
Pace Associates, 86
Paepcke, Walter, 182
Palazzo Farnese, Rome, 254
Palazzo Strozzi, Florence, 254
Palmer, Potter, 93, 98, 105
Palmer, Potter, estate, 122
Palmer, Potter interests, 27
Palmolive Building, 23, 242-247
Para Auto Tire Co., 300
Pardridge, A. J., 17, 18, 260
Park Tower, 236-237
Park Place Tower, 23
Parkway Hotel, 230
Parvenu, The, 30
Paschen Brothers, 27, 322, 334
Paschen Contractors, 126
Patrician, The, 308
Pattington, The, 292-293
Patton, James E., 292
Peabody Hotel, Memphis, 60
180 E. Pearson St., 250-253
200 E. Pearson St., 254-255
Pedgrift, Freeman & Co., 94
2800 N. Pine Grove Ave., 329-331
Plotke, Milton, 220
Poinsettia Apartments, 18
Porter, George, 268
Postle, David E., 292
Powers, Richard M., 334
Powhatan, The, 30, 64, 66-71, 304
Portfolio of Fine Apartment Homes, A, 17, 18
Pridmore, J. E. O., 16
Promontory Apartments, 22, 86-89
Quinn & Christiansen, 38, 42, 336
Quinn, Everett, 38, 336

Quinn, J. Edwin, 30, 46, 294
Radcliffe, Adelaide, 259
Raeder, Henry, 168
400 E. Randolph St., 256-259
Ranney, George, 98, 100, 103
Rapp, C. W. & G. L., 74, 82
Rasmussen, George, 300
Raymond Apartments, 132
Real Estate Indicator, 282
Rebori, Dewey, and Wentworth, 112
Rebori, Wentworth, Dewey & McCormick, 311
Rebori, A. N., 310
Reichert & Finck, 54
Reichert, William, 54
Reliance Building, 23
Renaissance, The, 337-338
Reynolds, Peter F., 27, 210, 290
Rindskopf, A.C., 213-217
Rissman & Hirschfeld, 296, 316
Rissman, Maurice B., 296
Robin, Albert, 27
Robin Construction Co., 184
Roche, Martin, 94, 188
Root, John, 14
Root, John, Jr., 105, 111, 188
Roxy Theater, 60
Rubloff, Arthur, 27
Ruthmere, 329
Saarinen, Eliel, 66
Sandburg Village, 27, 31
Sandegren, Andrew, 16, 27, 30, 288
Sanders, James, 21
Scher, Raymond, 27
Schiporeit, George, 164
Schiporeit-Heinrich, 164
Schmidt, Richard, 232
Schweikher, Robert Paul, 98
60-70 E. Scott St., 260-261
Searl & Associates, 31, 144
Seeds, Elise, 32
Seide, Wiliam H., 298
Selwyn Theater, 282
2666 E. 73rd St., 42-43
Sewell, Ike, 205
Sexton, Patrick J., 124
Schal Associates, 248
Shapiro, Berta, 84-85
Shaw, Howard Van Doren, 16, 190, 192, 318, 320-321
Shepard, Stuart G., 182
Sheraton Chicago Hotel, 336
3000 N. Sheridan Rd., 332-333
3100 N. Sheridan Rd., 334-335
5510 N. Sheridan Rd., 29, 336-337
5555 N. Sheridan Rd., 338-341
6033 N. Sheridan Rd., 23
6166 N. Sheridan Rd., 23

Index

Sheridan-Aldine Apartments, 296-297
Sheridan-Grace Apartments, 306-307
Sheridan-Melrose Apartments, 294-295
shirt front buildings, 19
Shoreland, The, 16, 74, 78-81, 82, 230
Shoreland Apartments, 162-163
Shoreline Homes, 29, 44-45
Singer Building, 23
2231 E. 67th St., 29, 44-45
Skidmore, Owings & Merrill, 126-129, 137, 178, 248
Smith, Clute & Brown, 58, 268
Smith, Charles B., 298
Smith, William Jones, 208
Smyth, John M. & Co., 29
Sollitt, Ralph & Sons, 44, 270
Solomon Cordwell Buenz, 30, 200
South Shore Country Club, 37
5454 South Shore Dr., 78-81
5490 South Shore Dr., 82-85
5530-32 South Shore Dr., 86-89
7000 South Shore Dr., 46-47
7321 South Shore Dr., 21, 48-49
Spoor, George K., 324
Standard Plumbing, 29
1320 N. State Pkwy., 268-269
1530 N. State Pkwy., 105, 270-273
1550 N. State Pkwy., 16, 17, 32, 194, 274-275
300 N. State St., 262-267
Steif, B. Leo, 18, 27, 306
Stewart Apartments, 194-195
Stewart, John K., 194
Stewart-Warner Speedometer Co., 298
Stock, Frederick, 112
Stockton, Walter T., 188, 206
1244 N. Stone St., 276-277
Stone, Charles D., Mr. and Mrs., 98
Stone, H. O. & Company, 25
5830-44 S. Stony Island Ave., 90-91
Strandberg, E. P. Co., 56, 105
Sudler, Louis, 270
Sullivan, Louis, 14
Swanson, Joseph, 288
Swanson, T. B., 288
Swayne, Albert W., 90, 326
Taft, Lorado, 56
Telford & McWade, 292
Terminals Building, 23
Thielbar & Fugard, 276
Thompson Starrett, 74
Thompson, William Hale, 334
Thorek, Dr. Max, 308
Thorne, Mrs. George A., 190
Thorne, Robert J., 310

Tigerman McCurry Architects, 31, 134-135, 252-253
Tishman Construction, 137
Tower Homes, 72-73
Treat and Foltz, 15
Trowbridge, Raymond, 31
Trumbull Park Homes, 22
Tucker, Preston, 182
Turner Construction Co., 196, 210
Turnock, Enoch Hill, 329
Union Carbide Building, 23
Union Trust, 25
University of Chicago, 56, 72, 74, 78
Urbain, Leon, 18
Van Osdel, John, 23
Vinci Hamp Architects, 31, 128, 193
Virginia Hotel, 15
Vista Homes, 90-91
Vitzhum & Teich, 288
Wahl Construction Co., 286
Walcott and Work, 31, 241, 272
Walker, Wiliam Ernest, 16, 31, 178, 200
Waller, Edward Carson, Jr., 27, 48
Waller, J. B., 292
Walsh Construction Co., 144
220 E. Walton Pl, 278-279
232 E. Walton Pl., 280-281
233 E. Walton Pl., 282-283
Warren, Clinton J., 15, 16
Warwick, The, 26
Water Tower Place, 250-253
Weber, Peter J., 300
Webster Hotel, 230
Weinzelbaum, Louis, 324
Weissbourd, Bernard, 27
442 W. Wellington Ave., 342-343
Wells Brothers, 168
Wendell, Barrett, 98
Westfall, Carroll William, 19, 186, 298
Wexler, Jerrold, 238, 256
Willett, Mr. and Mrs. Howard, 226
Wilson, Elsie Cobb, 102
Wilson, Horatio, 15, 16
Windermere, The, 34, 74-77, 78
Windsor Beach Apartments, 48-49
Wolman, Jerry, 137
Woodruff, George, 210, 212-217
World's Columbian Exposition of 1893, 48, 74, 238, 300
Wright, Frank Lloyd, 14, 66
Wrigley, William, Jr., 34, 210, 218-219
Zeisler, Claire, 150
zoning code of 1923, 188